Musical Childhoods & the Cultures of Youth

Music/Culture A series from Wesleyan University Press

Edited by Robert Walser, Susan Fast, and Harris Berger
Originating editors, George Lipsitz, Susan McClary, and Robert Walser

Also by Susan Boynton

Shaping a Monastic Identity:
Liturgy and History at the Imperial
Abbey of Farfa, 1000–1125 (2006)

From Dead of Night to End of Day:
The Medieval Customs of Cluny
(coedited with Isabelle Cochelin, 2005)

Musical Childhoods

& the Cultures of Youth

Edited by Susan Boynton & Roe-Min Kok

Wesleyan University Press ◆ Middletown, CT

Published by Wesleyan University Press,
Middletown, CT 06459
www.wesleyan.edu/wespress

Copyright © 2006 by Wesleyan University Press.
All rights reserved

Designed and typeset by Julie Allred, BW&A Books, Inc.
Printed in the United States of America

Library of Congress Cataloging-in-Publication Data
Musical childhoods and the cultures of youth /
edited by Susan Boynton and Roe-Min Kok.
     p. cm. — (Music/culture)
Includes bibliographical references (p.) and index.
ISBN 0-8195-6802-3 (cloth : alk. paper) —
ISBN 0-8195-6803-1 (pbk. : alk. paper)
1. Music—Social aspects. 2. Music and youth.
3. Music—Psychological aspects.
I. Boynton, Susan, 1966– II. Kok, Roe-Min.
III. Series.
ML3916.M883   2006
780.83—dc22   2005054696

Contents

Preface

Roe-Min Kok & Susan Boynton

This cross-cultural collection brings together ten essays that view music through the multifaceted lens of childhood. Music associated with children and adolescents has traditionally been the domain of ethnographers and pedagogues interested primarily in the cultural and educational aspects of living musical traditions as practiced by the young. Only very recently have scholars of music begun to view the concept of childhood as a historical, critical, and aesthetic framework for analyzing repertories traditionally associated with children.[1] With coverage spanning ten centuries, four continents, and many distinct repertories and cultural practices, this volume is unprecedented in its breadth and scope. The interaction between historical and social-scientific approaches is fundamental to the interdisciplinary spirit of the volume; the essays employ methods based on historical and ethnographic analyses alike and address music created both for and about the young. This collection thus embraces both the major intellectual trajectories that inform current scholarship on children and youth in the humanities: the ethnographic/sociological, with its focus on the cultural agency of teenagers and young adults (see Amit-Talai and Wulff 1995), and the historical/archival, with its focus on exploring children and their relations to families, institutions and public policies—or the "child as historical subject" (see Austin 2004; Fass 2004).

Our collection represents only the tip of the iceberg in a rich field of study, and all-inclusiveness is neither our goal nor our claim. We have instead focused on foregrounding and exploring repertories and areas that have received little attention up to now, including Western classical and folk musics that refer to childhood or children, historical sources that describe music and children, and childhood memories of learning or experiencing music, along with ethnographic studies of various children's musical cultures (the last has a longer intellectual history than the others; see Minks 2002). In part, the collection is a response from scholars of music to the widespread interest in the history of childhood sparked in the middle of the twentieth century by

Philippe Ariès's *Centuries of Childhood: A Social History of the Family* (1960; English translation, 1962). Following Ariès, though not uncritically, scholarly studies of children and childhood, youth, and adolescent cultures have blossomed in disciplines ranging from sociology, law, history, and psychology to literature, theology, and the visual arts.[2] Within this explosion of writings on children and childhood, the sheer diversity of thought and understandings applied to the seemingly common words *childhood* and *children* is often bewildering; we shall briefly clarify and explain their (admittedly flexible) use in this collection.

In its most commonly understood modern sense, *child* signals human presence and human subjectivity of a kind frequently associated with chronological age but also with a psychological state (occurring naturally or otherwise) that, depending on cultural and other contexts, may be considered desirable or laughable. Authors in this collection indicate the chronological ages of their subjects wherever possible; most often, their subjects include pre- and postpubescent youth. "Childhood," the notion of a phase in life, traces its existence to relatively recent historicist thought and is also a context-dependent sociocultural construct typically presented from an adult perspective (Calvert 1992: 3). Depending on where, when, and how it is used, the word *childhood* may be quite removed from the specificity and grounding implied by human presence (this is also the case for the metaphorical child). The historical and memory-based essays in this collection may be viewed as scholarly explorations or in some cases as reconstructions of childhood. The words *children* and *childhood* are bound by their respective theoretical spaces, even though they share an etymological root and overlapping domains—configurations of differences that fundamentally enrich the scholarly voices and approaches taken in this collection. Amanda Minks's afterword offers a critical synthesis of notions of difference as manifested in this collection's essays and discusses the essays' engagement with contemporary theoretical discourses.

When was "childhood" established in the adult imagination? Ariès proposed sixteenth- and seventeenth-century Europe as the birthplace of our modern Western differentiation between pre- and postpubescent life (1962: 33–43). His claim, rather dubiously based upon his reading of representations of the young in European visual art, has since been challenged many times (see, e.g., Hanawalt 2002, Kinney 1995, Pollock 1983). Notwithstanding numerous critiques of Ariès's work (see Cunningham 1998), Ariès identified the child as a historical subject and introduced topics in the study of childhood that scholars continue to investigate today. Arguably, the true significance of Ariès's contribution lay less in his identification of a "date of origin" for childhood than in his articulation of and quest for subtler problems: identification of the processes by which the child became established as a distinct entity in the consciousness and imagination of the adult public, and identification of forms or structures within which the child and its life were conceptualized by adults.

For instance, Ariès's insights into educational institutions as early breeding grounds for age-based and behavioral differentiation have far-reaching consequences for the essays in this collection, which illustrate the persistent presence and power of institutions, broadly defined, over musical repertories written for, performed, and consumed by the young. We have grouped the authors' contributions around three categories that might be viewed as flexible points of reference for the variegated outcomes that may or may not result from institutional power over the young and their music.

Part 1, "Ritual Performance," gleans new evidence for notions of childhood operative in medieval, early modern, and contemporary systems of belief and offers fresh insights into the activities of young musicians who had specialized roles in their communities. In the first essay, a music historian and a social historian join the ranks of those who have offered evidence to refute Ariès's much-debated claim that "in medieval society the idea of childhood did not exist" (1962: 128). Susan Boynton and Isabelle Cochelin investigate the role of child oblates in the Burgundian abbey of Cluny in eleventh-century France, correlating the oblates' musical duties with their functions within the monastery's fundamentally hierarchical structure. The essay offers a rare glimpse of music making by children in the cloister—a crucial site for educational endeavors in this period—as documented by adult supervisors under institution-specific circumstances. Todd Borgerding's study of choirboys in early modern Spain reveals pre-Enlightenment notions of children: they had distinct theological and rhetorical functions as bodily reminders of institutionalized ideals of purity, and their high voices shaped the musical style of the polyphonic repertory in significant ways. In both essays, the nature and practices of religious institutions emerge as cyclical entities into which children were musically, physically, and mentally socialized: adults transformed the religious beliefs that dictated and sanctioned their actions by choreographing children's sounds, bodies, and minds into living reminders of the very same beliefs.

The essay by Anne Dhu McLucas centers on the multiple meanings of ritual performance. Her analysis of a Mescalero Apache puberty rite for young girls reveals the unifying role of music and the conceptual breadth underlying the understanding of sound among girls undergoing the ritual. The girls' dancing is integral to their transformation from childhood to adulthood, as is, paradoxically, their silence, whose power has been prescribed by tradition.

Part 2, "Identity Formation," foregrounds the manifold associations of childhood with music in the minds of individuals who practice it. These four essays grapple with and explicate what may be described as the veiled influences of institutions on the psychological structuring of individual identity. Such structures form (and sometimes endure) as a result of how individuals interact with music and its communities during their formative years—interactions that are largely unquestioned, ubiquitous though they are over the globe. The essays in this part embrace social-scientific and historical approaches. Steven Huebner looks beyond traditional Freudian interpretations of Maurice Ravel's lyric ballet *L'Enfant et les sortilèges;* drawing upon theories of child development by Jean Piaget, Huebner probes the ballet's quasi-fairy-tale plot for clues of attitudes toward child-rearing and child development in fin de siècle Paris.

Autobiographical narrative can foreground the intersection of learning music and growing up in an ethnic community. The ex-colony Malaysia is the setting for Roe-Min Kok's memories of learning Western classical piano via the British-based Associated Board of the Royal Schools of Music. Using postcolonial theory, she addresses issues of reception and identity formation that resulted from the transmission of Western classical music into a specific non-Western society. This account draws upon childhood memories and highlights the informal and loose, yet highly complex and influential, relationships that develop between the institutions of family and society within which children are often doubly—and unwittingly—ensconced.

Patricia Tang's essay grapples with ways in which memories of childhood may be used in ethnographic case studies. In conducting interviews—Western-academy-style—with Senegalese griots (musicians by blood lineage), Tang finds that griots privilege and present information about their childhoods in ways that they think will ultimately buttress their musical significance and "authenticity" in the eyes of Western researchers, whose chronicles are perceived by griots as instruments of cultural validation.

Traditions acquire immense, if often veiled, power as they are institutionalized over the course of time and through long practice. They represent a force to which children and their experiences are often exposed, by which children may be silenced, or which they may eventually choose to silence as adults. Heather Willoughby delves into the role of tradition in the professionalization and ritualized coming-of-age of three Korean female *p'ansori* singers, one of them a character in a recent popular film. The strict social and musical conventions governing the training and practice of the singers' chosen art become standards of excellence to which they must measure up but also complicate the singers' personal life choices as young women in a traditional Confucian society.

The politics of youth identity and its role in shaping musical traditions link part 2 to part 3, "Musical Socialization." Part 3 comprises three essays on the inculcation of cultural-political norms in diverse geographic and historical contexts. These case studies highlight the transformations, appropriations, and displacements of musical traditions through which young people learn values in the process of engaging with music. Institutions in three continents (Asia, Europe, and North America) wield varying power over music in the lives of the young. The essays document the essentially unstable nature of such power, as youths tend to form their own particularized responses and behaviors to ideas received, thus proving to be active, unpredictable agents during and after the time they spend within the parameters of institutional control.

Joy Calico exposes the social-political motivations behind the creation of Hanns Eisler's *New German Folk Songs,* folk songs commissioned by the German Democratic Republic to inculcate socialist ideals in the young with the aim of constructing a "new" German identity. Calico's essay includes concrete evidence for the songs' reception history, collected from questionnaires she distributed among and collected from those who had sung the songs in their youth. Hermann Gottschewski and Machiko Gottschewski discuss the politically sanctioned importation of Western classical music into Japan since the end of the nineteenth century, the music's cultural impact on Japanese youth, and new Japanese musical genres that have resulted from the process.

Judah Cohen shows that youth recognize, participate in, circumvent but also manipulate the strictures of institutional pressures to suit their own needs. Drawing upon fieldwork in an American Reform Jewish summer camp in upstate New York, Cohen focuses on the religious-educational phenomenon of songleading, which he finds is (unusually enough) propagated and mediated by the young participants to shape their own musical-religious culture, and which thereafter plays a crucial role in their adult identities.

Diverse as they appear, the musical traditions in this book (which are often separated in traditional scholarly discourse) share connections in function, experience, and meaning that will be discussed here and in the afterword.

All the essays show that engaging with music as a child cannot be equated with exclusively sonic experiences. Along with musical sounds and knowledge, children absorb behavioral norms and cultural values within a process that has often been termed "enculturation," or more recently, "musical socialization" (see Minks 2002). The participation of young musicians directly and profoundly affects musical repertories and their social contexts. Several essays address this phenomenon in relation to national identities; other forms of group identity come into play as well. For instance, religious beliefs foster environments where identity and music are bound together in ritual performance. The first and last essays in this book (by Boynton and Cochelin, and by Cohen) illustrate the fusion of social and religious education with singing, while Borgerding and McLucas discuss the shaping of performer/audience identities through ritual. Thus learning music, and performing music in a ritualized context, often intersects with learning one's place in a group or in society as a whole. These observations confirm the current understanding of teaching and learning music as "a process that is embedded in social and cultural values and meanings" (McCarthy 2002: 563).

Another issue-at-large is the role of bodily discipline in the formation of children through music. Musical performance is a somatic act in which physical control is implicitly assumed as well as overtly displayed, and striving for such mastery is an essential component of musical training. The corporeal conditioning of the young via the practice of music (a practice that often involves ritualization in some form) emerges as a theme in several essays. For example, Willoughby argues that bodily suffering is a prerequisite to musical perfection for a Korean *p'ansori* singer. Kok demonstrates that learning physical gestures and linguistic phrases from another culture is part of the act of studying Western music in a non-Western setting.

Boynton and Cochelin show that children in a medieval European monastery assimilated their roles in the community and absorbed its rituals through imitation; similarly, the Senegalese musicians interviewed by Tang learned to play at an early age by creating their own instruments and ensembles in emulation of the adult ones they saw around them. Beating on drums is as much part of their basic physical experiences of childhood as learning to walk or discovering the limits of their strength. While drawn from different historical contexts, all these studies point up the ways in which musical knowledge and traditions come with values that are transmitted in sonic but also physical experiences. We may conclude that institutionalized mimicry is fundamental to musical apprenticeship, particularly in societies where learning consists primarily of observing and imitating other musicians. Children's bodies are repositories for the rituals of learning music; on a very fundamental level, the young represent embodied memories of their societies' culture.

Physical and/or social power does not necessarily accompany children's music, or music making, however. Hierarchical relationships are inherent to instruction that takes the form of rote learning with a master teacher, whether the students are medieval monastic oblates, *p'ansori* singers, or Colette's fictional child. While musical apprenticeship may ultimately result in the empowerment of the young learner (as detailed by McLucas, by Tang, and by Cohen), it can require subjection of the self so painful as to be physically or psychologically disturbing (see the essays by Kok, Boynton and Cochelin, and Willoughby).

All the essays grapple with issues of representation, as most extant historical sources are not written from a child's perspective. Indeed, the child may be considered among "history's most frustratingly mute agents" (Kok 2003a: 3). Even writers' reflections on their own youth, such as the famous reminiscences in the *Confessions* of Augustine and Rousseau, are by their very nature the fruits of maturity. For the most part, children have little or no power over how they are represented by adults. The essays in this collection represent, re-represent, and deconstruct representations of children and childhood, a topic that has long been of interest to art historians and literary scholars. Confronting their subjects creatively, authors in this book have used a diverse array of sources that mention children and/or childhood directly or indirectly: transcriptions of interviews, field notes, questionnaires, historical texts, musical scores, memory and autobiography, monastic regulations, ecclesiastical and governmental legislation, theories of child development, political theory, and propaganda.

Among the several methodologies represented here, ethnography or methods informed by ethnography prove particularly useful for avoiding exclusively adult perspectives and gaining insight into the elusive phenomenon recently termed "children's culture."[3] Patricia Shehan Campbell (1998) has studied the production and experience of music by young people who act as distinct agents in forming their own music cultures in addition to assimilating and reproducing adults' conceptions of music making, a view to which Cohen's study adds.

Childhood and adolescence have always been and continue to be meaningful sites for musical interactions. Given the interdisciplinary nature of the subject, the contents of this book will speak to ethnomusicologists, music educators, and music and social historians, as well as to scholars of cultural studies, anthropology, and psychology. We believe that the unusually wide range of subjects and diversity of approaches offered here will impart a fresh look at the vast potential inherent in the study of music and youth, expose links between living and past musical traditions, and point to manifold possibilities for future scholarship.[4]

◆ Acknowledgments

Our sincere thanks to each and every one of our contributors for their enthusiasm and patience, to Suzanna Tamminen, director of Wesleyan University Press, for her unflinching support and wise guidance, to the anonymous readers for Wesleyan University Press for their many helpful suggestions, and to Jaime Madell for his assistance with the musical examples. We are also grateful to our families, and to Christoph Neidhoefer, Jens Ulff-Moeller, Steven Huebner, Julie Cumming, and Lloyd Whitesell for their encouragement and belief in this project.

Notes

1. Recent examples include Kok 2003a, Pesic 2001–2, Knapp 1999, Appel 1998, Metzer 1997, Eicker 1995, and Appel 1994.

2. See Kok 2003a for an interdisciplinary bibliography.

3. Arnheim 1998, Fineberg 1997, and Golomb 2002 provide useful analogies in the field of child art. We thank David Rosand for bringing Fineberg's work to our attention.

4. This collection traces its origins to the panel "Discourse of Power, Discourse of Play: Music of Childhood and Its Institutions," organized by Roe-Min Kok for the Seventeenth International Congress of the International Musicological Society, August 1–7, 2002 (Catholic University of Leuven, Belgium).

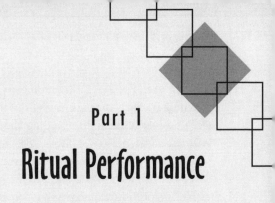

Part 1
Ritual Performance

Part 1 explores the roles of young people in the performance and meaning of ritual. Ritual is notoriously difficult to define.[1] For the purposes of this book, the term refers to repeated, structured actions following specific rules and endowed with symbolic meaning, and often with religious significance. The essays in this part emphasize the nonverbal elements that provide an essential ingredient in the perceived meaning of ritual performance, understood to include the sacred subdivision of ritual action known as liturgy. A recent definition of liturgy as "the arena of intense communication of cultural values and the negotiation of power within social formations at given historical moments" (Flanigan, Ashley, and Sheingorn 2001: 714) can be applied equally well to the diverse historical, social, and geographic contexts of these three essays.[2]

Ritual can communicate the fundamental concerns of a community as well as shape corporate and individual identity. As Catherine Bell (1992: 220) has pointed out, ritual is not an isolated phenomenon, for it cannot be entirely separated from other activities and takes on meaning in relation to them: "Ritual acts must be understood within a semantic framework whereby the significance of an action is dependent upon its place and relationship within a context of all other ways of acting: what it echoes, what it inverts, what it alludes to, what it denies."

While many see ritual as an expression or a sublimation of power, Bell (1992: 197–218) stresses the creative dimension of ritual performance, arguing that ritual engenders power rather than representing or constructing it. In performance, ritual realizes and reifies symbolic relationships that intersect with social structures. Performance was part of an ongoing process of study that was itself ritualized (Boynton 2000).[3]

Ritual performance also functions as a bearer of meaning for participant and observer alike. As Borgerding shows, the image of the choirboys in Seville was constructed not only by performers in religious ceremonies, but also by witnesses who were likely to be aware of their symbolic implications. In a living culture such as the one studied by McLucas, the content of ritual may be understood differently by participants defined as "insiders" and observers identified as "outsiders." Thus ritual is "a culturally constructed system of symbolic communication" that is performative in several ways, as noted by Tambiah (1979: 119): it is an action as well as a statement, its signification constructed by the participants.

Nonverbal communication in various forms is essential to the meaning of ritual. Gesture and dance, the physical appearance of the participants, and sound are all important elements in ritual performance. Although not usually identified as a distinct parameter in ritual theory, singing and other forms of sound create meaning in ritual as much as words or gestures. Studies of ritual that have addressed the role of young people have focused primarily on rites of passage without taking into account their musical dimensions. These three essays expand the field by bringing the musical role of young people to bear upon the ritual function of music.

—*Susan Boynton*

Notes

1. For an overview of theories of ritual, see Bell 1997: 1–92.

2. This was originally formulated as a description of liturgy in the European Middle Ages.

3. For another example of the ritualization of learning in a medieval religious community, see Marcus 1996.

The Sociomusical Role of Child Oblates at the Abbey of Cluny in the Eleventh Century

SUSAN BOYNTON AND ISABELLE COCHELIN

Life in a medieval monastery revolved around the celebration of the liturgy. Monks spent most of their waking hours singing eight offices and two masses distributed throughout the day according to a regular schedule. In addition to these daily rituals, processions and other ceremonies enriched the services on Sundays and important feast days in the church calendar. From the office of Matins in the dark hours before dawn to the final office of Compline in the evening before the monks retired to sleep, the monastic experience was shaped and articulated by liturgical performance. Singing together for several hours a day was not only the central activity of the community but also the formative experience of its members, who tended to grow up in the monastic environment from an early age.

From the earlier Middle Ages to the early twelfth century, the majority of the newcomers in male and female monasteries in Western Europe were children aged between three and fourteen who had been offered by their parents as a gift to God.[1] This offering was known as an oblation, and the young monks and nuns were called oblates.[2] In order to help his readers understand this phenomenon, which has become "repugnant to the feelings of western Europe,"[3] the medieval historian Richard Southern (1953: 162) used a vivid image: he compared the oblates to a conscript army and contrasted this group with the "volunteer army" that filled the male monasteries beginning in the twelfth century with the rise of adult vocations.[4] Female monasteries did not evolve in the same way, and their mode of recruitment remained both more stable and more complex; families went on using the nunneries as temporary or definitive abodes for their unmarried daughters as well as for their widows.[5] This study is centered on male oblates rather than on oblates of both

3

sexes, because the sources offer much more information on boys than on girls, and the transformation in the status of male oblates is inseparable from the evolution of medieval (essentially male) writings on childhood.[6] Our focus is the hundred years before the transformation that took place in male monasteries during the twelfth century.

Our discussion connects the status of oblates in the Burgundian abbey of Cluny to their liturgical activities from the end of the tenth century to the end of the eleventh. Although at the bottom of the hierarchical structure of the foremost monastery in medieval Western Europe, children played a fundamental role in its daily life, especially in its notoriously time-consuming and awe-inspiring liturgy. In order to contextualize our analysis of the role of child musicians at Cluny as well as to introduce the principal issues in the history of childhood, the first part of this essay surveys the historiography of medieval childhood along with the methodological problems it presents, followed by an introduction to the abbey of Cluny and its importance for the study of childhood. We then place the musical activities of Cluniac oblates within the context of liturgy and ritual, which constituted a form of education and training, and thus an integral part of the broader learning process that guided young monks to adulthood.

The education of young singers at Cluny relied heavily upon a comprehensive physical discipline that served to instill in them the structures of hierarchy within the monastic community. In the liturgy, as in the rest of monastic life, these structures were performed and thereby imprinted upon the oblates' minds and bodies. The theorist of ritual Catherine Bell has aptly characterized this process as "ritualization": "A ritualized body is a body invested with a 'sense' of ritual. . . . Ritualization produces this ritualized body through the interaction of the body with a structured and structuring environment" (Bell 1992: 98). A medieval monastery such as Cluny was a "structured and structuring environment" both in space and in time; movement through the buildings of a monastic complex was regulated according to ritual codes that endowed the architectural spaces with meaning.[7] In these spaces, the Cluniac oblates were continuously trained throughout days organized around the rhythms of liturgy and ritual, and their musical performance—distinctive and yet integral to the choir of monks—was at the center of the actions that articulated the social structures within the monastic community. The unusual combination of significant musical activity and abundant historical sources makes the oblates of Cluny a useful, even an ideal focus for a new, sociomusical assessment of medieval childhood and music.[8]

◆ The Historiography of Medieval Childhood

Since the 1960 publication of Philippe Ariès's *Centuries of Childhood*, medievalists have taken wildly opposite stands regarding childhood in the Middle Ages. Until the 1970s, they usually endorsed Ariès's point of view, which claimed that the Middle Ages had no real definition of childhood and treated children ruthlessly. Subsequent generations of scholars rejected this perspective, maintaining that there was little difference between contemporary and historical affection for the young. We offer a more balanced approach by drawing upon monastic texts that have been more or less ignored by scholars on both sides of the debate, even though they are among the richest sources for understanding medieval childhood prior to the twelfth century.

The social historian Barbara Hanawalt recently published a review of literature on the history of medieval childhood in the prominent medieval studies journal *Speculum* (Hanawalt 2002). She described the split dividing scholarship and gave a name to each side: under the heading "discontinuity thesis," she grouped Ariès and his followers, and she designated as proponents of the "continuity thesis" most medievalists who have worked on the issue since the late 1970s. Hanawalt ridiculed the arguments of the former group, accurately for the most part. Ariès and his followers were especially mistaken in their claim that, during most of the Middle Ages, childhood was not perceived as a distinct stage in the life cycle. In fact, since late antiquity, ecclesiastics such as Isidore of Seville (†636), including monks such as Bede the Venerable, defined *pueritia*, usually divided between *infantia* (up to age 7) and *pueritia* (up to age 14), as a stage clearly distinct from the rest of the human life cycle.[9] This conception of childhood was not limited to scholarly definitions of the ages, as seen, for instance, in the structural organization of monasteries: while seven was the average age at which children entered the community, fifteen was the age of profession and admission to the group of adult monks.[10]

Hanawalt, however, did not turn the same critical eye on her own "team": she and the other supporters of the continuity thesis have also made serious methodological errors. They have focused almost exclusively on the late Middle Ages but have generalized their conclusions to the entire thousand-year period;[11] they have picked and chosen their sources to support their arguments; they have studied children alone, without trying to understand them in regard to other age groups;[12] and they have overlooked or made unsupported statements regarding the monks' perception and treatment of children. A brief discussion of each of these flaws will demonstrate the complexity of the history of medieval childhood and clarify the rationale for the narrower focus we have adopted in this article.

Two wonderfully illustrated books have been published on medieval children in the last ten years (Riché and Alexandre-Bidon 1994; Orme 2002). Given the beauty of their illustrations and the simplicity of their texts, which praise almost unconditionally the tenderness of medieval parents for their children,[13] one cannot help but wonder whether the publishers of these books were not trying to attract the attention and spending power of modern parents in search of a mirror reflecting an idealized image of themselves from a distant past. Moreover, both books manifest a striking tendency to focus on the late Middle Ages and even the Renaissance while applying the conclusions to the whole medieval period. For instance, Orme rejects Ariès's claim that children were almost never depicted during the Middle Ages; he affirms instead that there were numerous medieval representations but does not provide specific references to these images.[14] The illustrations in Orme's own book come almost exclusively from the fifteenth and sixteenth centuries. Orme (2002: 4–10) admits occasionally that the perception and treatment of children might have evolved between the early and the late Middle Ages, but he does not reflect on this change or explicitly consider the period before 1200.

Except for a very few studies such as Sally Crawford's on Anglo-Saxon childhood (1999) and Didier Lett's on "French" childhood (although France did not yet exist at the time),[15] no serious attempt has ever been made to examine the history of medieval children before the "renaissance" of the twelfth century, even though historians agree that this century may have been a turning point in the medieval conceptualization of childhood.[16] Changes in spirituality during the twelfth century led to a new representation of childhood in ecclesiastical writings, and both these developments seem inseparable from the decline of oblation. From the twelfth century onward, during childhoods now spent more often in the lay world, monks had more time to observe children in the context of family love, and once cloistered, they had fewer occasions to ponder the great difficulty of molding children into angels. However, in the preceding centuries (in the early and central Middle Ages), most extant written sources come from monasteries, but attempts by scholars to decipher the medieval monastic conception and treatment of childhood have been superficial and inconsistent; as a result, the distinctive character of the depiction of childhood before the twelfth century has essentially gone unnoticed.

The two authors cited above, Crawford and Lett, included monastic texts in their corpus of primary sources, but not in a systematic manner.[17] Such a methodology tends to privilege texts that strengthen one's initial hypothesis. For instance, in order to demonstrate monks' regard for children, Lett mentioned the four positive traits associated with childhood by a handful of writers, mainly monastic. Jerome, later copied by the encyclopedist Isidore of Seville as well as by the monastic writers Columban, Bede the Venerable, and Smaragdus, had claimed that the child does not persevere in anger, does not remember offences, is not delighted by the sight of a beautiful woman, and does not say one thing and think another.[18] Neither Lett, nor Pierre Riché, in whose writings Lett had found this list of children's qualities, acknowledged that the simple repetition of a text can be symptomatic of limited interest in the issue it presents, nor did they try to understand the context of these statements (Hayward 1994: 76–77).[19] Rather than simply concluding that monks had a positive image of childhood, they should have pondered the fact that Jerome's list of qualities was actually an inventory of negatives, centered more on the potential sins of adults than on the qualities of children. Jerome sought to elucidate Christ's saying that one has to humble oneself like a child to occupy a significant position in Heaven: "So whoever will humble himself like that little one, he will be greater in the kingdom of heaven."[20] Thus he was explaining to his (mostly adult) readers how to behave.

This last observation leads us to the final methodological problem we wish to discuss: the tendency to focus on children while disregarding the role of adults. Such an approach would seem unthinkable were we to replace "children" with, say, "women." One cannot understand the conception and treatment of a group simply by collecting sentences dealing with its members. It is necessary to compare and contrast their situation to that of other groups, particularly the ones with which they interact regularly. The most interesting studies on childhood to date are the ones that have avoided this pitfall, such as Sally Crawford's chapter on cemeteries (1999), James Schultz's book on childhood in Middle High German texts (1995), or Doris Desclais Berkvam's work, too little known, on medieval children and mothers in twelfth- and thirteenth-century courtly texts (1981).[21]

In this essay, we analyze the treatment of and discourse on Cluniac oblates with reference to adults as well, particularly when discussing the issue of status. Moreover, having based our research on the entirety of one genre of sources of one monastic community (the customaries associated with the abbey of Cluny), we hope to avoid the dangers of picking and choosing information too selectively.[22] Finally, by studying this community primarily in the eleventh century, we wish to initiate the much-needed process of studying the medieval monastic conception of childhood before the twelfth century.

◆ The Abbey of Cluny and Monastic Childhood

In its wealth and political importance, Cluny was an exceptional monastery and therefore cannot provide a truly representative case of child oblation practices in the central Middle Ages.[23] Nevertheless, many other communities strove to imitate its way of life, so understanding the role of young male oblates in this eminent Burgundian abbey helps us to understand what the society of the central Middle Ages intended to do with these members of their religious communities.

Cluny was founded in 910 by William, Duke of Aquitaine. From the viewpoint of tenth- and eleventh-century onlookers, as well as of modern scholars, the Burgundian abbey was remarkable in two ways. First, it was independent from all exterior interventions, under the direct authority of Saint Peter and Saint Paul, and protected by the papacy: neither lay lord nor local bishop was allowed to interfere with its affairs. This first characteristic did not particularly affect the issues discussed in this essay, except for the fact that their sheltered cloister afforded the Cluniacs the necessary freedom to attempt to build their space into a threshold to Paradise and to transform themselves into terrestrial angels. Inseparable from this last concern, the second feature that distinguished Cluny from other monasteries was its remarkable customs or way of life. In the prevalently oral world of the tenth and eleventh centuries, the Cluniac customs were diffused inside and outside of Cluny primarily through direct observation and imitation. Oblates and novices imitated their elders, while monks from other monasteries came sometimes from far away to study the way of life at the Burgundian abbey and Cluniac monks were sent throughout Europe to reform other abbeys.[24]

The Cluniac customs were so sought out that they were also sometimes recorded; written descriptions of them were obtained in the eleventh century by several monasteries wishing to imitate or learn about life at Cluny. These customaries exist in four different versions, written for different audiences between approximately 1000 and 1080. No other medieval monastery can claim such a rich corpus of customaries, because none could boast such a renowned way of life. Written usually by anonymous authors for other monasteries in order to facilitate their attempt to imitate the Cluniac monks, the customaries are not purely prescriptive, but rather descriptive (Cochelin 2005). Therefore, they constitute an ideal window through which to view the Cluniac conception and treatment of children. The customaries are in fact one of our principal sources for the study of the Cluniac liturgy (see Boynton 2005) and particularly our main source of information for the study of the status and activities of the oblates.

In the earliest version from circa 1000, which scholars have designated the *consuetudines antiquiores* (the "older customs"),[25] the customary takes the form of a liturgical ordinal, listing the prayers, chants, and gestures performed throughout the year during the mass, divine office, processions, and other rituals such as the washing of the feet (*mandatum*). In the three more recent customaries, dated circa 1040 for the *Liber tramitis* (literally the "Book of the Path"),[26] and circa 1080–85 for the customaries of Ulrich of Zell and Bernard of Cluny,[27] about one-half to one-third of the contents comprise the ordinal, while the rest concerns the daily life of the monks. On this last issue, these sources are so detailed that they tell us, for instance, all the steps followed by the monks to cook their beans[28] or the measures taken by a brother after a wet dream.[29] Customaries explain most activities of the monks at all times of the day throughout the year, and passages dedicated specifically to the actions and treatment of children are numerous. Unlike the other important sources for the history of early medieval childhood (the lives of saints), the customaries are not centered on exceptional children but evoke the daily life of the average child in the monastic community.

On the basis of the information offered by the Cluniac customaries, it is possible to formulate an hypothesis on the percentage of children aged between three and fourteen in the community at Cluny, as well as observe their decreasing importance with respect to the overall monastic population over the course of the second half of the eleventh century. The *Liber tramitis* tells us that two days a week the children were in charge of the daily *mandatum* or maundy, a ritual foot washing of poor laypeople framed by the singing of chants and the recitation of prayers. It was performed by monks in remembrance of Christ doing the same service to the apostles on Maundy Thursday and asking them to repeat this gesture later on. The participation of the oblates in this ritual illustrates their total inclusion in the elect group of the brothers: they formed a distinct but integrated unit within the community. On Saturday and Sunday, two children washed the paupers' feet, accompanied by one adult (the abbot on one day, and the children's teacher on the other).[30] Given that responsibility for the *mandatum* rested equally on the shoulders of all the brothers at Cluny, the prescriptions in the *Liber tramitis* suggest that children represented approximately one-fifth of the community by the mid–eleventh century. This proportion is fairly typical of the population of other monasteries, both contemporary and earlier ones.[31] However, by the late eleventh century, according to the customary of Bernard, the children accompanied by an adult were now in charge of the *mandatum* only once a week.[32] This seems to indicate that their proportion had dropped to only a ninth or a tenth. Given that over the same period (from the mid–eleventh to the late eleventh century) the claustral population of Cluny apparently increased from one hundred monks to at least two hundred,[33] in the middle of the century there must have been about twenty children, or slightly more, and about eighty adult monks, while later on, the number of adults exceeded that of children by a far greater proportion. Cluny, with its children, its young adults (called "adolescents under surveillance"),[34] its adults, and even its very old monks, should be understood (like any other male or female monastery of the time) as an attempt to create a perfect world with (theoretically) no sex and all ages represented. Of this ideal microcosm, the children were an essential part, filling a specific niche—especially with regard to the liturgy.

Why did parents give their children to monasteries? In his book *The Kindness of Strangers,* John Boswell (1988: 228) offered an original explanation for oblation as an institution devised by the medieval church to take care of children who would have been otherwise abandoned or killed by their parents. It is intriguing that the best argument for this thesis appears in the introduction to one of the Cluniac customaries, the one written by the German monk Ulrich of Zell. In his prefatory letter, he violently criticizes parents who rid themselves of their physically or mentally handicapped children by giving them to monasteries.[35] However, one must treat this statement with caution, placing it in context and not generalizing it to the whole history of oblation. Ulrich had entered Cluny as an adult convert,[36] and his attack on oblation was partly motivated by his personal frustration that oblates, having reached adulthood, could monopolize some positions of prestige in the cloister. This monopoly was probably mainly due to their greater mastery of the customs and liturgical texts. Ulrich complains, for instance, of the power of the *armarius,* one of the most important officers, who was in charge of both the library and the liturgy, and who had to be an oblate.[37] Moreover, he was writing at the end of the eleventh century, at a time when the practice of oblation had already begun to be seriously challenged by the entrance in the monasteries of an increasing number of adult converts, all highly motivated and some very well educated, such as Ulrich himself.[38] In fact, these adult converts had become so numerous by the end of the eleventh century that the new orders that were founded at the time, such as the Carthusian and the Cistercian orders, were able to forbid entrance to children.[39] More and more often, these adult converts were able to appropriate positions of power.[40] Fewer offices were therefore left for the oblates once they became adults. Within this context of the decline of oblation as an institution, it is possible that "dumping" of unwanted children, especially mentally or physically handicapped ones, had become increasingly significant among the large array of reasons justifying oblation from the parents' point of view. However, in the previous decades and centuries, great piety inspired by the biblical story of Samuel, offered to the Temple as a child, or the desire to have a family advocate in the midst of a powerful religious, economic, and political institution were other predominant motivations downplayed by Boswell. Finally, whether an offering, an investment, or an abandonment, oblation to Cluny was not an option for the peasantry but was reserved for only the highest echelons of society.

The integration of the oblates inside the Cluniac community was grounded in the definitive character of their membership: even though they did not make their solemn monastic profession until puberty, they could not choose to leave the monastery once given to it by their parents. The oblation was accomplished in front of witnesses to make sure that the child would never "raise his neck from the yoke of the rule."[41] Occasionally, powerful parents could find powerful arguments to convince the monastery to let their son go, especially if circumstances had suddenly made him the sole heir of the family land, but the practice must have been rare for at least two reasons. First, in the Frankish world, courtiers' qualities were not yet in great demand, as royal and ducal courts had declined[42] and lords prized primarily warlike qualities in their heirs and faithful followers; noble parents gave to the church their sons who were the most inadequate to the secular world—those with poor physical ability.[43] Second, these sons, who had arrived in the cloister at a very early age, would have faced tremendous difficulties adjusting to the battlefield later in life. As monastic sources of the eleventh century proudly point out, the oblates did not learn skills such as hunting and going to war.[44] Child monks were trained instead for the life of terrestrial angels, unceasingly praising God, especially in chant and prayer, and kept ignorant of sexuality. According to the worldview of medieval monks, children in the monastery had to be molded carefully to overcome the stain of original sin and the tendencies of carnal beings, so that later on they might achieve monastic perfection.[45]

The most striking facet of the way the Cluniacs treated their oblates (as compared to the adults in the community) is the importance given their bodies, a multifarious phenomenon that can be explained in various ways. Medieval children formed the most fragile section of society, as they belonged to the age group with the highest mortality rate: between thirty and fifty percent of children died before the age of twenty. In this context, it is understandable that the Cluniacs paid close attention to the physical well-being of oblates, for instance by easing their entrance into the infirmary,[46] placing the coals heating the refectory in winter closer to them,[47] and offering them additional food during the day.[48] But the monks were also afraid of these prepubescent bodies that represented potential objects of desire in a world devoid of women.[49] The customaries show that the Cluniacs took great precautions to prevent physical contact between adult monks and oblates. In the sections of the texts dedicated to the oblates, this subject is second in importance only to the descriptions of their liturgical activities. Because Cluny tried to model its inhabitants into angels and make its space into the antechamber of Paradise, the monks sought particularly to avoid every possible form of sexual pollution. As a result, the movements of the children and their contact with the adults were under very close scrutiny by the teachers; the customaries of Ulrich and Bernard closed their chapters on children with the statement that no child of a king was raised with more supervision in a palace than the smallest boy at Cluny.[50]

This heightened sensitivity to the carnality of children[51] was probably inseparable from the fact that the Cluniacs usually placed them at the bottom of the hierarchical structure of the monastery.[52] At least until the middle of the eleventh century, hierarchy was based primarily on seniority: the longer monks had worn the cowl, the more admirable and angelic they were considered, having demonstrated in the long term their faithful observance of the monastic way of life (especially regarding chastity and obedience) and loyalty to the house they had entered (*stabilitas loci*). The children were considered by their fellow monks so far away from these higher ranks that they were partially excluded from the rule of seniority: they were placed below all adults, whether or not the latter were recent converts. In doing so, the Cluniacs contradicted the Rule of Saint Benedict, which asked that seniority be applied to all.[53] The system of seniority is of central importance because the spaces and activities of Cluniac daily life were structured according to hierarchy: children and adult monks sat in the refectory, in the choir, in the chapter house, and in the exterior world, walked in procession, went to the garden, and washed the feet of the poor all according to their order in the hierarchy.[54]

The assignment of status is not a static phenomenon, however. In the second half of the eleventh century changes in the system occurred as a result of the evolution of spirituality, which had led to the increasing numbers of adult converts and the greater importance attached to the celebration of the Eucharist, among other transformations. In the choir, for the greatest religious celebrations, and in most processions, another hierarchy became preponderant: on these special occasions, monks stood no longer according to their seniority within the community but according to their ecclesiastical rank. In this context, oblates who had become subdeacons were normally placed above new converts coming from the lay world.[55] In other words, from the late eleventh century onward, for the most important celebrations, child monks no longer occupied the lowest echelons of the community: age was now considered a less significant marker of inferior status than distance from the Eucharist and a close association with the lay world.

◆ The Cluniac Oblates in the Monastic Liturgy

Whether based on seniority or ordination, hierarchy played a fundamental role in the liturgy and oblates had to learn to master it.[56] The Cluniac customaries show that the hierarchies performed in church were continuous with the social structures and complex regulations and ritual codes that shaped the oblates' behavior at every moment of the day, through their interactions with the other monks. By singing and reading, as well as by executing prescribed gestures and actions, the community performed the structures of seniority that were inculcated through the discipline of monastic life described meticulously by the customaries. Even as the oblates assimilated this system, they were also perpetuating it and internalizing the rules and codes they would later pass on to others when they joined the ranks of the senior monks. The fact that the *armarius* at Cluny was chosen from among the monks who had been oblates, rather than from among the adult converts, is an illustration of child monks' superior ability to act as keepers and transmitters of customs over time.

Liturgical performance at Cluny illustrates Catherine Bell's interpretation of ritual as fundamentally creative and performative—not only representing, conveying, or constructing relationships of power, but actually engendering them. The customaries indicate the ways in which the performance of the office taught and reinforced the community's understanding of the relationships among its members, including among the children. The *Liber tramitis,* for instance, states that responsories were sung and lessons were read in the order in which the performers had arrived at the monastery: first the younger children, then those who had entered the community earlier. Preparation for the liturgy served to initiate oblates into the structure of the community, which could also be learned through nonmusical activities such as the daily compilation of the list of monks designated to perform the chants and readings.[57] Children participated in the writing of the list and announced it in chapter. They also read from the martyrology and the memorial book and thus were responsible for notifying the community when the thirtieth day after a monk's death had passed, and for telling the sacristan when the bells should be rung for the anniversary of a death.[58] On the first day of Lent, it was a boy who read aloud the chapter of the Benedictine Rule regarding the distribution of books to the monks.[59] A boy also read in chapter when the monks returned from performing manual labor. The children went ahead of the community as it processed from the workplace singing psalms. When they first reached the cloister, the boys raised their voices; thereafter one of the boys read from a book beginning at the place the *armarius* showed to the boy's teacher. This reading provided the theme for a sermon by the prior.[60]

Just as in communities outside the monastery, children in monastic communities must be studied as part of the larger group, not in isolation from adults. Even as they sang in the office with the rest of the choir, they had a distinct position as well as a carefully delineated musical role. According to the customaries of Bernard and Ulrich, the oblates were supposed to stand facing the west, between the two choirs of monks, so that they could be seen by the older monks who stood near them.[61]

The entire choir probably sang choral chants such as the ordinary of the mass and the hymns of the divine office, but for some other parts of the liturgical repertory younger and adult monks had slightly different musical functions. One can extrapolate these differences from the Cluniac customaries. The assignment of a chant or reading to a child represents the exception that needs to be specified. It seems that the choir of adults and adult soloists sang the majority of the more elaborate chants of the mass and office (such as alleluias, tracts, graduals, offertories, and great responsories). A senior monk was in charge of the direction of the choir during the principal mass of the day and the hours of the divine office. It is not clear whether the schola, or choir of the oblates, always sang with the adult choir in addition to the chants specifically assigned to them. The children must have participated in the psalmody of the office, but we do not know whether they sang in octaves with the men or in alternation with them.

The customaries from Cluny state that oblates intoned psalms and hymns, chanted litanies, and sang both simple and more complex chants. That the assignment of chants to specific groups or members of the community is for the most part not stated in liturgical books enhances the importance of customaries as sources of information on the performance of the liturgy. Bernard's account of the oblates' liturgical responsibilities concludes: "[They] pronounce the versicles of each psalm at all the canonical hours, intone the antiphons on ferial days, and intone whatever is sung at the morning mass, unless it is a major feast day; at Lauds and Vespers, they sing a responsory and say the versicles; in the summer at Matins they say the single short lesson; they always read in chapter, never in the refectory."[62] Several of the items mentioned by Bernard are among the simpler musical compositions, particularly the versicles sung during the office, brief responsories of Lauds and Vespers, the litanies, and the *Benedicamus domino,* a versicle performed at or near the conclusion of an office.[63] The performance of these chants by high voices must have created a particular aural aesthetic associating them not only with a certain kind of sound but perhaps also, by extension, with symbolic signification and contrast with the rest of the community. The *Benedicamus domino,* in particular, has a liminal function as a concluding chant. The boys themselves exercised a liminal function; the office could not begin until they arrived with their teachers, and they were the first to leave the choir, an embodied reminder of the temporal boundaries of the offices. This practice may have arisen from the fact that the oblates were the youngest group in the community and consequently the most volatile with regard to discipline.

While it might be assumed that child oblates sang primarily the simpler chants of the liturgy, monastic customaries of the central Middle Ages make it clear that they performed a wide range of musical genres (Boynton 1998).[64] The *Liber tramitis* refers to the oblates performing the fourth, eighth, and twelfth great responsories at the office of Matins on feasts of certain saints. The assignment of these responsories to oblates is significant because they were the ones that customarily received the greatest liturgical and musical emphasis.[65] Great responsories were not the only soloist chants sung by the oblates; according to the customary of Bernard, two boys sang the gradual at the morning mass for the dead.[66]

Some specific chants were assigned to boys on days of great importance in the church year. According to the *Liber tramitis,* during the night office on Christmas, the children sang responsories while carrying candelabra in procession to the oratory of the Virgin Mary. On Maundy Thursday, a single boy sang the antiphon *Calicem salutaris* ("I will receive the chalice of salvation, and I will call upon the name of the Lord") once all the brothers had assembled in their places for Vespers.[67] A single boy also sang the invitatory antiphon on the day after Easter.[68] The solo performance of these chants by a high voice must have had a special effect, perhaps heightening the solemnity of the occasion by use of a distinctive vocal timbre.

The use of boys' voices for special emphasis was particularly symbolic on Palm Sunday. The itinerary of the procession on Palm Sunday differed from church to church and imitated the triumphal entry of Christ into Jerusalem with stops during which the singing monks enacted symbolic gestures based on the scriptural narrative.[69] According to the earliest Cluniac customaries, the children sing the antiphon *Osanna filio David* at the moment in the procession that evokes the arrival of Christ at the gates of Jerusalem. The text of the antiphon is the words attributed to those greeting him: "Hosanna to the Son of David: blessed is he who comes in the name of the Lord." The performance of this chant by boys effectively represents the action described by one of the antiphons sung during the consecration of the palms: "The children of the Hebrews spread out their garments in the road, and were crying aloud, saying: Hosanna to the son of David; blessed is he who comes in the name of the Lord."[70] Thus the boys "impersonated" the "children of the Hebrews" mentioned in the antiphon text.[71] Later in the procession, a station takes place in which the oblates sing antiphons in front of displayed relics.[72]

Liturgical performance was one of the activities that integrated the oblates into the monastic community at Cluny even as it brought out their difference. The considerable time and energy that were devoted to teaching the oblates suggests that they were an intrinsic part of the Cluniac community aspiring to perfection and angelic status. The customaries sometimes indicate quite explicitly the didactic character of the oblates' participation in the liturgy, particularly in the description of their actions during the ritual performed during the death of a monk. While the rest of the community gathers in the infirmary reciting psalms as the monk dies, the customary of Bernard states that the child oblates should not mix with the monks but rather stand to one side with their teachers so that they can hear and say what the others sing. This provision may have been intended to enable the children to learn the ritual through imitation and limited participation.[73]

Learning to sing and read occupied every free moment of the day, a lengthy process that constituted most if not all of a monk's formal education. The oblates learned chant by listening and then repeating after their teacher, the traditional method of instruction specifically mentioned in the Cluniac customary of Ulrich: "The boys sit in the chapter house, and learn the chant from someone singing it before them."[74] Although the customaries mention that children had access to psalters and hymnaries, as well as other books, for learning texts, it seems that in the eleventh century they were not expected to learn melodies directly from notated chant books. The staffless neumatic notation used at Cluny in this period would communicate only certain kinds of information about the melodies, such as phrasing and text underlay, but not intervallic or pitch content.[75] Supervised practice took place at various times of the day with teachers (*magistri*) who seem to have been responsible primarily for surveillance of the children, demonstrating the importance that the Cluniacs attached to this task. The *armarius* was ultimately responsible for the education of the oblates as well as for the library and the organization of the liturgy. Presumably because of his full schedule, however, most of the instruction of the oblates was entrusted to an assistant, and the *armarius* listened to the children sing and read only after his assistant had already trained them (Cochelin 1996: 253–54). If they made mistakes, he would mete out appropriate punishment: "Every day at dawn, after the boys have read through three psalms, as is the custom, he comes to them without delay, so that he may listen to the one who is to read the lesson in chapter. And if at that time those same boys blunder in any way by singing or reading negligently, or if they learn the chant less diligently, they experience appropriate discipline from him."[76]

Teachers castigated the bodies of the children, who were perceived to be incapable of understanding other forms of punishment,[77] and corporal punishments such as whipping were common, if we are to believe the customaries.[78] Pulling the oblates' hair was also permitted, but no other methods were allowed that might be conducive to physical contact.[79] A fundamental part of the boys' education consisted of learning the proper physical composure and the gestures they had to perform at all times, inside or outside church. They learned chants, ritual words, behaviors, and gestures mostly through imitation of their elders, through physical mimicking, rather than by using books. In this regard, it is significant that the Cluniacs did not find necessary to write down their customs to ease the learning process of their oblates; this was finally accomplished only at the end of the eleventh century, by the monk Bernard, for the adult converts, whose numbers had increased. For the two different age groups, then, two different modes of education were applied (Boynton 2000). The bodies of Cluniac oblates were controlled and directed at all times both inside and outside the church. Surveillance had both negative and positive implications; the monks had to police the children, but they also had to train them in the "angelic" way of life that made Cluny famous in eleventh-century Europe.

◆ Conclusion

The textual sources from eleventh-century Cluny show that oblates' performance in the liturgy embodied their place in the hierarchical organization of the monastery. Even though they were at the bottom of the hierarchy, the children were far from marginalized but rather formed an integral part of the community, and to some extent they represented its future. Even though the oblates were perceived as carnal beings in need of rigorous training to become angelic, they were important participants in the most angelic of the monks' activities: the *opus Dei*.

While the bodies and voices of the child oblates at Cluny were central to liturgical performance, the sources do not tell us about their own perceptions of ritual. Their lives as the future monks of the community were shaped by institutional control. As earthly creatures in the process of a lifelong transformation into an angelic state, the oblates were perceived by adults as extensions of their institutional ideals and ideologies. Sources such as the monastic customaries used in this study provide a particular conception of childhood filtered through the needs and concerns of adults. It is typical of the history of childhood that the children themselves, even singing "angels in training," are ultimately silent.

Notes

1. On oblation and its importance in early medieval monasticism, see de Jong 1996, which states that oblates became the majority of the newcomers in monasteries from the ninth century onward, when Carolingians praised their sexual purity and put emphasis on monastic schools; see also de Jong 1998: 60. More research on this subject is needed, as it is quite possible that oblates were predominant in monasteries even before the ninth century.

2. The two substantives *oblatio* and *oblatus* and their English equivalents, *oblation* and *oblate*, derive from *oblatus*, the past participle of the verb "to offer." The substantive *oblatus* is normally used to designate the child given to the church, but it can also be used to name the same individual once he has become an adult. The same is true for the feminine *oblata*. Since the decline of male oblation, the term oblate has been used inside the Catholic Church for members of very different religious institutions; see Dubois 1973. A child given away to the church or to a lay lord to be educated was also called a *nutritus*, as he was "nourished" physically and intellectually in his foster home.

3. Interestingly enough, this negative remark on oblation comes from one of the greatest historians of English monasticism, a Benedictine contemporary of Southern, David Knowles (1966: 28).

4. On the decline of oblation from the late eleventh century onward, see Berend 1994 and Cochelin 1996: 215–28.

5. The well-known eighteenth-century story of *La religieuse* by Diderot offers a caricature of the practice of enclosing young girls in monasteries without asking for their point of view. On entrance into female monasteries, including oblates',

and the characteristics of female monasticism before the twelfth century, see Parisse 2004.

6. For the high and late Middle Ages, much relevant information on the musical role of girl oblates can be found in Yardley 2006.

7. For a useful introduction to the study of ritual in monastic space, see Bonde and Maines 2003.

8. For an analogous approach to boy singers in a later period, see Dumont 2004. Although Cambrai cathedral was a secular, not a regular religious institution, and the boys in the choir school there were not permanent members of the cathedral chapter, they lived in a communal residence, and their education and musical roles were comparable to those of oblates at Cluny.

9. See Sears 1986; Burrow 1986; and Cochelin 1996: 55–59 and annexe C.

10. This division of the life cycle was also meaningful for life outside of the monasteries, as the initiation of children into the world of adult activities would often start at home or in a foster home, around age seven, and by the age of fourteen boys could marry, an essential rite of passage into adulthood in the Middle Ages. On the importance of these two ages, especially male puberty (around the age of fourteen or fifteen) in medieval canon law, see for instance Metz 1976. Like most medievalists, Metz was struck by the lack of clarity in medieval vocabulary concerning the ages, but it is clearer, more realistic, and more logical than it appears; see Cochelin 1996.

11. Shulamith Shahar (1990: ix) avoids this pitfall by specifying in her preface (although not in her title) that her monograph concerns the twelfth through fifteenth centuries. However, she uses monastic sources from the ninth, tenth, and eleventh centuries, including Cluniac customaries, without reflecting on their relevance to a later period (84–203). More generally, whether because of a tentative use of psychology or a desire to be exhaustive, the contradictions and overgeneralizations limit the usefulness of the book for historians of medieval childhood.

12. Barbara Hanawalt avoided these three methodological errors in her first book dealing with childhood (1986); this work remains a remarkable study of age groups in the English peasantry of the fourteenth and fifteenth centuries. However, in "Medievalists and the Study of Childhood" (2002) she seems oversensitive to the debate between the continuity and the discontinuity theses and therefore defines her corpus of sources in order to substantiate her support for the former. See also Hanawalt 1993.

13. See, for instance, Alexandre-Bidon and Lett 2000, 52: "The child is born, and the whole family is moved. The mother, the nurse, and even the father gather around this small creature and give themselves over to the joys and cares of what will be called childraising" ("L'enfant est né, et la famille en est toute émue. Mère, nourrice et même père s'empressent autour de ce petit être et s'adonnent aux joies et aux soucis de ce qu'on appellera la 'puériculture'").

14. A much sounder criticism of Ariès's claim is found in Pastoureau 1997.

15. See Alexandre-Bidon and Lett 2000: 7–69.

16. On this issue, see especially Herlihy 1978 and Boquet 1999.

17. Another recent study with a chapter on childhood based partly on monastic sources is Real 2001. While Real offers a remarkable study of all the hagiographical sources of the Merovingian period, she did not try to understand the authors' worldview, including their perception of childhood, but rather bypassed the authorial issues to discuss the lay world as depicted in the texts. Methodologically speaking, this approach is problematic for the study of hagiography.

18. "Sicut iste paruulus, cuius uobis exemplum tribuo, non perseuerat in iracundia, non laesus meminit, non uidens pulchram mulierem delectatur, non aliud cogitat, et aliud loquitur, sic et uos nisi talem habueritis innocentiam et animi puritatem, regna caelorum non poteritis intrare" (Jerome 1979: 48–50). Comparable passages appear in Isidore of Seville, *Quaestio* 40 (*Patrologia cursus completus, series latina* [*PL*] 83: 207A); Columban, letter 2, paragraph 8 (2001: 42–43), Bede the Venerable 1960: 559; and Smaragdus (*PL* 102: 655–56). Most of these authors added at least one caveat to their list, that one had to be like a child regarding meanness (*malitia*), not wisdom (*sapientia*); see I Corinthians 14:20. See, for instance Jerome 1979: 48. Isidore alone presents the list as the totality of the qualities of children: "Tell me, how many virtues does a small child have? He answers, four" ("Dic mihi, infans parvulus quantus virtutes habet? Respondit IV").

19. See especially Riché 1995: 367, Riché 1976: 453–54; and Riché and Alexandre-Bidon 1994: 23.

20. "Quicunque ergo humiliauerit se sicut paruulus iste, hic est maior in regno caelorum" (Matt. 18:4).

21. See also Desclais Berkvam 1983; Paterson 1989; Rasmussen 1996.

22. Our study of the Cluniac oblates is also informed by the hagiographic and liturgical sources from Cluny, but this article focuses on the customaries, which represent by far the richest source of information.

23. On the history of Cluny, the two most comprehensive recent studies are Iogna-Prat 2002: 9–95 and Wollasch 1996.

24. For instance, in the tenth century, Odo, the first great abbot of Cluny from 927 to 942, was asked to reform important abbeys in France and Italy, such as Fleury in the Loire Valley and San Paolo Fuori le Mura in Rome; see the life of Odo of Cluny written by John of Salerno in 943, translated by Gerald Sitwell (1958: 3–87).

25. *Consuetudines Cluniacensium antiquiores* 1983: 3–150.

26. *Liber tramitis* 1980: 7–287.

27. Quotations of Bernard in this article are from the manuscript in Paris, Bibliothèque Nationale de France (BNF), lat. 13875, citing the chapter number and f. in the manuscript, followed by the reference to the relevant pages in Herrgott 1726. Susan Boynton and Isabelle Cochelin are preparing an edition (with English and French translations) based on the manuscript cited above, which is the ear-

liest copy of the text and was produced at Cluny. Unlike the other Cluniac customaries, Bernard's was produced for internal use: as he explains in the letter introducing the text, Bernard wrote in order to help the novices learn the proper rituals followed by the whole community; see Bernard, chap. 1, f. 6r (Herrgott 1726: 134–35).

28. Bernard, chap. 48, ff. 87v–88r (Herrgott 1726: 236–38).

29. Herrgott 1726: 175. The quire of Paris, BNF lat. 13875 containing this passage is lost.

30. *Liber tramitis* 1980: 183, 254.

31. See, for instance, Brooke 1974: 88; Leclercq 1936; de Jong 1995: 642.

32. Bernard, chap. 29, f. 6or (Herrgott 1726: 204).

33. On the increase in claustral population in the second half of the eleventh century, see Ulrich, book I, chap. 18 (*PL* 149: 668A, 691D). By the twelfth century, Peter the Venerable (1975: 55, 85), the ninth abbot of Cluny, mentions some three hundred to four hundred monks at Cluny.

34. See Cochelin 2000a and 2000b.

35. Ulrich (*PL* 149: 635).

36. On the life of Ulrich, see Tutsch 1996: 16–22.

37. Ulrich, book III, chaps. 4 and 10 (*PL* 149: 738, 748–49).

38. The religious fervor that led so many adults into the monasteries and permitted the decline of oblation in the late eleventh and twelfth centuries is inseparable from the changes in spirituality mentioned above, in relation to changes in the contemporary perception of childhood. Many medieval men and women now wished to come closer to a Christ whose human frailty was more and more a source of admiration and a cause for conversion.

39. On the decline of oblation, see Lawrence 2001: 121.

40. When Peter the Venerable (1975: 66, 97) wrote statutes for Cluny and its dependencies in the first half of the twelfth century, he deplored the fact that the oblates occupied no more significant office inside the monastery.

41. Inside the charter signed by the child and the witnesses, it was specified that "from this day may he not be allowed to remove his neck from beneath the yoke of the rule" ("ut ab hac die non liceat illi [the child] collum de sub iugo excutere regulę"); Ulrich, book III, chap. 8 (*PL* 149: 742A); Bernard, chap. 28, f. 56v (Herrgott 1726: 201).

42. On these courts in the ninth century, see Innes 2003.

43. Two examples are offered in the two earliest Cluniac Lives: the life of Gerald of Aurillac written by Odo of Cluny (*PL* 33: 645) and that of Odo of Cluny written by John of Salerno (*PL* 133: 45–47). Both texts are translated in Sitwell 1958.

44. See, for instance, Odo of Cluny (*PL* 33: 645) and John of Salerno (*PL* 133: 47A–B).

45. On the late-antique conception of conversion as a lifelong process (and not a sudden illumination) that concerns the body as well as the mind, see Elm 2003.

Even though this essay deals with the central Middle Ages and conversion to monastic life (not to Christianity), a similar conception of conversion prevailed, at least up to the late eleventh century.

46. Ulrich, book III, chaps. 8 and 27 (*PL* 149: 746, 769–70); Bernard, chaps. 25 and 27, ff. 43v–44v, 63v (Herrgott 1726: 186–87, 208). See also Cristiani 2000: 783–84.

47. Bernard, chap. 9, f. 21r (Herrgott 1726: 152).

48. For instance, on the custom of serving a sort of snack (*mixtum*) in the middle of the day to the children as well as to the recently bled adult monks, see *Consuetudines Cluniacensium antiquiores* 1983: 12; *Liber tramitis* 1980: 165, 178.

49. Odo of Cluny (*PL* 33: 652C) observed in his Life of Gerald of Aurillac that prepubescent boys have the face of their mothers, while they later look like their fathers.

50. "Et ut tandem de ipsis pueris concludam, difficile mihi uidetur ut ullius regis filius maiori diligentia nutriatur in palatio quam puer quilibet paruulus in Cluniaco"; Ulrich, book III, chap. 8 (*PL* 149: 747D); Bernard, chap. 29, f. 65r (Herrgott 1726: 210).

51. On the perception of childhood as "paradigms of physicality and willfulness," see Nelson 1994: 84–86. However, the rest of this article demonstrates that the medieval church's perception of childhood cannot easily be summarized and was rich in paradoxes.

52. On the fact that the groups of individuals placed at the bottom of social hierarchies are "more closely tied to, and defined by, the body" see Farmer 2002: 40.

53. However, Cluny was not the only community that disregarded this Benedictine regulation. See, for instance, Hildemar 1880: 576; de Jong 1983: 110.

54. On the importance of hierarchy in the Cluniac daily life and its evolution at the end of the eleventh century, see Cochelin 2000a.

55. On subdeacons, see Reynolds 1999.

56. Hierarchy played a similar central role in the education of the young noble warrior in the Carolingian court; see Innes 2003: 72–74.

57. The *Liber tramitis* (1980: 238–39) specifies that the group compiling the *brevis* included a child writing the incipits of the responsories: "Die sabbatorum debent esse quattuor qui breuem faciant quorum infans qui scribat capita responsoriorum. . . . In duodecim lectiones sint tres: armarius, cantor, infans."

58. "Et quia ipsi cotidie legunt in codice martirologii, et fratrum memoriali, ab ipsis sciendum et notandum, quando trigesimus cuiusque defuncti sit consummatus, ab ipsis elemosinario pronunciandum quantorum sit anniuersarius fratrum, ut tot quoque accipiat prebendas, et secretario quando sint omnia signa pulsanda pro anniuersario cuiusque quod bene notandum est in regula"; Bernard, chap. 29, f. 64r (Herrgott 1726: 208).

59. Bernard, chap. 77, f. 135r (Herrgott 1726: 304).

60. Bernard, chap. 77, f. 159r (Herrgott 1726: 281).

61. Bernard, chap. 29, f. 57v (Herrgott 1726: 208).

62. "Ad horas omnes regulares singulos psalmorum uersiculos pronuntiare in priuatis diebus antiphonam inponere, et quicquid cantatur ad missam matutinalem, nisi sit aliquot magnum anniuersarium, ad matutinos et uesperos responsorium decantare, uersus dicere, in estate ad nocturnos, illam minimam et unicam lectionem legere. In capitulo legere semper, in refectorio nunquam, ad collationem per uices"; Bernard, chap. 29, f. 63v (Herrgott 1726: 208).

63. On the performance of the *Benedicamus Domino* by boys, see Walters Robertson 1988: 5–9; Boynton 1998: 201–4.

64. The important musical responsibilities of medieval monastic oblates constitute an early example of a widespread phenomenon seen later in cathedral choirs; for recent studies of cathedral choristers and their musical roles, see Demouy 1993; Dobszay 1995; Dumont 2004; Reynaud 2002.

65. *Liber tramitis* 1980: 123; Boynton 2002.

66. Bernard, chap. 41, f. 83r (Herrgott 1726: 229).

67. *Liber tramitis* 1980: 20, 77.

68. Bernard, chap. 77, f. 46v (Herrgott 1726: 320).

69. On the liturgy of Palm Sunday, see particularly Graef 1959. For a study of a particular Palm Sunday procession, see Wright 2000.

70. Hesbert 1968: number 4416: "Pueri Hebraeorum vestimenta prosternebant in via, et clamabant dicentes: Hosanna Filio David; benedictus qui venit in nomine Domini." See also Boynton 1998: 207. Boys also sang these antiphons during the Palm Sunday procession in other places.

71. The later customaries from Cluny, however, do not contain a passage corresponding precisely to this one. Perhaps the early customaries containing this text reflect the procession as performed in the monasteries for which the manuscripts themselves were copied rather than at Cluny itself, or perhaps the assignment of this chant to the oblates was an implicit, continuous tradition.

72. *Consuetudines Cluniacensium antiquiores* 1984: 65.

73. "Neque ipsi infantes debent cum aliis mixti esse in infirmaria, sed seorsum ad unam partem cum magistris suis manere, ita ut audiant et dicant quod dicit conuentus"; Bernard, chap. 26, f. 50v (Herrgott 1726: 193–94).

74. "Pueri sedent in capitulo, et per aliquem praecinentem cantum addiscunt"; Ulrich (*PL* 149: 687).

75. Such notation can be seen in a manuscript that was notated at Cluny, the breviary Paris, BNF, lat. 12601.

76. "Omni die diluculo postquam pueri tres psalmos, ut mos est, perlegerint, continuo venit ad eos, ut illi, qui lecturus est in capitulo auscultet lectionem. Ea etiam vice si ipsi pueri aliquid offendunt cantando vel legendo negligenter, vel si minus diligenter cantum addiscunt, dignam ab eo disciplinam experiuntur"; Bernard, chap. 15, f. 31r (Herrgott 1726: 163). The corresponding passage in the customary of Ulrich (*PL* 149: 749) is almost identical.

77. Cluniac customaries do not offer any explanation, but it is to be found in

the Rule of Saint Benedict that they followed and read daily; see Benedict of Nursia 1972: chap. 30.

78. Ulrich, book III, chap. 8 (*PL* 149: 742D, 744B, 747A); Bernard, chap. 28, ff. 57r–58v, 64r (Herrgott 1726: 201–3, 208).

79. Ulrich, book III, chap. 8 (*PL* 149: 749C); Bernard, chaps. 15 and 28, ff. 31r, 58v (Herrgott 1726: 163, 203).

Imagining the Sacred Body

Choirboys, Their Voices, and
Corpus Christi in Early Modern Seville

TODD M. BORGERDING

Among the features of the public religious rituals that took place at Spanish cathedrals during the sixteenth century, none was as unique, nor so closely identified with Iberian religious practice, as the dances of the choirboys. At Seville, which, with Toledo, was the leading cathedral center on the Iberian peninsula, the choirboys, or *seises,* attained renown for their participation in the great feasts of the church, such as the Nativity, Corpus Christi, Easter, the Assumption, and, in the seventeenth century, the Immaculate Conception. The celebrations of these feasts, which included masses, solemn Vespers and Compline, together with processions through the cathedral and the streets of the city, grew during the sixteenth century to extraordinary proportions, involving the participation of virtually all the ecclesiastic, monastic, confraternal and civic organizations in Seville. By far the most elaborate of these spectacles were those for the feast of Corpus Christi, the celebration of which attained a new splendor following the Council of Trent.[1] Historians generally understand the spectacular fiesta of Corpus, with its dances, floats, *autos* (religious plays), triumphal arches, and music, as a means of redirecting popular and pagan festive traditions toward the ends of Counter-Reformation display and the expression of civic pride.[2] Indeed, the language of the Tridentine sanctioning of the feast, "to celebrate a triumph over falsehood and heresy, that in the sight of so much splendor and in the midst of so great joy of the universal Church, her enemies may either vanish weakened and broken, or, overcome with shame and confounded, may at length repent," gave license to cathedral authorities to outdo themselves with elaborate displays of religious authority that promoted the mysteries of Corpus Christi (Schroeder 1941: 76). The dances and songs of the *seises,* a tradition that still survives today, were an essential element in the promotion of the feast.

In this essay, I propose that the display of choirboys and their voices on the feast of Corpus Christi developed during the sixteenth century in tandem with a theological understanding of childhood that made it possible for the dancing *seises* to be understood as signifiers of Christian virtue and purity, and, by association, as symbols of the transfigured Host. Focusing on the practice at Seville, I argue that a repertory of music that displayed the talents of boy singers grew out of this epistemological tradition during the second half of the century and contributed to the expression of orthodox Catholic doctrine. This music, which survives largely in Francisco Guerrero's *Canciones y villanescas espirituales* (1589, transcribed in García and Querol Gavaldá 1957), was performed in highly public settings, so that much of the music heard during feasts such as Corpus Christi was the music of boys. Clearly the *seises* were bodies—and voices—that mattered.

Why they mattered, and how they mattered, are questions that invite us to think anew about the place of boys in the musical establishments of early modern Europe. The early modern body has been the focus of scholarly inquiry in recent years.[3] While much of this work has focused on adult female and male bodies, some scholars, especially those working in the area of English Renaissance theater, have noted that the bodies of boys were richly polyvalent signifiers. Michael Shapiro (1994: 199), for example, argues that for early modern playwrights and their audiences, "the primary cause of . . . attraction to the figure of the boy actor/female character/male persona was their sense of the excitement of watching a young performer project the illusion of multiple identities and deftly maneuver among them." Similarly, Lisa Jardine (1992: 28) argues that, in terms of erotic potential on the streets of London around 1600, "the bodies of boys and the unmarried woman elide as they carry the message of equivalent sexual availability." Peter Stallybrass (1992) has argued that cross-dressing boy actors were the focus of an intense gaze that negotiated the tension between the female prosthetics of costumes and the body that existed beneath them.[4] The voices of boys, too, took part in the construction of their transformative identity: Linda Austern (1994 and 1998) has argued that these voices, in theatrical contexts, played an important role in the construction of their erotic bodies, since they shared with women both a vocal range and a potentially sexual body.

While I wish to position my study of choirboys within the context of these recent studies on the early modern body, I suggest here that the mutability of the Renaissance child-body and voice worked in a different way when put on display during the religious rituals of Counter-Reformation Spain. Boy singers were not in themselves unusual in medieval and early modern choirs, but evidence suggests that their presence became more prominently displayed as the sixteenth century came to a close. Their numbers increased in cathedral choirs such as the one at Seville, and they took an increasingly important role in the performance of chant and polyphony.[5] Because of the church's growing preoccupation with display and theatricality during the second half of the sixteenth century, boy singers were increasingly visible and audible in public rituals. In the context of an exegetical tradition regarding boys and childhood that focused on their purity and potential for religious transformation, boys became ideal vehicles for the promotion of Catholic dogma (Trexler 2002). By drawing connections between the sacred epistemology of childhood, the contexts in which the bodies and voices of boys were put on display, and the music they performed, I propose here new ways of understanding the importance of child musicians to the Counter-Reformation church.

Singing choirboys were a feature in Spanish cathedrals from the fifteenth century, and in some places before that, when a system for their education was established.[6] In Seville, a 1439 bull of Eugenio IV established a school for the training of six choirboys who would sing "certain responses and verses." The 1454 bull of Nicholas V established the position of master of the choirboys, mentioning that their voices added "brilliance and splendor" to the service (Gonzáles-Barrionuevo 1992: 271–73, 281–82). These six choirboys, or *seises* (the name comes from their number), who entered the choir at about age seven and typically served until their voices changed, around age fourteen, were trained in grammar and music—chant, and by the sixteenth century, counterpoint, and polyphony as well.[7] In addition to the *seises*, younger *cantorcicos* processed with the choir, sang chant, and occasionally joined in the performance of polyphonic music. The number of *cantorcicos* increased during the sixteenth century, so that by 1565, ten of them joined the *seises* in the processions of Corpus Christi (Gonzáles-Barrionuevo 1992: 37–39). Numbers varied of course from place to place, and from year to year, but it is safe to assume that on large feasts at Seville, sixteen boys may have joined the typical cathedral choir of twelve adult men, doubling the *tiple* (soprano) and alto voices.[8] Apart from their regular duties, choirboys were called upon to perform on the great feasts of the church, where they normally occupied a prominent position. They sang in the popular Matins services at Christmas, they appeared in any number of processions during the year, and, of course, they sang and danced during Corpus Christi. A typical procession on Corpus Christi, which became the topos for all religious processions in Seville, was led by the confraternities, followed by the religious orders and the crosses of the approximately thirty parishes of the city. Then came the *custodia*, or processional monstrance containing the

Host, which was borne among the cathedral clergy, followed by the Inquisi-
tion, with the *ayuntamiento,* or City Council, bringing up the rear (Brooks
1988: 54–69). In these processions, the musicians and dancers were positioned
near the *custodia,* so that they shared with it the focal point of the procession
(61). During other moments of the weeklong festivities, boys danced before
the local authorities and in front of the monstrance and sang or acted in tab-
leaux that were borne in processions.

Occupying as they did such a visually prominent position in festival rituals, the costume and appearance of boys was treated as a serious matter
by the cathedral authorities. In many of these appearances the boys sang in
choir vestments, and in the dances they often were costumed as courtly pages
(Gonzáles-Barrionuevo 1992: 235–36), or as the event demanded, as various
religious characters. From at least the middle of the fifteenth century and
throughout the 1500s, the cathedral accounts record payment to choirboys
who performed in the *nube,* or cloud, a float borne during the procession on
the feast of Corpus Christi, and describe their costume in detail.[9] Typical is
the entry for the procession of 1536:

> ITEM: three hundred seventy-five *maravadís* are discharged to pay a
> man who was in the cloud the day of Corpus Christi speaking [the
> part] of Jesus.
>
> MARIA: Item one hundred thirty-six *maravadís* are discharged to pay a
> boy who was in the cloud dressed as Mary.
>
> ITEM: Paid to two other boys who were in the cloud dressed in the
> habit of St. Francis and St. Dominic six *Reales.*
>
> ITEM: Paid to four choirboys who were singing in the cloud twelve
> *Reales.*
>
> ITEM: Paid two *Reales* to the two boys who were dressed as angels in
> the cloud.[10]

This record suggests that four choirboys, probably *seises,* attended to the singing, while six other boys, no doubt drawn from both the *seises* and the *cantorcicos,* were costumed characters in what was apparently a form of *auto sacra-
mental.* The *nube* of the Corpus Christi procession, then, was a platform for
the display of both the bodies and voices of boys. As was the case in English
theatrical contexts, these bodies seemed to have been seen as richly mutable.
Boys played both adult male and female roles, they represented angels, and, of
course, they played the role of choirboys. But their presence in the *nube* raises
questions: why, if an adult male was portraying Jesus, did not adults also play
St. Francis and St. Dominic? For that matter, why should a boy be employed to

represent the mother of Christ, when an adult male (women being, of course, expressly excluded from such ritual roles) might just as well have performed that role?

We can arrive at a better understanding of this by exploring these voices and bodies in the context of the church's traditional view of boys and youth. Early modern cathedral culture, drawing upon scriptural and patristic traditions, developed an iconography of boys that focused on several aspects of their preadult status, presenting them as models of purity and Christian virtue. Indeed, in the gospels, Christ continually held up children, or the childlike state, as an ideal for his followers. Quoting from Psalm 8, he located the childlike simplicity needed for prayer when he said, "From the lips of children and infants you have ordained praise" (Matt. 21:16). Christ suggested that the simplicity of children was essential to understanding the mysteries of heaven with the words "I praise you, Father, Lord of heaven and earth, because you have hidden these things from the wise and learned, and revealed them to little children,"[11] and he instructed his followers, "I tell you the truth, unless you change and become like little children, you will never enter the kingdom of heaven" (Matt. 19:14). And, famously, Christ urged his followers "Let the little children come to me, and do not hinder them, for the kingdom of heaven belongs to such as these."[12] In all of these cases children, or those like children, were identified as the heirs of the eternal kingdom, precisely because of their simplicity, the purity of their minds and beings. Unlike adults, the naïveté of children, the simplicity of their thoughts, their trusting nature, allowed them to understand the mysteries of Christ's teachings and made them ideal models for adults who sought the same end.

The scriptural topos of the child was popular among the patristic writers, who expounded on the ideal of purity associated with children in the Gospels. Origen, for example, explained why Christ compared the great to little children.

> One, expounding the word of the Saviour here after the simple method, might say that, if anyone who is a man mortifies the lusts of manhood, putting to death by the spirit the deeds of the body, and always bearing about in the body the putting to death of Jesus, to such a degree that he has the condition of the little child who has not tasted sensual pleasures . . . then such a one is converted and has become as the little children. . . . the same might also be said in regard to the rest of the affections and infirmities and sicknesses of the soul, into which it is not the nature of little children to fall. (Origen 1896: 484)

Children, then, unblemished by worldly desires, were predisposed to spiritual health. Expanding on this topic of purity were others such as Clement of Alexandria, who in his *Paedagogus* offered an exegesis of Gospel passages related to children. Referring to the passages in Matthew (18:3 and 19:14), Clement argued that Christ was not speaking figuratively of regeneration but rather calling on his followers to imitate the simplicity that is in children. Childlike simplicity, however, suggested not spiritual stasis, but rather a dynamic state of faith:

> In contradistinction, therefore, to the older people, the new people
> are called young, having learned the new blessings; and we have the
> exuberance of life's morning prime in the youth which knows no old age,
> in which we are always growing to maturity in intelligence, are always
> young, always mild, always new: for those must necessarily be new, who
> have become partakers of the new Word. And that which participates
> in eternity is wont to be assimilated to the incorruptible. (Clement of
> Alexandria 1903: 214)

Thus the native curiosity of children mapped onto the ideal Christian faith, which exists in a permanent state of pure childhood that continually is in a state of transformation, of growth in faith and spirituality.[13]

The early church and the patristic community of writers did not of course have an unanimously positive attitude toward children,[14] but such views as those expressed by Clement and Origen were certainly known in early modern Spain and would have met with approval. Patristic writings were not only transmitted to early modern audiences in printed books but also formed an integral part of Catholic ritual, since lessons of the Office were typically drawn from the likes of Clement. In Spain, children enjoyed a high degree of care and attention during the 1500s: many new hospitals were established for the care of orphans by such churchmen as Saint Tomás de Villanueva (1488–1555) and Fernando Contreras (1470–1548), and new medical techniques for the treatment of children were developed by Pedro Ponce de León (1510–84) (Morales 1960: 91–94). Illustrious peninsular humanists contributed to the early modern understanding of children as well: Antonio de Nebrija's *De liberis educandis libellus* (1509) was an important work on education, and two major works by Juan Luís Vives, *De institutione feminae Christianae* (1523), and *De subventione pauperum* (1526), contain important chapters on children and child rearing. Child saints grew in popularity in all ranks of Spanish society; Saint Leocadio of Toledo was a favorite of the royal family, Saints Justo and Pastor received particular devotion from Phillip II, and the patrons of Seville cathedral, Justa and Rufina, were also children (Morales 1960). It is not surprising, then, that missionaries in the New World—arguably the most important arena for early modern evangelization—looked to children not only as objects of conversion, but also as tools for the conversion of adults, embracing a concept expressed by Torquemada when he said "a little age is a lot, for through the power of God you have no age, but only will" (Trexler 2002: 251–54).

Early modern Spanish commentators, such as the evangelizing archbishop of Granada, Hernando Talavera, brought this positive view of children to bear on the bodies of boys who were seen by congregants in early modern ritual. Talavera's 1496 *Cerimonias de la Misa*, a guide to the mysteries encountered in the Latin mass, maintains a visual focus throughout, explaining the vestments, furniture, and movements of the liturgical actors, with particular emphasis on their bodies. In his preface Talavera explained, "The mass heard with devotion is the best and most acceptable offering and gift that one can offer to our redemptor. For principally in it are represented the mysteries and acts, so worthy of remembrance, that our redemptor and master Jesus Christ, true God and true man, performed. . . . And for this reason I wanted to compile, briefly, the images and thoughts that should occupy our spirit during the celebration of the mass."[15] In chapter 3, "On that which is represented by the boys who normally assist at the altar," Talavera explains, "the boys who normally minister and carry the candles before the priest when he goes to the altar represent the prophets who came before the coming of our Lord, as well as the holy angels who serve him diligently in all their works."[16] At work here is a transformation of physical position into historical position: the physical position of the boys in the procession, before the priest-Christ, allows them to represent the prophets, who came temporally before Christ. In addition, as unformed adults, they are apt symbols of the prophets, who were, after all, not partakers of the spiritual maturity of Christianity. On the other hand, the actions of the acolytes, who assist the priest during mass, are analogous to the servant role of the angels. If not mentioned specifically by Talavera, the boys projected the ideal state of Christian purity, while at the same time functioning as polysemic icons—they were prophets, and they were the pure, sinless, asexual soul matter of the angels. They were, in fact, ideal material for the construction of sacred symbols, since their underlying purity could be molded and directed by costume, context, and text, to communicate specific messages.[17]

Such images became part of the vocabulary of Counter-Reformation artists who made visible the teachings of the church. According to one Spanish iconographer, the early seventeenth-century Sevillian Jesuit Martin de Roa, religious ideas were represented in various ways: directly (according to objects directly observable in nature); at one remove (according to verbal descriptions from history and scripture—the angel Gabriel was described as a beautiful youth, and so he is depicted); and via "mysterious figures" or symbols (Roa 1623). Presenting angels as boys draws on the latter two of these categories, as Roa explains:

> All of these things are represented by the brush according to how history paints them with words. Not because the angels have any form, nor because their nature of invisibility is able to receive any color, but rather because thus [represented] the people are able to know about them. . . . For this reason Angels are always painted as boys, in an eternal spring of youth, not subject to the prices of time, nor to old age, because of the vigor and perpetuity of their being, which remains always in one state, without breaking nor diminishing their virtue. The eyes [are painted] bright and lively, to represent the liveliness of their understanding, full of divine enlightenment.[18]

Talavera, who invites the congregation to imagine altar boys as prophets and angels, and Roa, who offered detailed guidelines for the depiction of angels, both remind us of the costumed choirboys of the Corpus Procession, where nothing was left to the imagination. Indeed, the essential problem of the artist depicting angels was directly applicable to the Feast of Corpus Christi: both objects, angel and transubstantiated Host, were by nature invisible. And yet, as with angels, it was necessary to make visible mystery of Corpus Christi, so that the people would know of it.

◆ Boys' Voices and Their Music

If the bodies of boys were potent symbols of purity, and of the ideal Christian, their voices contributed to this image. Few descriptions of the quality of boy's voices from the Renaissance survive, but evidence suggests that the ideal voice was that described by Isidore of Seville in his *Etymologies:* "The perfect voice is high, sweet, and clear: high, to be adequate to the sublime; clear, to fill the ear; sweet, to soothe the minds of the hearers. If any one of these qualities is absent, the voice is not perfect."[19] Indeed, during the seventeenth century, a prospective choirboy at Seville was criticized because his voice lacked clarity and vibrance (Brooks 1988: 99). Writers on the art of public speaking, who often relied upon musical analogies, described the ideal voice in terms very similar to those of Isidore (Borgerding 1988). Luís de Granada, undoubtedly the most important sacred rhetor of the late sixteenth century, described the ideal preaching voice as one that is "projected with clear sweetness, not in an affected or effeminate manner, but in a masculine and natural manner. The same things that flatter and entertain the ear in singing do so as well in oratory."[20] Granada held up children's voices as ideal models for speakers, since they have the most natural and unaffected voices (Borgerding 1998: 588). Another Spanish rhetor, Francisco Terrones del Caño, suggested that the high voice was appropriate for specific uses when he described the three styles of speaking used by orators: "For the masses, use cries and groans, for a noble audience use reasoned and measured speech, and for royalty, speak almost in falsetto and with great submission."[21] The last of Terrones del Caño's voice classifications is striking; it seems odd, even absurd, to imagine addressing a king with a high, falsetto-like voice. But, if one remembers the role of angels as intercessors before God, and takes into account the close identification of God with kings in early modern culture, his intent becomes more clear. When addressing a king, or speaking to God, one should assume the voice of an angel-like boy. In addition, singing boys were commonly compared to angelic choirs, as in historian Alonso Morgado's sixteenth-century description of the *seises* of Seville: "[These] are the boys with the best voices that can be found. Thus, in this Holy Church, the gentleness of the Music is absolutely heavenly" (Brooks 1988: 99). The clarity and naturalness of boys' voices, then, projected an aural image of purity, so that the voices of choirboys approached the sound of angels.

In their regular performances with the musical chapel of the cathedral, the *seises'* voices were heard in concert with adult male voices, but in the music that was heard on the feast of Corpus Christi and certain other public feasts of the church year, boys' voices were put on prominent display. The only substantial collection of this kind of music is Francisco Guerrero's 1589 *Canciones y villanescas espirituales,* the last printed collection of Spanish-texted songs of the sixteenth century, and the first devoted exclusively to settings of sacred texts. This collection has been studied from a variety of points of view,[22] but what has yet to be addressed is perhaps the collection's most striking feature: the predominance of works that feature high voices—specifically the voices of boy choristers. While there is nothing in the print itself that clearly indicates the liturgical or ritual functions of these pieces, it seems safe to assume that they were collected as an anthology of Guerrero's best compositions for the feasts that demanded this kind of music.[23]

The *Canciones y villanescas espirituales* consists of sixty-one pieces: thirty-three are for five voices, twenty for four voices, and eight for three voices (see table 2.1). The collection reflects the type of liturgical ordering that was common in Spanish motet books of the second half of the sixteenth century, a practice that seems to have been developed in Spain by Guerrero himself (Borgerding 1997). The individual pieces do not bear rubrics indicating the feasts on which they were to be performed, but in most cases the texts clearly indicate religious themes that coincide with the feasts of the liturgical calendar upon which Spanish-texted music would be sung.[24] Thus, those designated in table 2.1 for the Nativity would have been performed at the services on Christmas Eve and Feast of the Three Kings, those for Mary on the Marian feasts, including the Assumption, the Annunciation, and the Conception, and those for the Sacrament during the feast of Corpus Christi. The pieces labeled "moral" and "passion" are more difficult to assign to a liturgical function and may have been intended for performance in private devotional settings. The pieces in the collection were organized first by vocal scoring, probably to facilitate the publication of the partbooks,[25] but among each grouping of five-, four-, and three-voiced works can be found clear groupings for the feasts of the Virgin Mary, the Nativity, and the celebration of the Blessed Sacrament on Corpus Christi. This is more clearly shown in table 2.2, which organizes the pieces according to theme.

A closer look at the vocal scorings shown in table 2.2 shows that boys' voices are featured in a high proportion of these works: all of the three-voice pieces are scored for two *tiples* and alto, and eleven of the four-voice pieces are scored for two *tiples*, alto, and tenor; the remaining four-voice pieces are scored for *tiple*, alto, tenor, and *baxo*.[26] If we take into account the fact that many of the five-voice pieces were composed in the typical ABA form of the *villancico*, with reduced vocal scoring for the *copla*, several more "boys' pieces" can be added to the list, since eight of the *a 5 canciones* feature coplas for two *tiples* and alto, five of them feature *coplas* for solo *tiple*, eight for two *tiples* and alto, and two for two *tiples*, alto and tenor. Two more of them, numbers 20 and 23, have *coplas* for five voices, but the lower two voices participate minimally (these voice parts are indicated in parentheses in tables 1 and 2). None of the pieces features lower voices on the *coplas*. Taken together, then, thirty-eight of the sixty-one pieces, or more than half of the collection, can be said to feature prominently the high voices of boys, and while there does not seem to be a higher percentage of these pieces assigned to any one feast, it is significant that nearly all of the three-voice pieces are for the Virgin Mary or the Blessed Sacrament. This suggests that, apart from the tradition of featuring boys' voices in *canciones*, Guerrero found high voices especially appropriate for Corpus Christi and the

Marian feasts, which together make up the two largest groups of *canciones* in the collection.

The musical style of the *canciones* that feature boys' voices is also distinctive. Many of the works in the 1589 collection feature passages of imitative polyphony, which, while not as complicated as that sometimes found in Latin-texted religious music such as motets and masses, nevertheless shares with it the problem of making the texts less intelligible in performance. In those pieces or *coplas* that feature boys' voices, however, the texture is nearly always homophonic (see ex. 2.1).

Homophony is less difficult to perform, of course, and this may have been a factor in Guerrero's decision to compose these passages in a simpler texture. But homophony also allows the text to be heard more easily, and this fact, too, must have guided Guerrero's compositional decisions. In any case, the texts sung by boys in pure harmony would have been clearly understood by audiences in the cathedral and the streets of the city.

The texts for the *canciones* for Corpus Christi convey typical themes for the feast, including adoration of the Host and descriptions of its benefits to communicants. In almost all cases, however, the emphasis is on the identification of the Host with God (or Christ's body), and the effect that consuming the Host has. Number 33, for example, asserts the veracity of the dogma of transubstantiation through repetition of the notion that God exists in the Host:

Quiere Dios que le ofrezcamos,	God desires that we offer him
para aplacarse de nos,	in order to bring him to us
esta hostia que llevamos	this Host which we raise up
y es la hostia'l mesmo Dios.	and the Host is the same God.
Aquesta hostia que vemos,	This Host which we see
que adora nuestro sentido,	that our senses adore,
por nos a Dios la ofrecemos	we offer to God for ourselves
y Dios es el ofreçido.	and God is that which is offered.
I esta hostia que llevamos	And this Host which we raise up
en ella vemos a Dios;	in it we see God
pareçe que la llevamos,	it seems that we raise it
mas la hostia lleva a nos.	but the Host raises us.

No. 61 similarly mentions the benefits of the Sacrament, while at the same time pointing out that the communicant must be in the proper state in order to enjoy those benefits:

Example 2.1 **"Dios los estremos condena,"** *Canciones y villanescas espirituales*

Franciso Guerrero (Venice, 1589), no. 31

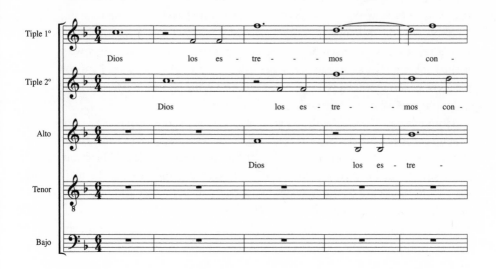

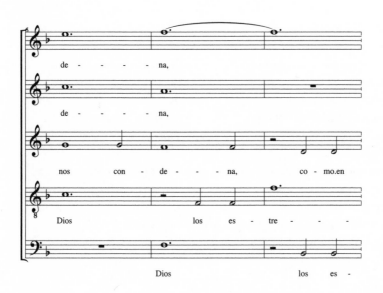

Qual - quier es - tre - mo.es vi - cio - - so, y.el

Qual - quier es - tre - mo.es vi - cio - - so, y.el

Qual - quier es - tre - mo.es vi - cio - - so, y.el

me - dio.es la rec - ti - tud, pe - ro.en es - te pan sa -

me - dio.es la rec - ti - tud, pe - ro.en es - te pan sa -

me - dio.es la rec - ti - tud, pe - ro.en es - te pan sa -

[d.c.]

bro - so, los es - tre - mos son vir - tud.

bro - so, los es - tre - mos son vir - tud.

bro - so, los es - tre - mos son vir - tud.

Es menester que se açierte	It is necessary to be in the right state
a comer desta comida,	to eat of this food
que al malo da pena y muerte	which to the bad gives sorrow and death
y al bueno da gloria y vida.	and to the good gives glory and life.
El que fuere conbidado	He who is invited
a comer deste manjar,	to eat this delicacy
primero se á de provar	first he must prove
que el manjar aya provado.	that he has tried the delicacy.
Porque's justo que se açierte	Because it is just that he be right
a comer deste comida,	to eat this food
que al malo da pena y muerte,	which to the bad gives sorrow and death
y al bueno da gloria y vida.	and to the good gives glory and life.

The singing choirboys of Spain, then, if they dressed the part, did not sing the part of angels, prophets, or the Virgin Mary; their words, the texts of Guerrero's 1589 collection, are not scriptural utterances of angels or prophets. Instead, their bodies and voices functioned to deliver doctrinal messages while at the same time representing the invisible: prophets long dead and lost to human view, as well as angels, invisible by nature. Most importantly, perhaps, they gave bodies, lively, singing, pure, and human bodies, to the mystery of Corpus Christi. They enacted the invisible, nearly ineffable mystery of transubstantiation that was the crux of the feast and embodied Christ's presence.

◆ Lively Bodies

The display of boys and their voices on the feast of Corpus Christi was expanded in Seville during the seventeenth century, when in 1613 Matheo Vazquez de Leca, canon of the cathedral, endowed celebrations on six days of its octave—raising the splendor of the feast considerably. The language of the endowment shows the concern he had for the performance of both music and dance:

> On the designated Sunday before the feast the chapel master of the Cathedral will be called and given the order in which the six days of the octave of the Most Holy Sacrament will be sung, and [instructed] that the manner of singing be varied so that the same thing is not sung one day after the other, and that the following order is kept: Each afternoon the choir must attend at the first verse of the *Pange lingua* and likewise

sing two *chansonetas* with the boys dancing in their costumes. A good motet is to be performed by the two chapels of singers and instrumentalists together, and between the motet and the *chansonetas* a singer with good voice and perhaps the instrumentalists alone [i.e., without the participation of the full choir] will perform some motet. [All this is done] because with this variety the public will be moved to greater devotion.[27]

If greater devotion was the goal, this endowment also heightened the visibility of the choirboys—already visible in the processions—during the octave of Corpus Christi. The songs and dances of the *chansonetas,* as noted above, generally took place before the monstrance, which was located outside the confines of the choir. Thanks to the peculiar design of most Spanish cathedrals, including Seville, this was in fact a visually important physical motion, since the *coro* of these cathedrals was enclosed on three sides, open only on the side facing the altar. The choir, then, was heard but rarely seen. When dancing and singing *chansonetas,* however, the voices, and specifically the voices of choirboys, were literally embodied for the congregations.

That this act of embodiment should take place on the feast of Corpus Christi seems significant in Spain, where bodies and embodiment of the sacred became increasingly important as the seventeenth century approached. This was true not only in the mystery of Christ's taking on human flesh, celebrated in the massive displays for Corpus Christi, but also in the rapidly growing devotion to the doctrine of the Immaculate Conception. This doctrine, which held that Mary had been conceived in the womb of her mother without sin—in effect, that she, like her son, had been miraculously created in the womb of her mother—was one of the defining dogmas of sixteenth-century Spain. What had historically been pious tradition became in Spain a dogmatic battleground (Sebastian 1958), and by the end of the century the church in Spain, indeed the Spanish faithful in general, held the purified bodies of Christ and his mother to be so closely linked that the motto "praise to the Immaculate Conception and to the most Holy Sacrament" became a password for Spanish Catholic orthodoxy. In 1578 the chapter at Seville demonstrated its allegiance to the Immaculate Conception and at the same time associated it with Corpus Christi when it declared that "the instrumentalists and singers shall celebrate the octave of the Conception of our Lady [December 8] in the same manner as the octave of Corpus Christi."[28] Seville claimed for itself leadership in the Immaculist movement (Ros 1994), and, as the early seventeenth-century master of ceremonies at Seville cathedral reported, all preachers, after stating the text of their sermons, were required to recite the phrase "Praised be the Most Holy Sacrament and the Immaculate Conception of the Most Holy Virgin Mary our Lady, mother of God, conceived without original sin."[29]

The pure body figured prominently in explaining these mysteries. In his 1492 tract "How we must take communion," Talavera painstakingly details the actions that a Christian must perform to purify his or her body in order to be prepared to receive communion. Talavera's "Ceremonies of the Mass" describes communion as the mingling of Christ with the communicant, an idea echoed by Luis de León, the sixteenth-century mystic who tells us that "it is an accepted fact, for all faithful, that Christ's body, as the Holy Wafer, received in communion, becomes part of our flesh and body, and this means that we become one and the same with Christ, flesh of his flesh, and not only in spirit but also in body we are one and the same. Let no one doubt these conclusions" (Luis de León 1984: 243). The mystery of Corpus Christi presented bread transformed into the bright purity of Christ's being, that of the Immaculate Conception offered a purified mediatrix; and in the celebration of both of these, boys were present. The significance of boys' voices and their bodies on Corpus Christi, and, indeed, on other feasts such as those devoted to the Virgin Mary, then, may well have been in their performance of a symbolic discourse that communicated a message of embodiment.

Revealing mysteries such as the transubstantiation (whereby bread and wine become the real body and blood of Christ), the Incarnation (where God takes on human form), or indeed the Immaculate Conception, presented the church with a crisis of representation: the essence of these mysteries defies direct representation, and other, more subtle approaches had to be used. In art, as we have seen, iconographers justified the representation of the invisible by means of symbol or imaginative depiction, and several scholars have shown how, in painting, the unrepresentable was placed before the eyes of the people. Leo Steinberg (1996), for example, has shown how the exposition of puerile genitalia, common in early modern nativity scenes, functioned to display the sex and thereby the real humanity of Christ. In the case of the Immaculate Conception, historians have shown how an accretion of Old Testament texts and images, when applied to a painting depicting the Virgin Mary, was construed to signify her Immaculate Conception (Stratton 1994). The doctrine of transubstantiation posed no less a challenge, and the church responded not only with the ubiquitous image of the chalice and host, but also with the aggressive promotion of the feast of Corpus Christi, with public ritual displays. The voices of boys, and the bodies from which they emanated, were rich signifiers with the potential to make apparent these complex mysteries. This was possible in a culture that believed in the transforming power of religion and words, when transubstantiation had not yet been wholly reduced to hocus pocus, and before rhetoric had become empty words. By presenting texts that stressed transformation through the efficacy of the Host, the pure bodies and voices of boys had the effect of representing the purity of the Host itself, while at the same time the sight of the dancing *seises* presented a vision of spiritual transformation.

Notes

1. On the tradition of Corpus Christi processions in Spain, and more specifically in Seville, see Brooks 1988; Lleo Cañal 1975; Reynaud 1974: 133–68; and Very 1962.

2. See Brooks 1988: 145; Very 1962: 8–9.

3. See, for example, Bynum 1995 and Elam 1996. Much of the discourse has been fueled by explorations of Ovidian texts and their impact on early modern literatures (Stanivukovic 2001), as explored in Enterline 2000.

4. See also Orgel 1989.

5. On the development of the choir in Seville during the sixteenth century, see Gonzáles-Barrionuevo 1992: 38–47, and Gonzáles-Barrionuevo 2002: 121–38.

6. The education of choirboys at Seville is discussed in Gonzáles-Barrionuevo 1992: 75–94. See also Reynaud 2002 and Bertos Herrera 1988.

7. Gonzáles-Barrionuevo 1992: 44–50. The experience of choirboys was similar in Granada (Lopez Calo 1963: 143–45) and at Barcelona cathedral (Gregori i Cifré 1988).

8. Gonzáles-Barrionuevo 2002: 121. See also Bowers 1995; Fallows 1985: 43–46; and Reynolds 1989.

9. The records in question are held at the Archivo de la Catedral de Sevilla (hereafter ACS), sec. IV (cargo y descargo). The earliest record of payment to boys dressed as these characters is dated 1458. Although references to the *nube* are scarce after the 1540s, it is clear that the tradition continued in Seville, since an inventory from 1550 lists "la nube que se solia sacar el dia de Corpus xpi. con sus aparajos" (the cloud that is usually taken out on the day of Corpus Christi, with its apparatus). See ACS, sec. O, lib. 53, "Inventario antiguo del 1550 de los bienes de la fabrica," f. 20v.

10. ACS, sec. IV, lib. 59 (1536), f. 44v.: "Iten se le descarga trezientos y setenta y cinco m[a]r[avadí]s q[ue] pago a un ombre q[ue] fue en la nuve el dia de corpus x[rist]i diziendo el Jh[es]u[s] [f.] 45 maria. yten se le descargan ciento y trienta y seis m[a]r[avadí]s q[ue] pago a un niño q[ue] fue en la nuve vestido fecho la maria yten pago a otros dos niños q[ue] furero[n] en la nuve vestidos del abito de sa[n]. fraco. y s[a]nt[o] domingo seis Reales q[ue] valen dozientos y quatro

mrs. yten pago a quatro cantorcicos q fueron cantando en la nuve doze Reales q[ue] falten qutrcioto y ocho mrs. yten pago dos R[ea]l[e]s a dos niños q[ue] fueron fechos angelicos en la nuve." Such references in the cathedral pay records stop around 1540, but this is likely because of changes in the way records were kept. Choirboys dressed as angels appear in Granada later in the century, as a document dated 1568 shows. See Lopez Calo (1963: 242). A similar reference appears in documents from Toledo cathedral, where in 1561 instrumentalists accompanied boy choristers dressed as angels in the procession on Corpus Christi. See Reynaud 1974: 159.

11. See also Luke 10:21. This, of course, stands in contrast to Paul's use of the child topos in his first letter to the Corinthians, 13:11: "When I was a child, I talked like a child, I thought like a child, I reasoned like child. When I became a man, I put childish ways behind me. Now we see but a poor reflection as in a mirror; then we shall see face to face. Now I know in part; then I shall know fully, even as I am fully known." Here the notion of physical and emotional maturity is used as a metaphor for fuller understanding of the Christian mysteries.

12. Matt 18:3. See also Mark 10:14; Luke 18:16.

13. Clement, unlike Paul, does not see the metaphorical children of God as ever growing old, but rather assimilating new ideas by virtue of the childlike state. See chapter 6: "The name children does not imply instruction in elementary principles."

14. Nor is it within the scope of this essay to present a full account of the development of patristic and medieval religious thought on children and childhood. See, however, the essay by Susan Boynton and Isabelle Cochelin in this volume.

15. Talavera 1496: preface: "La misa devotamente oída es de las mayores é más aceptas ofrendas é presentes que á Nuestro Redemptor se pueden ofrecer; ca en ella principalmente son representados los misterios é actos muy dignos de continua memoria que Nuestro Redemptor é maestro Jesucristo Dios é hombre verdadero hizo. . . . E por eso quise compilar brevemente las imaginaciones é pensamientos en que nuestro espíritu se debe ocupar en tanto que la misa se celebra."

16. Ibid., chap. 3: "De lo que representan los mozos que comúnmente ministran el altar. Los mozos que ende ministran é llevan cirios encendidos ante el sacerdote cuando va al altar representan á los profetas que ante Nuestro Señor venieron é á los santos ángeles que en todas sus obras con diligencia le servieron."

17. My view of the polyvalence of symbols follows that of Robert Weimann (1996) and others, who see the symbolic language of the Renaissance not as the ossified replication of signs (pace Foucault) but as one in which symbols were open to a variety of interpretations.

18. Roa 1623: ff. 20v–21v: "Todas estas cosas se representan assi por el pinzel, porque assi las pinta la Historia por las palabras. No porque tengan figura alguna los Angeles, ni su naturaleza invisible sea capz de recibir algun color: sino porque assi se mostraron, i se dieron à conocer à los onbres. . . . [f. 21'] Pintanse por esta

razon sienpre mancebos, en una eterna primavera de juuentud, no sujeta à gastos de tienpo, ni de vejez, por el vigor, i perpetuidad de su ser, que permanece sienpre en un estado, sin quiebra, ni menoscabo de su virtud. Los ojos claros, vivos, por la viveza de suentendimie.to lleno de ilustraciones Divinas."

19. Translation from *Source Readings* 1998: 19.

20. Granada 1848: 613: "Salga con cierta suavidad, no afeminada ó affectada, sino varonil y natural; lo cual asi como en el cano, asi tambien en la oracion halaga y entretiene los oídos."

21. Terrones del Caño 1617: 151: "Al vulgo, a gritos y porrazos; alauditorio noble, con blandura de voz y eficacia de razones; a los reyes, casi en falsete y con gran sumisión."

22. Questions of genre, texts, and musical style are discussed in Stevenson 1961: 216–24. Further discussion of the texts and genres, and the relationship of Guerrero's collection to other sixteenth-century Spanish-texted music, is found in García and Querol Gavaldá (1957: 9–47).

23. The cathedral's financial records list payments to Guerrero and other composers for *chansonetas* produced for Corpus, the Nativity cycle, and various feasts of the Virgin Mary.

24. I have, for the most part, followed the themes assigned to the pieces by Garcia and Querol (1957). While noting the variety of themes and their possible connections to the feasts I discuss here, Querol does not note the liturgical organization of the collection. On the development of sacred vernacular song in Spain, see Laird 1997: 17–21, and on the texts and musical forms of Guerrero's collection, see Laird 1997: 25–29.

25. This is typical too in motet publications. By printing the five-voice pieces first, the bass and tenor part books, which necessarily contain fewer pieces, can maintain the same numbering system as the other part books, which contain all sixty-one works.

26. I refer to the vocal ranges using the terms listed in the print. The *tiple* parts were written either in C1 or G clef, the alto in C2 or C3, the tenor in C3 or C4, and the *baxo* in C4, F3, or F4. The cleffing system used by Guerrero seems not to indicate any sort of transposition, a common Renaissance practice explained in Kurtzman 1994 and Cramer 1976, and in any case the labels of the voice parts make clear the vocal types and ranges desired.

27. ACS, sec. IX, leg. 146, no. 7: Iten mandara el do[mingo] Diputado antes de la fiesta llamar al maestro de Capilla de esta Santa ig[lesi]a y le dara horden que lo que se Cantare en los seis dias de la octava del Santiss[i]mo sacramento se Varie del modo que no se cante en un dia tras del otro una misma cossa y que en ello se tenga el orden que se sigue. A de entrar cada tarde al Principio la Capilla de Cantores con el Primer Versso de Pange Lingua y ansse de Cantar dos chanssonetas Baylandos los muchachos con sus bestidos de Danza un motete bueno que canten las Capillas Juntos de ministriles y Cantores y entre el motete y las chanzonetas

una vez se tocara la Corneta al horganillo y otra vez al mismo cantara algun cantor de buena voz y tal vez los ministriles solos tocasen algun motete Para que con
esta variedad el Pueblo Pueda ser movido al Mayor devoccion.

28. ACS, actas, lib. 31, f. 56: "Este dicho dia mandaron que los menestriles y
cantores celebren el octavario de nuestra señora de la concepcion segun y como se
celebra el octavario del corpus christi."

29. ACS, sec. 3, Liturgia, lib. 35, f. 40': "Alabado sea el santissimo sacramento, y
la immaculada conçepçion dela virgen sanctissima maria nuestra señora, madre
de Dios, conçebida sin pecado original."

Table 2.1 Works in Francisco Guerrero, *Canciones y villanescas espirituales* (Venice, 1589)
t=*tiple*, a=*alto*, T=*tenor*, B=*baxo*

Number	Incipit	Voices	Copla	Theme
1	Quand'os miro, mi Dios	ttaTB		Passion
2	Claros y hermosos ojos	ttaTB		Christ's eyes
3	Baxóme mi descuydo	ttaTB		Christ's eyes
4	En tanto que de rosa	ttaTB		Moral
5	Dezidme, fuente clara	ttaTB		Moral
6	La gracia y los ojos bellos	ttaTB		Mary
7	La luz de vuestros ojos	ttaTB		Mary
8	O dulçe y gran contento	taTTB		Moral
9	Sabes lo que heziste? 2 *parte* Llorad vostras ninphas	ttaTB		Moral
10	Pluguiera a Dios 2 *parte* Ay! No lo quiera Dios	ttaTB		Penitential
11	Mi offensa's grande	ttaTB		Penitential
12	Si el jardín del çielo	ttaTB		Mary
13	¡O qué nueva, o gran bien!	ttaTB	TtaT	Nativity
14	¡O qué plazer!	ttaTB		Nativity
15	Vamos al portal	ttaTB	Tta	Nativity
16	¡O grandes paces!	ttaTB	T	Nativity
17	Apuestan zagales dos	ttaTB	TtaT	Nativity
18	Virgen sancta	ttaTB	T	Nativity
19	Oyd, oyd una cosa	ttaTB	Tta	Nativity
20	La tierra s'está gozando	ttaTB	tta (TB)	Nativity

Number	Incipit	Voices	*Copla*	Theme
21	Pastores, si nos queries	ttaTB	Tta	Nativity
22	¡Hombres, victoria, victoria!	ttaTB	TtTB	Nativity
23	Zagales, sin seso vengo	ttaTB	tta(TB)	Nativity
24	Mi fe, vengo de Belén	ttaTB	TtTB	Nativity
25	Al resplandor d'una	ttaTB	T	Nativity
26	A un niño llorando	ttaTB	T	Nativity
27	Pues la guîa d'una estrella	ttaTB	Tta	Nativity
28	Jucios sobre una estrella	ttaTB	T	Nativity
29	Alma, si sabes d'amor	ttaTB	Tta	Sacrament
30	Alma, mirad vuestro Dios	ttaTB	Tta	Sacrament
31	Dios los estremos condena	ttaTB	Tta	Sacrament
32	Estraña muestra d'amar	ttaTB	TtaTB	Sacrament
33	Quiere Dios que le ofrezcamos	ttaTB	Tta	Sacrament
34	Ojos claros, serenos	ttaT		Passion
35	De amores del Señor	ttaT		Christ pastor
36	Dexó del mundo	ttaT		Magdalen
37	Adiós, verde ribera	ttaT		Moral
38	Esclareçida madre	ttaT		Mary
39	¿Qué te dare, Señor? *2 parte* Un grande abismo	ttaT		Passion
40	Prado ameno, graçioso	ttaa		Nativity?
41	Acaba de matarme	ttaT		Passion
42	Sanctíssima María	ttaT		Mary
43	Pan divino, gracioso *2 parte* El pan qu'estás mirando	ttaT		Sacrament
44	Vana sperança	ttaT		Moral
45	Huyd, huyd	taTB		Moral
46	Dios inmortal	taTB		Sacrament
47	¡O qué mesa y qué manjar!	taTB		Sacrament
48	¡O celestial medicina!	taTB	taTB	Sacrament
49	Todo quanto pudo dar	taTB	taTB	Sacrament
50	Antes que comáis a Dios	taTB	taTB	Sacrament
51	Oy, Joseph	taTB	taTB	Nativity
52	Los Reyes siguen la'strella	taTB	taTB	Nativity

Number	Incipit	Voices	*Copla*	Theme
53	Niño Dios d'amor herido	taTB	taTB	Nativity
54	Si tus penas no pruevo	tta		Passion
55	Pastor, quien madre virgen	tta		Mary
56	O virgen, quand'os miro	tta		Mary
57	¡O venturoso día!	tta		Sacrament
58	Qué buen año	tta	tta	Sacrament
59	Tan largo á sido	tta	tta	Sacrament
60	¿Qué se puede desear?	tta	tta	Sacrament
61	Es menester que se açierte	tta	tta	Sacrament

Table 2.2 Guerrero, *Canciones y villanescas espirituales,* Arranged by Theme
t=*tiple*, a=*alto*, T=*tenor*, B=*baxo*

Number	Incipit	Voices	*Copla*	Theme
35	De amores del Señor	ttaT		Christ pastor
2	Claros y hermosos ojos	ttaTB		Christ's eyes
3	Baxóme mi descuydo	ttaTB		Christ's eyes
41	Acaba de matarme	ttaT		Passion
36	Dexó del mundo	ttaT		Magdalen
6	La gracia y los ojos bellos	ttaTB		Mary
7	La luz de vuestros ojos	ttaTB		Mary
12	Si el jardín del çielo	ttaTB		Mary
38	Esclareçida madre	ttaT		Mary
42	Sanctíssima María	ttaT		Mary
55	Pastor, quien madre virgen	tta		Mary
56	O virgen, quand'os miro	tta		Mary
44	Vana sperança	ttaT		Moral
45	Huyd, huyd	taTB		Moral
4	En tanto que de rosa	ttaTB		Moral
5	Dezidme, fuente clara	ttaTB		Moral
8	O dulçe y gran contento	taTTB		Moral

Number	Incipit	Voices	*Copla*	Theme
9	Sabes lo que heziste? *2 parte* Llorad vostras ninphas	ttaTB		Moral
37	Adiós, verde ribera	ttaT		Moral
13	¡O qué nueva, o gran bien!	ttaTB	ttaT	Nativity
14	¡O qué plazer!	ttaTB		Nativity
15	Vamos al portal	ttaTB	tta	Nativity
16	¡O grandes paces!	ttaTB	t	Nativity
17	Apuestan zagales dos	ttaTB	tta(T)	Nativity
18	Virgen sancta	ttaTB	t	Nativity
19	Oyd, oyd una cosa	ttaTB	tta	Nativity
20	La tierra s'está gozando	ttaTB	tta(TB)	Nativity
21	Pastores, si nos queries	ttaTB	tta	Nativity
22	¡Hombres, victoria, victoria!	ttaTB	ttTB	Nativity
23	Zagales, sin seso vengo	ttaTB	tta(TB)	Nativity
24	Mi fe, vengo de Belén	ttaTB	ttTB	Nativity
25	Al resplandor d'una	ttaTB	t	Nativity
26	A un niño llorando	ttaTB	t	Nativity
27	Pues la guîa d'una estrella	ttaTB	tta	Nativity
28	Jucios sobre una estrella	ttaTB	t	Nativity
40	Prado ameno, graçioso	ttaa		Nativity
51	Oy, Joseph	taTB	taTB	Nativity
52	Los Reyes siguen la'strella	taTB	taTB	Nativity
53	Niño Dios d'amor herido	taTB	taTB	Nativity
1	Quand'os miro, mi Dios	ttaTB		Passion
34	Ojos claros, serenos	ttaT		Passion
39	¿Qué te dare, Señor? *2 parte* Un grande abismo	ttaT		Passion
54	Si tus penas no pruevo	tta		Passion
10	Pluguiera a Dios *2 parte* Ay! no lo quiera Dios	ttaTB		Penitential
11	Mi offensa's grande	ttaTB		Penitential
29	Alma, si sabes d'amor	ttaTB	tta	Sacrament
30	Alma, mirad vuestro Dios	ttaTB	tta	Sacrament
31	Dios los estremos condena	ttaTB	tta	Sacrament
32	Estraña muestra d'amar	ttaTB	ttaTB	Sacrament

Number	Incipit	Voices	*Copla*	Theme
33	Quiere Dios que le ofrezcamos	ttaTB	tta	Sacrament
43	Pan divino, gracioso 2 *parte* El pan qu'estás mirando	ttaT		Sacrament
46	Dios inmortal	taTB		Sacrament
47	¡O qué mesa y qué manjar!	taTB		Sacrament
48	¡O celestial medicina!	taTB	taTB	Sacrament
49	Todo quanto pudo dar	taTB	taTB	Sacrament
50	Antes que comáis a Dios	taTB	taTB	Sacrament
57	¡O venturoso día!	tta		Sacrament
58	Qué buen año	tta	tta	Sacrament
59	Tan largo á sido	tta	tta	Sacrament
60	¿Qué se puede desear?	tta	tta	Sacrament
61	Es menester que se açierte	tta	tta	Sacrament

Silent Music

The Apache Transformation
of a Girl to a Woman

ANNE DHU MCLUCAS

As told in the creation story of the Mescaleros, as well as other Apache groups,[1] a coming-of-age ceremony was originally given to the Apache deity Isdzanadl'esh[2] ("White-Painted Woman") by her parents when she was an adolescent.[3] She then passed it on to the people as a way of initiating young girls. It is believed that when the goddess grows old, she has only to walk westward and meet a girl running eastward at the end of her ceremony to return herself to youth.[4] During the ceremony, the girl is said to become Isdzanadl'esh and hence has her healing powers. At several points during the ceremony, the girl is asked to bless tribal members, and throughout it she is identified as Isdzanadl'esh and is enjoined to think of the well-being of the tribe. She retains these powers during the whole of the ceremony, and the memory of her power, as well as the learning that goes on during the ceremony, is meant to remain with her throughout her life. As Talamantez (2001: 300) writes: "This deity whom the initiate has *been* for a while is also everything that a woman can hope to be. She is wise; she is powerful; she heals; she provides effective tools for living a life of harmony and balance. . . . All a woman has to do when she meets obstacles in her life is to remember how she felt during her ceremony when she was Isanaklesh." In earlier days, the ceremony meant that a girl was now ready for marriage and childbearing. While such early marriage seldom happens now, it is still expected that the girl who has had a ceremony is ready to behave as an adult Apache female.

The girls of many of the traditional families on the Mescalero Apache Reservation of southeastern New Mexico take part in this rite of passage, which brings them from girlhood to womanhood in the space of five days.[5] The girls' puberty rite, which is the most important and central ceremony of the tribe,[6] is held together in large part by music, chanted to the accompaniment of rattles by a healer, or, as translated from the Apache *gutaal,* "singer," and his assistants. That the girls themselves remain silent during this ceremony is both an important and a paradoxical fact. Except for the characteristic sound of the jingles on their dresses as they dance and the occasional talking necessary to carry on daily tasks, they are meant to remain largely silent while a great deal of music and speech goes on around them. How are we to interpret this silence, and what purpose does it serve? In examining some of the musical details of this ceremony, I aim to reveal how it serves to represent important Apache values—including that of silence—and hand them on to the next generation.

On the present-day Mescalero reservation, the girls' feasts (as they are commonly referred to in English by tribal members) are held privately all summer long in various locations throughout the reservation, as well as in one large, public ceremony, held on and around the Fourth of July.[7] This public ceremony is tribally sponsored and is celebrated in an arena near the rodeo grounds, complete with bleachers, a loudspeaker, and ample grounds for camping. It is attended not only by the families of the several girls going through the ceremony, but also by Native Americans from other tribes from around the country, the Mescalero, Chiricahua,[8] and Lipan Apaches who occupy the reservation, and by tourists who have come to attend it or the nearby rodeo that occurs at around the same time. Although the atmosphere of the public ceremony is somewhat carnival-like, with the loudspeaker, food and other vendors, and many distractions for visitors, the actual performance of the ritual is carried out with care and dignity, amid all else that is happening. This observation contradicts, in part, Sonnichsen (1973: 34), who writes:

> The puberty ceremony . . . is becoming increasingly commercialized.
> The first three days are still more or less private and sacred, but the fourth
> day, arranged to fall on or near the Fourth of July, is strictly for tourists.
> Visitors jam the bleachers at the rodeo ground and eat hamburgers around
> the dance plaza, staring uncomprehendingly at the Mountain Gods
> when the dance begins, poking at Indian babies, and taking pictures of
> everything. The Mescaleros forgive them for their bad manners as they
> pocket their money, and seemingly do not regret the decay of their most
> sacred ceremonial.

The private feasts, held by individual families throughout the summer, are done without all the ancillary activities, making it possible to focus solely on the ritual itself. Data for this article are drawn primarily from the private feasts attended in the years 1985–2003, although reference will be made as well to the public ceremony from time to time.[9]

As a rite of passage, this ceremony joins many others in the world that celebrate girls' coming of age.[10] Its closest relatives are those of the other Apache tribes and of the *kinaaldá* of the Navajo people.[11] The Navajo are related to the Apache in origin and language as descendants from the original northern Athapaskans, who came to the Southwest sometime in the early sixteenth century.[12] Other Athapaskan-speaking tribes have similar ceremonies, even though long separated in time; for example, the "sunrise ceremony" of the Tolowa in southern Oregon and northern California, which is held for their adolescent girls.[13] Some of the elements commonly included in Native American puberty rites in the western United States are the number four, some form of seclusion, the use of a drinking tube, a scratching stick, the acts of running and dancing as part of a public ceremony, and the use of hoof rattles.[14] The elaborate and beautiful symmetry of the Mescalero ceremony, however, as well as its extensive use of music, is to my knowledge unmatched in any other group.

The absence of a similar public ceremony for adolescent boys is often remarked upon. The way that adulthood and the blessings of supernatural beings are received by Mescalero boys appears to be much more personal and individual. As Opler (1969: 24) writes in his classic description of traditional Mescalero life, comparing normal religious life to that of the central girls' puberty ceremony: "The essence of Mescalero religion, however, was the individual power quest . . . The acquisition of supernatural power at some point in life was considered a normal Mescalero experience; the Mescalero was taught that he was infinitely better prepared to cope with danger if he had a supernatural helper." The young man's acquisition of supernatural power could occur through a dream, which often leads to the youth's initiation into certain rites by a mentor, who might lead him into the woods to learn appropriate songs and prayers. The lack of a public ceremony for the boys may have to do in part with the matrilinear and matrilocal nature of Apache life. Since it is the women through whom inheritance occurs, their strength should be publicly acknowledged and celebrated.

The girls' puberty rite of the Mescaleros has been described in detail by both insiders and outsiders to the culture.[15] What follows is a summary of the principal actions of the ceremony, made from personal observation, with emphasis on the musical portions and who is performing them, followed by an analysis of the importance of music and silence.

◆ The Ceremony

Preparation for the ceremony begins often years in advance of its actual celebration, since traditional families who have daughters know its importance and will begin to save the money and ritual items that will be necessary. One of my Mescalero friends, whose daughter recently went through her ceremony at age 13, said they had been saving since the day she was born so that they could have a proper feast for her. When the onset of a girl's menses begins, a small private ceremony, often referred to as "the little ceremony," will be held and the preparations for her big feast begin in earnest. Because of the harsh winter weather at Mescalero, the season for feasts is usually the summer and early fall.

The family finds an appropriate singer[16] as well as an older woman who will serve as the girl's sponsor (*nadekleshen* or *naaikish* in Apache)[17] and who will help her in preparations as well as throughout the ceremony. Both of these people must be knowledgeable about not only the ceremony and its songs, but also traditional Apache ways and lore, since it is their job to prepare the girl for womanhood, as celebrated in the ceremony. The girl's deerskin dress and boots must be made, enough cattail pollen gathered to last the entire ceremony (this gathering process is usually started several seasons before the feast), and the gifts for the various participants in the feast must be bought. Meanwhile, the girl is instructed in proper Apache ways by her sponsor, in preparation for the feast. Most important is that the girl understand the significance of this ceremony for the Apaches. Beginning from her "little ceremony" and throughout the actual feast, instruction is given to her in many forms. Each element of her dress and accessories is explained, following the origin myth. For example, in the myth (as retold in Talamantez 2000), the deerskin dress is assembled in sections, since as Isdzanadl'esh was pulled from the water, the medicine men covered first her upper half so that she would not be cold. There was a red mark on her from the red earth, which is reproduced on the dress. Rattles of deer hooves and shells were attached to her dress (small tin cones have now replaced the deer hooves), and eagle feathers decorate her hair. Likewise the skirt (a separate garment) is decorated with fringe, and the girl drinks through a reed tube, as did Isdzanadl'esh, who at first did not know how to drink. Most striking is the final painting of the girl with white clay, which happens at the end of the public ceremony, done in imitation of the white stains left by minerals of water as it recedes. In the myth she is found covered in water up to her nose; the painting of the lower half of her face reproduces the residue left by the white minerals on her face (Talamantez 2000: 147–54).

For private ceremonies, the family and the singer select a site; for the public feast, the site is above the rodeo grounds near the center of the reservation, where there is a permanent set of bleachers for spectators. In both cases the large cooking arbor is constructed from brush; tepees are erected for the girl, her relatives, and the singer and sponsor. Several days in advance, the men of the extended family start to gather wood, water, and the twelve long pine poles with their green tops left on that will be used to erect the ceremonial tepee. Four of these will be used as the main structural poles; to be added are eight additional tepee poles, to complete the beautiful and natural home in which the girl as goddess will dance. All of these preparations are completed in time for dawn of the first day of the feast, when many people of the tribe will have gathered at the feast grounds, camped in their tepees, vans, and tents. At dawn the singing begins, and the four main poles are raised by the male members of the family, in the order east, south, west, north, each to a verse of the song sung by the singer and his assistants, while the female relatives stand nearby, ready to make their ritual cries as each pole is raised.

The sound of this cry, which is the only public sound that the women make, is considered very holy, and has been explained in various ways in the literature.[18] It is a wordless glissando on the syllable *oo,* starting quite high and descending in pitch over a period of several seconds. Because it is emitted from behind the raised shawls of the women, it is often hard to discern where it comes from when first heard. So distinctive is the sound that the sponsor, who leads the other women in the glissando, has sometimes been identified in Apache as "she who makes the sound."[19] Several authors have stated that the sound is emitted whenever the name of the deity Isdzanadl'esh is mentioned (Opler 1965; Farrer 1994). However, as can be seen from a musical analysis of the songs, since the cry occurs regularly at the same point in a song's structure and is often heard independent of these names, it actually emphasizes the structure of the music.[20] The sponsor, who leads the cry, must know the music of the ceremony well in order to make the sound at the appropriate time. In fact, one of the singers revealed to me that he counts on the ritual cries of the sponsor and others to keep track of where he is in the song. I have observed in several ceremonies that hand signals are also made by the sponsor to the singer to indicate how many verses have been sung. In the long nights of singing, keeping track of the repetitions is difficult; the sponsors know the music as well as the singers and help the latter by means of their ritual cries and their hand signals.

In the dawn construction of the tepee, the ritual cry is emitted as each structural pole of the sacred tepee is raised, coinciding, as it will later in later

Diagram 3.1 **Ceremonial Tepee**

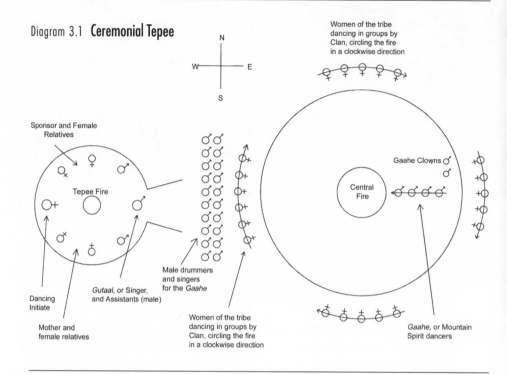

Women of the tribe
dancing in groups by
Clan, circling the fire
in a clockwise direction

Sponsor and Female
Relatives

Tepee Fire

Gaahe Clowns

Central
Fire

Male drummers
and singers
for the *Gaahe*

Gutaal, or Singer,
and Assistants (male)

Dancing
Initiate

Mother and
female relatives

Women of the tribe
dancing in groups by
Clan, circling the fire
in a clockwise direction

Gaahe, or Mountain
Spirit dancers

songs, with the end of the "verse" of the song.[21] Since there are four main poles, and since almost all of the songs have four verses, the songs are also a reaffirmation of the number four, the sacred number for Apaches,[22] a number that permeates the ceremony. Although several authors have written that a new song is sung for each pole raised, my observations have shown that instead one song with four verses is used; other songs are sung as the rest of the twelve poles are put into place.[23]

After the completion of the tepee with its opening and a runway to the east, a fire hole is dug in the center of the tepee (see diagram 3.1). The tepee top is covered with a canvas, while the sides are filled in with green brush and the floor strewn with green tule leaves. In front of the runway, the girl kneels on her buckskin and, after receiving a blessing from the singer, gives an individual pollen blessing to each tribal member who comes forward. This is done in silence, but with careful attention to the needs of each person.[24] After an offering of ritual food to all the guests present, songs are sung as the girl is "molded" by the sponsor; that is, as she lies on the buckskin spread for the purpose, she is massaged to insure a healthy body. Afterward the singer draws four footprints in pollen on the buckskin and a basket holding sacred objects is placed at a distance of some yards to the east of the tepee. As the girl steps into each of the four footsteps, the verse of the appropriate song is sung and a ritual cry is emitted. She is then "trotted off" by the singer to run around the basket four times. For each of her four runs the basket is moved closer in toward the tepee, and each time the sponsor and other female relatives make the ritual cry. After these morning events, the girl's relatives shower her with candy and fruits dumped from a basket. Then the girl and her sponsor go back to her private tepee, and the spectators are treated to a giveaway, in which gifts are thrown from the back of a pickup truck.

During the afternoons of the four feast days, various activities unrelated to the feast itself go on. There is often powwow dancing, with one or more drums hired by either the tribe or the host family.[25] Sometimes competition dancing by the young Mescalero residents is held in conjunction with the pow-wow music. While all of this goes on, the girl is resting and taking instruction in her tepee, often visited by relatives or by people who have an illness or infirmity that they wish her to bless. At some point during the afternoon, the girl and her relatives will come to the ceremonial tepee to start a fire in the fire pit by means of twirling a stick against another piece of wood. It is ideal and a good sign if the fire can be started so, but at many ceremonies these days, the fire ends up being started with a match.

At about dusk another, larger fire is lit in the center of the grounds to the east of the ceremonial tepee (see diagram 3.1) and the Gaahe, or Mountain Spirits, come out to dance, having already blessed the campground. They have also blessed and been blessed by the girl, who visits their campsite before they appear in public. The Gaahe are masked, painted dancers, who dance in teams of four, with one or two "clowns" (Gaahelibaye)[27] trailing them. The Gaahe carry long, flat sticks and have yucca headdresses. They wear deerskin kilts adorned with tin-cone jingles and leather moccasins with bells wrapped around their ankles. Because of these sounds, one can hear their approach from afar. The clowns wear loud cowbells attached to their backs. As they dance toward the fire, the Gaahe make the sounds of turkeys and owls. Their appearance is always presaged by the characteristic sounds of their various jingles and bells. As the Gaahe dance in their dramatic, heavy-stepped style, slapping their sticks against their thighs, the women form a broken circle around them, and, grouped by clans, they dance silently in small, delicate steps with their shawls moving rhythmically with their steps. Often the girl initiate will dance for a short while with her clan members before returning to her tepee.[28]

Late in the evening, the girl reappears with her sponsor and is led ceremonially into the tepee, which is now the home of the goddess. She grasps the tip of an eagle feather held by the singer, who pulls her into the structure as a song of four verses is sung. As each verse is sung and the ritual cry emitted, the girl takes one large step into the tepee. In four steps, she is inside, where the rest of the ceremony will take place. She, her sponsor, and female relatives walk to their sitting places in a clockwise direction; they sit inside the tepee facing the fire pit. The singer and his assistants sit on the other side of the fire, facing the girl, and with their backs to the entrance (see diagram 3.1). Much time is spent preparing the place where the girl will dance, making sure the fire is well stocked, supplying water to the singer and the others, but eventually the singing and dancing begins. The girl lays her rawhide down and dances across it from side to side in four sliding steps, with her elbows bent and her hands held in the air, the tin cones and shells on her dress jingling softly. The singer accompanies her in sets of four songs, with the sound of the fawn-hoof rattles, shaken in regular single pulses with no accent. Between the sets of songs, the girl rests and drinks water; the sponsor will often use this time to explain the meaning of the songs to her, since they are sung in an archaic Apache that few can understand. The content of the songs, as it has been explained to me, is to "sing the Apache world into being." That is, on the first night they sing of all the things that crawl on earth; the next night of the trees and growing things; the third night of the flying things; and the final night, of everything. Many of the texts also allude to the actions currently under way in the ceremony.[29]

After each set of four songs the singer and his assistants sing a short smoking chant and smoke sacred tobacco. Occasionally the girl switches to a different, forward-kicking so-called resting step with hands on hips for one set of songs.[30] The singing and dancing will go on from one to three hours, depending in part on the stamina of the girl and the wishes of the singer. Before or around midnight, the girl retires to her tepee.

For the first three nights of the ceremony this is the structure, but on the fourth night the singing and dancing extend for the whole night and many of the songs that have been heard the other three nights are recapitulated. As each song is sung, a hand-hewn stick (usually made by the girl and her family) is hammered into the ground around the fire pit, with a marker laid after each group of four. By the end of the night, the marking sticks surround the entire fire pit. The girl continues to dance without a break (other than the short pauses after each set of four songs) until the early morning, when she goes to her tepee, has her hair ritually washed with yucca root, and reappears in the tepee just before dawn.

In a single song, sung just as the sun rises, the singer and his assistants paint an image of the sun on the palms of their hands with clay and galena, a shiny black mineral that gleams in the sunlight. At the appropriate moment in the song, the singer turns his hand toward the sun, then rubs it onto the top of the girl's head.[31] After this, the singer paints the girl with red and white clay while the ceremonial tepee is being dismantled, except for the four structural poles.[32] The singer then blesses the members of the community with red and white clay while the girl sits in the sunlight.

The final actions of the ceremony, shortly after dawn of the fifth day, occur rapidly and are a reversal of those of the first morning. Following the blessing the singer leads the girl out of the tepee with the eagle feather (to a different song than that of the first day). He once again paints footsteps on the buckskin and a basket is placed to the east of the tepee, in this case nearer to the tepee than on the first day. The girl is once again "trotted off" and runs around the basket four times, accompanied by the four verses of the song and the ritual cries. This time, the basket is moved further and further eastward each of the four times, and on the last run, the girl does not return, but runs far past the basket, rubbing off the white clay as she runs. It is at this moment that it is said she meets Isdzanadl'esh, who returns to her youth. It is also at this moment that the girl becomes a woman. Simultaneous with this last run, the remaining tepee poles crash to the ground and the singer and assistants finish their last songs. The ceremonial gravity is broken by a giveaway, in which all manner of presents are thrown from a truck to the waiting spectators, once again mirroring the actions of the first morning.

◈ Analysis

From this description of the girl's puberty rite, you will notice that the girl has remained largely silent throughout the ceremony, while much music and talk has gone on around her. Except for the soft jingling of the tin cones on her dress, she makes no sound except to speak quietly and in private to her relatives, the sponsor, and the singer. In fact, it is considered important that the girl behave seriously, that she not be seen to be laughing and socializing with her friends during the time of the ceremony. The sound of the jingles, however, is crucial. Already in 1868, John Cremony (1868: 245) described the dresses as having small bells hung to the skirts and bits of tinsel profusely arrayed over her attire. When the sound is altered in any way, the onlookers notice. In 1996, at a private feast the girl wore a necklace with small bells, which added a new sound to that of the tin cones. Comments were made by many of the female onlookers that the sound had changed; opinions differed on whether that was a good or a bad thing.

It is traditionally only the men who sing and play rattles or drums,[33] while the women help, largely behind the scenes, providing the ritual food and sitting with the girl inside the ceremonial tepee (where no men except the singer and his assistants are allowed). I have seen but one exception to this all-male rule: at a private ceremony in 1987, one of the singer's assistants, although dressed as a boy and with hair cut like that of a boy, turned out to be a girl of about sixteen years who had had her ceremony several years before and wanted to study the songs. She sat with the male singers, and performed all the traditional functions of a young assistant, singing along quietly and in the same range as the men, fetching wood and water when required. She was an anomaly, though in a characteristic Apache way, accepted by the tribe in this role. She later left the reservation and went to join the circus!

The further participation of women in the visible portions of the ceremony is limited to dancing in a large circle surrounding the teams of *Gaahe,* as they dance around the central fire—and this they do silently, although, as mentioned above, the swaying of their shawls adds a powerful visual rhythmic element in stark contrast to the bold movement and loud noises of the *Gaahe.*[34]

This silence on the part of women is not an unusual situation in Native American tribes, but it cannot be equated with having "no voice" in the larger sense of being disempowered. For example, in the early Iroquois League, described by Martha Rendle (1951), gender roles could be described as "separate but equal" in the sense that women had their own well-defined spheres of influence, both political and religious. Both men and women were Keepers of the Faith; both could practice medicine and join medicine societies, and in the area of politics, while men did play the important public roles in the hereditary longhouse and league, it was the matrons who had the ultimate right to appoint and depose leaders, and the culturally crucial death feasts were the responsibility of the women. Yet men led the ceremonial singing, then as now, a fact which Rendle explains by using R. E. M. Wheeler's (1950: 127–28) classic description of male versus female roles in many tribal societies: the woman working unceasingly in the time-consuming duties of gathering, preparing, cooking, clothing, and child care versus the male, whom he describes in one hyphenated word as "man-with-time-to-think-between-meals," who often used this free time to create major religious and aesthetic roles in society. This division of labor with different but equally important roles for the genders is a familiar one in many Native American contexts. Rendle 1951 and Shimony

1980 document the absence of women as musicians for the Iroquois, McAllester 1954 and Frisbie 1967 for the Navajo, Tedlock 1980 for the Zuni, and Roberts 1972 for various pueblo groups. Likewise, in the total context of the Apache ceremony, which celebrates reaching womanhood, women do have important roles, albeit not overtly musical ones. In fact, it is clear that a balance of genders is achieved in the overall layout of the ceremony (see diagram 3.1), and that the silent and musical roles are a part of this balance, as well as those of gender.

Why are the women silent in the ceremonial context? It is quite certain that the meaning of their silence is not subservience. The adult women of Mescalero are neither passive nor silent in the affairs of their tribe, and the girls' puberty rite is the central ceremony of the entire tribe. Women continue, as in the past, to play active roles as tribal council members, practitioners of traditional medicine, heads of family, property owners, and even, in times past, as warriors.[35] The Apaches had a matrilinear and matrilocal social organization before the reservation period and the superimposition of white governmental structures, and much of this way of life continues at an informal level. As pointed out eloquently in an article by Inés Talamantez (1991: 133), the strong position of traditional Apache women in their society could be a model for a "post-patriarchal" society. Describing Mescalero society, she writes:

> Women usually have control of the household food supply and have primary roles in the inheritance of property. Mothers with adult children are especially powerful and are accorded respect by children who feel for them a strong and life-long bond. The hope is that a woman will complete the circle of life in beauty and balance by taking care of herself in all aspects: mental, physical, and spiritual, and by obeying ceremonial traditions and the laws of nature. Special ceremonies are performed to ensure that young girls will mature safely, adjust to life easily, become secure and self-confident women in order to propagate the traditions of their culture.

Of these special ceremonies, the one marking their change from girls to women is most important to traditional Mescaleros. Yet, in this central and highly musical tradition of ceremonial life, women's voices are scarcely heard. The reasons for this may become clearer on examining the value of silence in Apache culture.

◆ The Value of Silence

In Apache life overall, much more value is given to silence than in the dominant white world. As Basso has pointed out for the Western Apaches, silence serves a social purpose in dealing with uncertainty. According to him, the types of social situations in which Apaches refrain from speech are those in which the social identity and/or position of at least one participant is ambiguous. Under these conditions, "fixed role expectations lose their applicability and the illusion of predictability in social interaction is lost. . . . In short, keeping silent among the Western Apache is a response to uncertainty and unpredictability in social relations."[36] In the case of the Mescaleros, silence may thus signal the uncertainty and unpredictability of a girl about to enter womanhood. Her potential—for becoming a valuable member of Mescalero society, or for the opposite—is what is at stake in the ceremony.[37]

Silence was noted as a particular quality of Apache women as early as 1892 in this quote by Captain John Bourke, which also attests to the power of women in Apache life: "In all tribes the influence of the women, though silent, is most potent."[38] Claire Farrer (1994: 28) describes the importance of silence for both men and women in Mescalero society:

> The interplay between sound and silence is of immense importance throughout Apachean daily and ritual life. At times Power is manifest through song while simultaneously being present in silence, as some participating in an event have the role of voice and others have the role of no-voice. . . . Proper Apachean speech is characterized by periods of quiet. . . . A proper person leaves spaces in speech—times of no sound for listening to the universe and one's own inner voice, times of no sound for contemplation, times of no sound for framing the next utterance, times of no sound to allow wisdom to descend upon one.

The girl's silence in the ceremony gives her the dignity of the goddess at a period of life in which her identity is fluctuating. Her silence can be interpreted as a form of power, part of her new identity as a woman, and may encompass, as stated in the quote above, listening, contemplation, and "allowing wisdom to descend." Instructions given to the girl by the singer and sponsor include helping her contemplate how with her power she can help the tribe as she dances—by thinking of their health and well-being, by literally "sending sickness over the mountain," as one singer put it.[39] None of these instructions call for her to say anything; all of her important actions—blessing, dancing, and running—are done in silence.

◆ Conclusion

An investigation of this ceremony reveals several vital, but subtle musical roles played by the girls and the women who mentor them and are knowledgeable in tribal traditions. Among these are:

◆ the girl's dancing and the associated sounds of tin-cone jingles as an indispensable element of a musical performance

◆ the punctuation and guidance of male ritual singing by female ritual experts by means of their ritual cries

◆ the silent but rhythmic dancing of all the females, from the smallest girls up to the elders

◆ supportive subliminal singing, done by many women who have themselves been through the ceremony, know the rituals, and sing quietly along.

This last point has not yet been mentioned, but has been observed at various ceremonies; women who are watching the ceremony will sometimes quietly sing the songs under their breath—remembering them, perhaps, from their own feast, or from the many other feasts they have witnessed over the years. This is a quiet, scarcely observable phenomenon, but it attests to the power of the music and its memorability.

These musical roles—as well as the powerful silence—form a vital part of the girl's ceremony. By looking carefully at the totality of what constitutes a complete musical performance or a complete musical culture—including its silent or supportive roles[40]—we gain important information about the values imparted to girls about Apache womanhood through this highly evolved ceremony.

Notes

This article and the others I have written would not have been possible without the help and friendship of Dr. Inés Talamantez, Professor of Religious Studies, University of California, Santa Barbara, who has freely shared her invaluable knowledge and experience and has been my companion on many trips to Mescalero.

1. The Mescaleros are one of six principal Apache tribes in the Southwest; each of them has a form of this ceremony as well as a myth of its origins. These differ in many details; what is described in this article applies only to the Mescalero Apaches.

2. This transliteration of the Apache represents an approximation of how it is said; there is no dictionary of the language (unlike Navajo). The accepted phonetic transcription is ʔisdzanatlʔeesh, but most readers will find that hard to sound out. Goddard 1909 gives her name as IsdjanaLijn; Hoijer 1938 as ʔÌszánáλè.šń; Nicholas 1939 as Esdzandeha; Farrer 1980 as Isdząnatłʼeesh; Shapiro and Talamantez 1986 as Isdzanadlʼesh; Talamantez 1991 and 2000 as ʻIsanaklesh or ʻIsánáklésh; and Boyer and Gayton 1992 as Istún-e-glesh, but these are all the same deity.

3. There are other versions of how the ceremony originated; see Goddard 1909: 386, which states that it was the son of Isdzanadlʼesh, whom Goddard identifies as Nayenezganin, Child-of-the-Water, who first built a sacred lodge and celebrated the ceremony.

4. The most extensive and beautiful retelling of the myth as given to Inés Talamantez by the singer Willeto Antonio is found in Talamantez 2000: 147–54. Another version is found in Nicholas 1939: 193–94.

5. The ceremony begins at dawn on the first day and ends shortly after dawn on the fifth day, and is therefore often described as a four-night ceremony. However, the girl is also expected to stay at the campground and contemplate her experience for four days after the ceremony; therefore it could also be termed a nine-day ceremony, although the public portion lasts five days.

6. Its importance and long history are born out by its mention in Cremony 1868: 245–46; and its observance even in exile at Mt. Vernon Barracks, Alabama, as reported in Opler 1969: 154.

7. Presumably, the Mescalero tribe chose the Fourth of July when the government policy required that Native Americans celebrate only one ceremony, and that on a national holiday. Since summer is the best time for these outdoor ceremonies, the Fourth of July was a logical choice, and by tradition it has continued to be used for the tribally sponsored event.

8. The Chiricahua girls also go through the ceremony, but with significant departures from the practices of Mescalero, according to Boyer and Gayton (1992: 340–44). The most visible difference is in the moccasin toes, which for the Chiricahua bend upward at the end, but the most significant, according to Boyer and Gayton, is that the Chiricahua girls do not dance in the sacred tepee, but instead with the Mountain God dancers for the duration of the four evenings. I have, however, witnessed Chiricahua girls at the public ceremony dancing in the tepee all four nights.

9. Since the families of these girls would prefer anonymity, I am not at liberty to reveal their names; except for one feast in 2000, they were all conducted by the singer Willeto Antonio.

10. See, for example, articles in Lincoln 1981, concerning ceremonies in North Kerala in South India, the Navajo's Kinaaldá, Tiv scarification, and the Tukuna of the Northwest Amazon. For comparisons among Native American groups, the most thorough study is Driver 1941.

11. Charlotte Frisbie (1967) has written a book-length study of this important ceremony. The Navajo deity Changing Woman, 'Esdzą́ą́nádleehé in Navajo (note the name's resemblance to that of Isdzanadl'esh) is sometimes called White Shell Woman and is an equivalent figure to the Apache Isdzanadl'esh, or White-Painted Woman.

12. The timing of the migration to the Southwest of Athapaskan people from the north (their probable origin was in west-central Canada) is in dispute. It has been put as early as 1000 (see Jett 1964), but it is more generally agreed to be no earlier than 1525, which is when archeologists have dated the earliest Apachean sites. See Gunnerson 1979: 162.

13. The Tolowa girls' puberty ceremony is described briefly in the article "Tolowa" in Gould 1979: 134, and more comprehensively in Drucker 1937: 262–64, where Drucker describes a ten-day ceremony to celebrate the coming of age of a daughter of a rich man, or to ward against an oncoming illness, in the belief that "at this time a girl possessed a tremendous magical potency, which might thus be used in behalf of the people."

14. Information from Driver 1941. A deer-hoof rattle similar to those used by the Mescalero Apache is pictured in W. Wallace 1978: 644, and it is stated that "over much of California the deerhoof rattle figured in rites held when girls attained the status of women"; however, for the Tolowa the same article holds that it was used to accompany gambling songs, not for the puberty rites.

15. See Farrer 1980, 1994; Fergusson 1931; Goddard 1909; McLucas 2000; Shapiro and Talamantez 1986; and Talamantez 1991, 2000, 2001, and forthcoming.

16. The singer is traditionally male, as is true in many Native American tribes. While there are some women healers and even shamans among the Apaches, the puberty ritual is always led by a male singer. Perhaps the balance of male and female in the ceremony seen in diagram 1 has something to do with this.

17. Talamantez 2000 uses *nadekleshe;* Farrer 1980 uses *naaikish.* She refers to the sponsor as "godmother"; Boyer 1992 uses "chaperone" and "sponsor." Many girls continue to call their sponsors "mother" long after their feasts.

18. Various terms have been used for the sound: "cry in reverent recognition" appears in Nicholas 1939: 202; "high-pitched cry" in Opler 1965: 84 and Boyer 1992: 48; "high-pitched ululation" in Farrer 1980: 130; "ritual marker" in Shapiro and Talamantez 1986: 89n7; and "long, slow, glide" or "noise" (a translation of the Apache term) in McLucas 2000: 202.

19. Opler 1965: 84. Opler adds that the first use of this cry is attributed to White-Painted Woman when her son returned to her after vanquishing the monsters.

20. See Shapiro and Talamantez 1986 and McLucas 2000 for musical analyses.

21. The terms *verse* and *refrain* used in this article are not indigenous to the Apache, but they have been readily accepted by the singers with whom I have worked as a way of communicating about the structure of the music. Their definitions—*verse* as the flexible bearer of new words; *refrain* as repetitive of both

text and tune, and often using nonlexical syllables—are quite compatible with the way in which the Apaches structure their songs. Dan Nicholas (1939), who is Mescalero Apache and an informant for Opler and Hoijer, uses a similarly borrowed terminology: *chant* and *burden.*

22. The number four has been called one of the base metaphors for Mescalero Apache by Claire Farrer (1980). Shapiro and Talamantez (1986: 80–87) describe its multileveled use in the songs.

23. See Shapiro and Talamantez 1986 for the precise timings of the pole-raising songs.

24. For example, an infant will have both its head and feet blessed to encourage good growth; someone with a lame arm can indicate that it should be specially blessed.

25. A powwow "drum" means the large central drum as well as the group of four to eight men who beat on it and sing. Although originating in Plains tribes, it is now a pan-Indian phenomenon. However, well-known drums are often hired for the ceremonies from Plains states, such as Oklahoma.

26. Once again, nomenclature varies: Farrer 1980 refers to them collectively as *Baanaaich'isnde;* Talamantez 2001 as *hastchin;* Nicholas 1939 as *Gahan.*

27. Farrer (1994: 101–27) uses the term *Libayé* for the ritual clown, whose role she discusses in a chapter titled "Clowning and Chiasm." I have most often heard them called *Gaahelibaye.*

28. Farrer (1980: 140) makes the point that only the Gaahe, the clowns, and the girl make noise, and, as she writes, "those sounds are perceived as music." According to her, all other women remove any jewelry that might make noise as they dance.

29. Pliny Earle Goddard (1909) offers several texts from the ceremony given to him by a man he terms "the last priest of the chief rites of the ceremony"; clearly, however, the ceremony has continued and perhaps changed. Hoijer 1938 prints in poetic translations several texts that are still used; Farrer 1980: 145–46 offers several partial texts; and Shapiro and Talamantez 1986: 83–84 contains one complete text in a literal translation of a song sung at dawn on the final morning.

30. Talamantez 2000: 154 quotes Willeto Antonio in a charming rationale for the two kinds of steps from the myth, saying that at first her walking was shaky, as in the first step; the jumping step she learned later, showing her pride in how well she had learned to walk.

31. Shapiro and Talamantez (1986) provide a translation of this song (based on Hoijer 1938) and a more detailed description of the actions.

32. In particular, her legs and arms and the bottom half of her face are painted white, emulating the chalky residue left on Isdzanadl'esh when she was pulled from the water.

33. The *Gaahe,* or Mountain Spirit dancers, are accompanied by groups of men

playing small water drums and singing loudly (in contrast to the rather soft chanting of the singer in the ceremonial tepee).

34. Farrer (1980: 140, 157) has also described this silent dance, as have Shapiro and Talamantez (1986: 81).

35. In a rather fanciful account, based, however, on historical documents, Peter Aleshire (2001) tells the life story of Lozen, the sister of Victorio, who went on many Apache raids and was famed as both a horse stealer and an effective warrior.

36. Basso 1990: 96. Whether this larger social observation about a different group of Apaches can apply here, it is at least food for thought.

37. McAllester 1954 describes a similar value placed on silence in Navajo culture (Navajos are a related Apachean culture).

38. Bourke 1892: 180. Bourke was an army captain during the Indian wars, an aide-de-camp of Brigadier General Crook. His experience and interest in Indian life resulted in his becoming a respected ethnologist of Apache life in particular.

39. Shapiro and Talamantez (1986: 86) describe a conversation with one of the singers: "The Singer instructs her to think in images about the tribe—to think, for instance of a sick grandfather, and to send his sickness over the mountain away from the tribe—images of motion and healing."

40. For more examples of silent roles as a crucial part of musical performance, see A. Shapiro 1991.

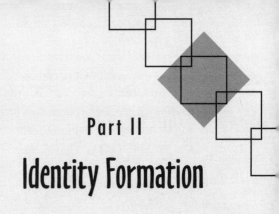

Part II

Identity Formation

The self is not something ready-made,
but something in continuous formation
through choice of action.
　　　　　　　　—J. K. Rowling

How is the self formed during youth? Although identity formation is a lifelong process, from chronological and psychological standpoints childhood represents a key phase in the development and definition of individual behaviors and outlooks. Few if any children are able to explicate the process of identity formation while undergoing it, however, and will more commonly reflect on memories of their youthful experiences as adults, naturally with added perspectives of age and maturity.

Part 2 presents four studies in music, youth, and the formation of individual identity under specific historical, social, and cultural conditions. Three essays (by Kok, Tang, and Willoughby) expound on and analyze memories of identity-forming choices made in their subjects' youths under various circumstances, while Huebner's essay probes the applicability of Jean Piaget's child-development theories in "the making of" the identity of the Child, jointly created by Colette and Ravel.

Youth identity scholar Mark Liechty has pointed out that "identity refers to a person's sense of inclusion in (or exclusion from) a range of social roles and ways of being, both 'real' (those derived from lived experience) and 'imagined' (those encountered in realms beyond the everyday: tales, religious epics, mass media, etc.)" (1995: 167). All the essays focus on individual resolutions and solutions in relation to realms real and imagined; music strikingly occupies both realms to a degree largely determined by the individual.

Liechty continues: "As a person's frame of reference expands beyond the boundaries of his/her own lived experience, via such avenues as education, travel and consumption of mass media, categories of being multiply into a plethora of 'possible lives' [Appadurai 1990: 9] . . . a person may have many identities encompassing many ways of being, within and between which there is no *necessary* consistency or logic" (1995: 167). Liechty's and Appadurai's formulations resonate in these essays. Music is shown to play various roles in shaping identity: as a bridge between lived and imagined ways of being, an avenue for articulating and exploring change, a way of expanding experience in individual lives, and a tool for the maintenance or disruption of values in interaction. In short, music emerges as a flexible, open-ended, and powerful element in "identity work" during which individuals "make sense of their lives" (Mueller 2002: 595).

—*Roe-Min Kok*

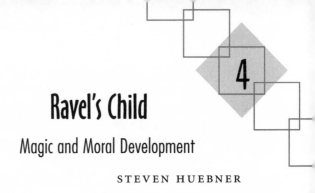

Ravel's Child

Magic and Moral Development

STEVEN HUEBNER

◈ Trauma and Smiles

A bored child, homework, an insistent mother: the beginning of *L'Enfant et les sortilèges* (1925) by Colette (Sidonie-Gabrielle Colette) and Maurice Ravel replays a familiar situation. Yellowing wallpaper peopled with rococo shepherds and shepherdesses, covered armchairs, and a floral-faced grandfather clock combine in a silent chorus of bourgeois domesticity. Protective and nurturing, one might say. Or, perhaps, oppressive.

The Child learns by rote imitation, and the lesson of the day is the expression "J'ai envie" (colloquially, "I feel like"). His first words in the opera simultaneously expose the mechanistic method of his instruction and subvert it:

J'ai pas envie de faire ma page,
J'ai envie d'aller me promener.
J'ai envie de manger tous les gateaux.
J'ai envie de tirer la queue du Chat
Et de couper celle de l'Écureuil.
J'ai envie de gronder tout le monde!
J'ai envie de mettre Maman en penitence.

I don't feel like doing my homework,
I feel like going for a walk,
I feel like eating all the cookies.
I feel like pulling the cat's tail,
and cutting off that of the squirrel.
I feel like scolding everyone.
I feel like putting Maman in the corner.

The Child's music meanders in organum-like parallel fourths and fifths on the oboes, a metrically variable and largely pentatonic passage. It promises extension ad infinitum just like the verbal sequence, and not without a disquieting hint in a blue note (F natural) whispered by a solo double bass harmonic. Mother cuts him off during the third iteration. Seen are the bottom of her apron and giant scissors on a chain, then her large hand—that is, according to Colette's libretto (and not most stage productions). The Child sticks out his tongue and is punished with sugarless tea and dry bread, and isolation. The mere verbal subversion of earlier erupts into a dizzy rampage. He breaks teapot and teacups, impales pet squirrel, tips kettle, rips wallpaper, disgorges pendulum, and careens into a maximal point of musical dissonance. And then, famously, the household objects spring to life. Wanton destruction has its price, they tell him. Furniture, clock, even books occult the familiar and perforce withdraw the pleasures they habitually provide. The succession of different musical styles and genres produced by the animated objects challenges the comfortable familiarity of the environment. After objects, animals: the Child follows two mating cats into the garden. To a despondent dragonfly, he reveals the fate of its mate pinned against a wall. His record of sadism unfolds, yet the animals—squirrels and toads and moths—momentarily forget his lethal past as they join in a choreographed celebration of nature, freedom, and love. "Ils s'aiment . . . Ils m'oublient . . . Je suis seul . . . (*malgré lui il appelle:*) Maman!" (They love each other . . . They're forgetting me . . . I'm alone [*in spite of himself he cries out:*] Maman). The word seems strange and threatening to the animals: they rush to attack the child and in their savagery injure one of their own, a tiny squirrel. The Child, also hurt, is moved to pity and binds the wound. General surprise. With mystical reverence for the unknown, the animals chant "Maman" and hoist the Child: "Il est sage . . . Il est bon" (He is well-behaved . . . He is good-hearted). A light appears in a window. The Child intones "Maman" to the same harmony that had accompanied scissors and apron at the beginning, and the curtain falls.

Initiating an influential tradition of interpretation in an essay celebrating the composer's fiftieth birthday in 1925 (the year that *L'Enfant et les sortilèges* was premiered), critic and composer Alexis Roland-Manuel (1925) maintained that Ravel's art was founded on an "esthétique de l'imposture" fueled by objective distance, allusive play, and calculated manipulation of opposites. The characters in a comic opera such as *L'Heure espagnole* behave like mechanical automatons, the objects and animals of *L'Enfant* like humans. This interpretive stream made its way through the Ravel criticism of Vladimir Jankélévitch (1956: 89–98) and, recently, into the reflections of Carolyn Abbate (2001: 185–

246) on the uncanny effects of music emanating from robots, machines, and other contraptions. Pursuing an analogy between the genre of the *tombeau* and music boxes of various kinds, Abbate argues that *L'Enfant et les sortilèges* is "a tombeau, even though it does not declare this by name. In an opera that concerns lifeless objects and their animation, music reflects the idea of mechanical reproduction [of something alive]" (192). Although her *tombeau* metaphor as applied to the *whole* opera seems somewhat reductive, Abbate does brilliantly explore the bizarre and disquieting intersections between humans and objects in the first part, where the composer reanimates "broken but useful things" such as minuets, musettes, and fox-trots. Ravel's impassiveness masks a range of troubling negotiations between the animate and inanimate, and the real and unreal, negotiations that engage "vulgarity, melancholy, stupor" (241). Music emerging from objects such as music boxes often sounds simultaneously foreign and as part of the subject's innermost being, a trace of past culture where a strange-sounding artifact of collective tradition melds with a personal identity carved out of that tradition. "Alien" voices may therefore produce a sense of longing for an irretrievable past, or intuitions about a lost corner of the psyche. Children try desperately to find a soul in their toys and even in surrounding objects, notes Abbate, echoing an essay by Baudelaire titled "Morale du joujou" (1925; Abbate 2001: 240). Scratch, turn, poke, and prod as they might, they only meet with failure, an event that inevitably marks the beginning of surprised deception and *tristesse*.

Abbate has not been the only critic to feel discomfort. Indeed, the opera has also sometimes invited interpretation as an unnerving allegory. For Marcel Marnat (1986: 571), an important biographer of Ravel, the explosion of blind chaos among the animals after the child's initial appeal to Maman represents a microcosm of "the incident at Sarajevo [in 1914] and its planetary consequences"—perhaps a bit of a stretch. For the *metteur en scène* Oscar Araiz (1989), environmental depredations spoil the garden paradise. He has worked on the premise that "this child is not a child, it is an adult with the head of a child. He also represents contemporary humanity marching forward to its ultimate destruction, calmly unaware." Baudelaire writes in "Morale du joujou" that the mighty effort to locate a soul in toys initiates a "tendance métaphysique" in the child, and eventual disenchantment. An adult, therefore, seems to hover here as well. Nevertheless, we might legitimately ask how the distinction between soul and matter can be meaningful to the child. To what extent does early exposure to, and comprehension of, this distinction mark a descent into a melancholy abyss, as Baudelaire (and Abbate) would have it? More broadly: is the opera as bleak as has sometimes been suggested?

The creative worlds of Colette and Ravel provide additional contexts for pondering these questions. Alexis Roland-Manuel (1926; 1938: 124) noted in an early review of *L'Enfant,* and later as well, that he could scarcely imagine two artistic temperaments more opposed than those of Colette and Ravel: the writer who in her earlier prose had so often unfurled sensuous reminiscences of her own mother and childhood versus the composer who manipulated objects, musical and otherwise. This much appears confirmed by Colette's (2001: 167) anecdotal recollections of her early impression of Ravel's setting. "How to describe my emotion at the first vibrations of the little drums that accompany the cortege of the [wallpaper] shepherds? . . . 'Now there, isn't this amusing?' said Ravel. Nevertheless, a knot of tears constricted my throat." Colette's compressed account suggests that she was deeply moved by the musical projection of the final reconciliation. And in view of the many parallels of *L'Enfant* to her own childhood reminiscences recorded in *La Maison de Claudine, Sido,* and many journalistic vignettes (Milner 1991: 151–69), one might be forgiven for suspecting a wellspring of nostalgia behind the tears. Ravel, for his part, savored his own humor. An impassive figure once again. Perhaps the contrast between the impressions of Colette and Ravel demonstrates Abbate's tension between genuine subjectivity and those curious and humorous-but-troubling little simulacra.

Yet the opera actually concludes with genuine feeling subjects and a protagonist who communes with nature and internalizes compassion. Sentient animals, so often anthropomorphized in Colette's writing, come after the objects, after those broken musettes and minuets. The boy's story is partly the listener's own story—also partly Colette's, partly Ravel's—a tale that results in implied harmony and a prospective new beginning for a young protagonist who has attained a new condition of awareness. Such extension of moral insight would seem to invite approval. Moreover, despite the trauma experienced by the Child, listeners—children and adult—never seem invited to relinquish a position of superiority toward him that is characteristic of the comedic mode. In this way of thinking, an empathetic smile seems more apposite than dystopic angst. Because the narrative of the opera is driven by the child's development as a human being, the literature of psychology and psychoanalysis offers useful schemas for a critical understanding of the work. In the remainder of this essay I consider how two models might be applied, those of Sigmund Freud and Jean Piaget. The investigation is not into authorial intent—I do not mean to suggest that either Ravel or Colette had particular theories of child development in mind—nor does it seek to extrapolate general conclusions about child rearing in the period of the opera's creation. Instead, I employ child development theories as narrative constructs, on the premise that these are transposable to many different times, places, and social classes. Critics of *L'Enfant* have followed Freudian paths before, and my purpose will be to review these and to suggest ways that the musical text may be folded into such arguments. The opera has never, I believe, been examined as an instantiation of Jean Piaget's theories. I intend this application to have real critical purpose, a response to the conceptual challenges it presents. For a Piagetian interpretation not only is particularly convincing in its own right but also furnishes a compelling counterweight to recent pessimistic interpretations of the opera that I have outlined. Nevertheless, regardless of the critic's temperament and preferences, that *L'Enfant* can sustain interpretations based on such radically different models serves as an eloquent tribute to its richness.

◈ Freudian Paradigms

As long ago as 1929, Melanie Klein (1950), a Viennese disciple of Freud, published an essay on Ravel's opera after reading a detailed plot summary that she came across in the *Berliner Tageblatt*. Two critics of Colette's work have fleshed out Klein's arguments in distinctive ways, Christiane Milner (1981, 1991) on two occasions, and most conspicuously Julia Kristeva (2002) in a recent book on Colette's work. Among musicologists, Richard Langham Smith (2000) has proffered quiet endorsement, as has the French commentator Jacques Dupont (1990). Details among critics differ, but the broad outline of the psychoanalytical argument is clear enough and deserves more extended attempts to explore its musical ramifications than offered in the past.

The beginning of the work recalls a primal crisis in the Child's earlier life, the separation of the infant from total fusion with the mother. Oral deprivation (sugarless tea and dry bread) signals the rupture and, at an even deeper level, apprehension of the mother's body with the father's penis in it: squirrel released from cage, pendulum wrenched out of clock. The music of the injured clock begins in a burst of futile martial virility, only to trail softly off into flaccid fecklessness, a decrescendo collapse from high G-flat to low B-flat in the baritone voice. Separation fuels the Child's rage, which he directs against the primary object of his desire, that is against the mother's body as represented by the house and later the garden (or against an image of *his own* body fused with that of the mother from whom he violently seeks to separate, as Kristeva would have it). As the Child boils over with anger, he also intuits, indeed fears, punishment for his acts. He projects this anxiety onto household objects, which do spring to life to exact retribution—and also seem to continue the work of deprivation.

Latent from the beginning, the genital phase of the child's development becomes more clearly articulated as the work unfolds. Wallpaper shepherds with their sleep-inducing vocalizations ("zzz") drift away, night descends, the boy lies outstretched, and the Princess emerges from his fairy-tale book in a quasi-hypnotic trance to remind him of how he had once called to her from deep in his sleep. At this point, is the child awake? As Milner points out, the dream world intersects with the subconscious. The dreamer and his subject seem to meet in a haze of somnolence colored by a wash of harp arpeggios and the Princess's first seductive pianissimo high G over magical octatonic harmony. Their ensuing dialogue produces arguably the most passionate music of the score. The accompaniment ripples, a profusion of half-diminished harmonies lend an erotic tint, and the vocal lines of the two characters pick up fluidly from each other at the penumbra of the Child's sexuality.[1] The vision fades away to leave him merely with "les debris d'un rêve" (the residue of a dream), an antipode to Ravel's brilliant apotheotic conclusion to the Sleeping Beauty story in *Ma mère l'oye*. Ravel's child now sings an aria redolent of Manon's "Adieu notre petite table" and shares with Jules Massenet's famous character a sense of loss, hollowness after communing with the object of his desire.

Following the slapstick relief of the arithmetic episode—asexual in the extreme—the nuptial tryst of the cats recalls the primal moment of parental coitus jealously apprehended by the Child. The felines create a frame around the first part of the garden scene. At their initial appearance they sing an extended, and comically sexy, duet where passion builds up over an extended F-sharp pedal that finds release by slipping down a semitone onto the initial F major harmony of the garden scene (just as the walls of the house separate). When the cats return several minutes later, they join the libidinal ambience of Ravel's *valse americaine* (see ex. 4.1a), better known as the "Boston," a more languid, hands-on-hips waltz than the Viennese variety. Not only is one of the main motifs of the cat duet related to the music of the waltz (compare "X" of ex. 4.1a with the waltz strain shown in 4.1b), but on their postcoital reappearance the felines also reshape their music, previously in 5/4, into the prevailing ternary meter. A strong cadence (in A-flat) follows, accompanied at the final iteration of the tonic by the descending perfect fourth associated orchestrally with the Mother in the first scene of the opera, now sung by the Child for the first time. In short, the musical assimilation of the amorous cats with both the gently sensuous garden animals and the vocal utterance of *Maman* produces a

Example 4.1 **L'enfant et Les Sortilèges**

Libretto by Gabrielle COLETTE
Music by Maurice RAVEL

Example 4.1a

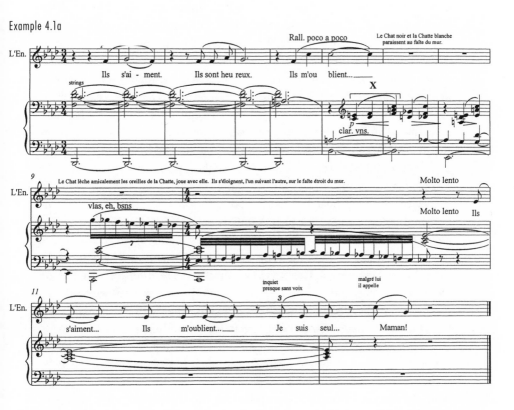

Example 4.1b

critical moment in the formation of identity.[2] The Child experiences profound isolation ("Ils s'aiment . . . Ils m'oublient . . . Je suis seul . . . Maman!") and sensing his vulnerability, the animals turn against him. Retribution for his earlier sadism continues, now colored by the terror of castration characteristic of the genital phase. Once again this is punishment that the boy has willed in order to allay his anxieties. In the context of more explicit representation of sexuality, it is much harsher than that meted out before.

In psychoanalytic theory, the final separation from the mother as well as the overcoming of anxiety in an ultimate trial and punishment create the necessary context for object love. The viciousness of the animals produces such a defining moment. The child situates his mother in his conscience, rationally recognizes her altruistic nature, and heals the squirrel. Kristeva, for her part, takes the argument to a different conclusion than Klein and Milner, suggesting that the Mother does not become *pensée* (thought, and by extension an "object") at the end, but rather *a-pensée* (a-thought), for the mother can never be divorced from the senses. Despite the trauma of separation, the child will forever be enveloped by nostalgia for the bodily, the olfactory, the tactile. This argument hinges strongly on Colette's initial conception of the *L'Enfant* project as a "Divertissement pour ma fille," shortly after the closely proximate death of her mother and birth of her only child. Kristeva continues her study with extended ruminations on Colette's quasi-incestuous relationship with the son of her second husband. Yet for an example of *a-pensée*, perhaps we need look no further than Colette's tears when she was together with Ravel many years later. Or her normally visceral style grounded in childhood memory.

The *L'Enfant et les sortilèges* libretto is not in itself a characteristic example of that visceral style. Compared with much of Colette's writing it is laconic and relatively flat, perhaps a result of tapering the material of her "Divertissement pour ma fille" for children. In doing this, she might well have intended to create space for Ravel to explore the hidden crevices of instinct. Among those privileging the psychoanalytical interpretation, Milner (1991: 1335) has most forcefully advocated the role of music in creating "d'énergies pulsionnelles souterraines" ("instinctive subterranean energies," though without specific illustration). Colette (2001: 163) herself admitted surprise at the emotional impact of Ravel's "vague orchestrale" at the end of the opera. On the other hand, while the epithet of "orchestral wave" would be quite appropriate for an opera by Wagner (which for this reason, among others, makes his work a *locus classicus* for psychoanalytical approaches) or even Verdi or Puccini, many will feel that it does not quite ring true for Ravel's mosaic of stylistic allusions and quick-paced turnover of episodes.[3] The composer himself (Ravel 1989: 46) spoke of an aesthetic goal in this period to pare down his writing. Notwithstanding some of the more lyrical passages that I have mentioned, he seems just as terse as his librettist. Is Colette's dubious reference to "vague orchestrale" merely a refraction of her own intuitions about the hidden implications of her text, waves emanating from deep in the child's psyche? Whatever the case, Milner (1981: 41) congratulates the writer for her "génie divinateur" in harmonizing with Freudian models. Thus, implicitly for Milner, Colette was ingenious for having intuited Freud's theory, Melanie Klein ingenious for having applied it. Few critics can escape such circularity in value judgment and it should not be judged too severely. Milner does imply that both the writer and analyst negotiated with irrefutable truths. One need not necessarily accept this to observe that according to their own terms of reference, Freudian approaches to L'Enfant do seem internally coherent. These account eloquently not only for the crisis at the beginning of the work, where sheer violence betrays primal energy and/or anxiety, but also for the alienation of the child from the amorous cats and the garden paradise. Nevertheless, although the Princess calls herself a "bien aimée," and the harmonic language at that moment brims with languorous half-diminished chords, perhaps the Child merely mimics her. In other words, not everyone will be inclined to believe that the typical child of six or seven is motivated by sexual desire, however subliminally. This would seem reason enough to call upon other theoretical archetypes for child development.

◈ Piaget's Paradigm: The Preoperational Child

Most operas are not about children, and whereas Freudian theory accounts for defense mechanisms and anxiety in adulthood—hence its wide relevance to all kinds of literary and musical criticism—Jean Piaget's most influential research was into early cognitive development. Although not without profound epistemological ramifications that Piaget himself considered, the relatively self-contained reference to childhood and adolescence in his method accounts for why it has not been marshaled often by critics in the humanities. Commonplace warnings about the "real life" truth value in Freudian critical theory seem especially relevant to appropriation of Piaget's model because of its potentially deceiving aura of science (due to more developed experimental routines) and the many challenges that have been directed at his methods. In short, the validity of Piaget's claims and procedures will not be a concern here (although in the context of the present collection of essays, caveats about cross-cultural applications of his analysis do seem worth bearing in mind).

Enough of what he proposed has achieved consensus to produce a credible interpretive strategy in criticism.

Colette and Ravel shaped the narrative of *L'Enfant et les sortilèges* around the development of compassion in its protagonist—object-love as some Freudians would have it, cooperation and reciprocity according to Piaget. Piaget gave extended attention to reciprocity in *The Moral Judgment of the Child* (1932), a book building upon premises elaborated in the previous decade, that is, roughly contemporary to *L'Enfant,* and these must first be succinctly reviewed (Langford 1995; Pulaski 1980; Rich and DeVitis 1994; Richmond 1970). For Piaget, moral development does not occur merely by independent logical inference—he specifically challenges Kantian thinking on this point—but as a result of adaptation, assimilation, and adjustment to society, a set of biological metaphors that characterizes his thinking more generally. Piaget proposes that cognition develops through four major periods: (1) sensory-motor thinking, from birth to approximately two years; (2) preoperational thinking, from about two to seven; (3) concrete operational thinking, from around seven to about twelve; (4) formal operational thinking. The many defining characteristics of each stage occur at different times in different children, not to mention that each stage comprises a succession of fluid substages. *L'Enfant,* as we shall see, portrays the transition from the second to the third stage, with pronounced overlap of both, as happens in real life.

For Piaget, egocentric thinking dominates the decisions and actions of the preoperational child. He does not mean this in the limited sense of calculated self-serving action but more broadly as "the confusion of the self with the non-self" (1932: 251). Literalness, unilateral perspective, juxtaposition of objects without account of functional relationships, disinclination to introspection, and melding of the objective and the subjective characterize this phase. The preoperational child does not realize that he or she even has an ego and is "unable to distinguish the part played by his subjectivity from that played by the environment" (1932: 95). He or she conceives of the world as "a continuous whole that is both psychical and physical at the same time" (1926: 236). Thus, the characteristic remark of a four-year-old: "I haven't had my nap, so it isn't afternoon" (Richmond 1970: 22). The child will not necessarily draw objects placed before her as she sees them, but as he or she "knows" them to be. Objects that appear together are assumed to have a functional relationship ("What makes the engine go?" answer: "The smoke"), a phenomenon that Piaget calls *syncretism.* Piaget employs the term *realism* as an overarching concept for the preoperational stage. Whereas in aesthetic theory realism usually refers to a mode of communication or perception that purports to minimize subjective intervention, the psychically flattened perspective of the child reads everything as real because everything is essentially concrete. Thus, even names are thought to be intrinsic to objects: "Where is the word 'lake'? answer: 'It is inside it because of the water'" (Piaget 1926: 73).

Because the preoperational child does not understand the internal nature of thought, she believes that her dreams are real. Even late in the preoperational stage, the child continues to attribute dreams to factors outside of herself, perhaps to the night, to her room, to God, to parents. One seven-year-old in Piaget's inquiries explained a bad dream about robbers as punishment from God because "I'd been naughty. I'd made Mother cry. I'd made her run round the table" (1926: 100). Closely related to this status of the dream is the preoperational child's conviction that everything in the world is alive, endowed with consciousness, emotion, and purpose, a phenomenon that Piaget called *animism*. As the child matures, the focus of this belief becomes gradually narrowed, first attributed to all objects, then merely to ones that move (like the sun or water), followed by living entities such as plants, and finally only to animals. The subphases are often not clearly distinguished. One eight-year-old asserted that the clouds feel the wind and the heat of sun, but would not feel a needle's prick as would an animal (1926: 174). As with dreams, objects may assume real agency in effecting punishment, as when a bridge gives way beneath a thief who has stolen apples from the other bank:

> For nature, in the child's eyes, is not a system of blind forces regulated by mechanical laws operating on the principle of chance. Nature is a harmonious whole, obeying laws that are as much moral as physical and that are above all penetrated down to the last details with an anthropomorphic or even egocentric finalism. It therefore seems quite natural to little children that night should come in order to put us to sleep, and that the act of going to bed is sufficient to set in motion that great black cloud that produces darkness. . . . In short, there is life and purpose in everything. Why then should not things be the accomplices of grown-ups in making sure that a punishment is inflicted where the parents' vigilance may have been evaded? What difficulty should there be in a bridge giving way under a little thief, when everything in nature conspires to safeguard that Order, both moral and physical, of which the grown-up is both the author and the *raison d'être*? (1932: 257)

The objects in *L'Enfant* exhibit feelings and *really* move, as they might in a dream (or perhaps, in this case, a nightmare) to enact what Piaget calls a justice of reciprocity, and to which I shall shortly return. The Child is not literally asleep all the time—that is, animist perceptions dominate—but as I have already suggested in connection with the Princess episode, sometimes it is hard to tell. Where Freudians see a path into subconscious sexuality, from Piaget's perspective this ambiguity seems to represent the natural alliance between childhood animism and dreams under the umbrella of realist thinking.

One might fancifully imagine that in his future life (after the events of the opera) Ravel's Child would be unlikely to experience the morphing of objects into humans with such intensity again. For the opera telescopes the progression of the preoperational child through various phases of animism. Near the beginning, the pendulum-less clock spouts a particularly pronounced example of preoperational reasoning. After recalling how he used to mark the regular and unchanging sequence of events in each day (sleeping, waking) he laments:

> Peut-être que, s'il ne m'eût mutilée,
> Rien n'aurait jamais changé
> Dans cette demeure.
> Peut-être qu'aucun n'y fût jamais mort . . .
> Si j'avais pu continuer de sonner,
> Toutes pareilles les unes aux autres,
> Les heures!

> Perhaps had he not mutilated me nothing would have changed in this house. Perhaps no one would have ever died . . . if I could have gone on sounding the hours, each the same as the next.

Why shouldn't life go on forever if the clock continues to ring its perpetual succession of chimes? Time is the clock, the clock is time. To damage the instrument is to broach mortality. For a production at the Opéra in 1979 the metteur-en-scène Jorge Lavelli (1979) tapped into a morbid vein of the opera and conceived the presence of the wallpaper shepherds primarily to exhibit their lacerations at the "moment of death." Soon the dreamy storybook princess will be swallowed up by an evaporation of a dream, night as a simulacrum of eternal darkness. A nightmare some parts of L'Enfant may well be, but to grasp the nature of death is also to grasp the nature of life. The opera ends in the organic world of the garden and its animals. And there, significantly, broken objects no longer play a role.

Whereas a sense of narrative and a "functional" relationship among events develops by the end of the opera—the animals' tales of woe and simultaneous exhibition of peaceful harmony produce the Child's redemptive action—

during the initial phases actions seem juxtaposed in syncretic fashion. Episodes tumble rapidly upon one another with no apparent organic connection and in a succession of heterogeneous styles (by the standards of Wagnerian opera, Debussy's *Pelléas et Mélisande*, or Fauré's *Pénélope*). A generic factor lies behind. Although Ravel (1989: 46) referred to the work as beholden to *opérette américaine* (inaccurately, as it turns out, for he meant vaudeville entertainment and not Victor Herbert), Parisian music hall was also a fertile influence. The armchair, clock, and teapot and teacups are a succession of "acts" in a variety show. Colette had given up her notorious career as a music hall entertainer shortly before writing the libretto and brought some of that world to her "Divertissement pour ma fille." Pursuing the music hall idea, in one letter to Ravel she even envisaged the incorporation of acrobats (which remained unrealized) and actually suggested the wild polka for the arithmetic episode (Ravel 1989: 172). The resulting juxtaposition of the boy's languid Massenet-like *ariette* "Toi le cœur de la rose" with the arithmetic polka produces as wide a stylistic rupture as any enacted on the opera stage at this time. The verbal text shifts from the poetry of "les debris d'un rêve" to the workaday, and also distorted, prose of arithmetic problems:

> Deux trains omnibus quittent une gare
> A vingt minutes d'intervalle,
> Valle, valle, valle.

Ravel, for his part, shifts from carefully crafted prosody around common-tone chord successions to nursery-rhyme music. Earlier, the Wedgwood teapot and Chinese cup famously mix it up in a cultural hodgepodge of ragtime and pentatonic *faux chinoiserie*, a tired cliché that to our ears today seems, if not vulgar, particularly lowbrow. Colette's use of the term *divertissement* suggests another generic tradition: the French opera ballet, with its relatively discontinuous episodes around a general theme. The initial commission of *L'Enfant* came from Jacques Rouché, director of the Opéra, and Ravel of course left a significant amount of space for choreography, so significant that the leading choreographers of the day were hired for early French productions. (*L'Enfant* was premiered in Monte Carlo in 1925 and first performed in Paris at the Opéra Comique at the beginning of the following year.) Thus, music hall meets French *divertissement* meets the syncretism of the preoperational child.

Preoperational syncretism makes for a natural analogue to the modernist impulse. Many of the characteristics that Piaget describes—mystical animism, flattening of the psychical and physical perspectives, isolation of the part at the expense of the whole, and concentration of one mode of perception at a time—apply equally well to avant-garde art of the early twentieth century. The child's perceptions are, of course, unintentional in the artistic sense. Yet the child subject manipulated by an adult creator—or artist, or even critic, who self-consciously assumes a child's perspective—seems a natural, and little-explored, vehicle for modernist expression. Ravel's *Ma mère l'oye*, Stravinsky's *Renard*, and Satie's *Parade* are good candidates for investigation from this angle. The controversial generic subtitle of the latter as a *ballet réaliste*—with its gunshots, lottery wheels, sirens, chorale, rag, and vapid oriental effects—might receive a special spin when considered against Piaget's little realist. For to place noise and orchestral music on the same aesthetic plateau would probably seem quite "natural" to the preoperational child—as natural as Picasso's cubist sets.

This argument is worth pursuing a bit further. Modernist artists at the beginning of the twentieth century challenged conventional frames: institutional, generic, syntactical, architectural. Although Ravel hardly occupied the forefront of the avant-garde when *L'Enfant* was premiered, few among his contemporaries called it a conservative or retrograde work. A. Mangeot (1925) noted in *Le Monde musicale* that "Colette's novelties and boldness could only suit Ravel's adventurous spirit," a critical view that certainly was not idiosyncratic in its day. In her letter to Ravel about acrobats and polkas, Colette cheered "Qu'une terrifiante rafale de music-hall évente la poussière de l'Opéra!" (May a huge gust of music hall whip up the dust in the Opéra!). Their challenge to institutions (be it Opéra or Opéra Comique), as in the work of Satie and his admirers among *Les Six,* seems clear enough. *L'Enfant* tests boundaries in another important way: it is impossible to stage as written. It explores a space between film—Disney, some have suggested—and opera (Jourdan-Morhange 1945: 125). Now this is a condition of other famous operas as well, but with human actors of roughly the same size in the roles of child, armchair, squirrel, and dragonfly—not to mention the difficulty in showing mother's huge apron and scissors on a chain—Colette is especially challenging. Jacques Rouché (1939), who eventually produced the work at the Opéra in 1939, bemoaned this fact at length in the press. He opted for allegorical actors whose costumes suggested the object they embodied, "just as Louis XIV's painters depicted allegorical costumes: gardening, painting, clockmaking"—another link to the venerable tradition of *la grande boutique.* But Piaget's preoperational child, able to concentrate on only one dimension or state-of-being at a time, will not necessarily be troubled by various and sundry impossibilities. Big or small, dragonflies move their wings, squirrels their tails. Both sing. The realist child will be enthralled by the immediacy of the sensual experience, with scant regard for incompatibility among physical attributes that might disturb those with broader perspectives.

◆ Piaget's Paradigm: Moral Development

According to Piaget, the analogue to the preoperational child's entwining of ego with the external world is moral realism. The child understands that there are rules, but these have a transcendental quality on "the same plane as actual physical phenomena" and emanating from higher authority. He continues: "One must eat after going for a walk, go to bed at night, have a bath before going to bed, etc., exactly as the sun shines by day and the moon by night, or as pebbles sink while boats remain afloat. All these things are and must be so; they are as the World-Order decrees that they should be, and there must be a reason for it all. But none of it is felt from within" (1932: 191). The child does not separate the operation of her ego from the operation of a world order whose objective reality encompasses both her own perceptions and the environment. Decrees cannot be felt "from within" because they are all felt "from without" at the same time. As a moral realist, the child holds that rules are "revealed by the adult and imposed by him" (111). He or she feels impelled by duty and has little awareness that rules are subject to interpretation or communal effort for their enforcement. She sees no role for herself in changing or even inflecting moral rules. Piaget (98–99) theorizes an essentially circular and mutually reinforcing relationship between first- and second-order moral precepts, or what he calls "constitutive" and "constituted" rules—the first deals in broad enabling principles (thou shalt not steal) and the second in particulars (a game of checkers where the two players apply a set of rules). But the distinction has no bearing on the preoperational child's acquiescence of moral constraints imposed by adults. The letter of the law is paramount. Comportment may be either right or wrong, and correct behavior exists as "pure duty" as distinct from what "moralists have called 'the good'" (195), altogether too abstract a concept for the preoperational child as it relates to the application of rules. Conformity is celebrated, nonconformity deemed worthy of punishment. Disobedience may be triggered by an "esprit de contradiction," a cogent expression of the complete powerlessness of the child in face of the imposed moral order (92). As far as the child is concerned, the justice delivered need not be materially related to the misdemeanor, but merely of sufficient severity to expiate the misdeed. Hence Piaget's distinction between expiatory justice and the justice of restitution at a later stage, where the punishments relate to the matter at hand and aim to produce an analogous effect upon the perpetrator of the misdeed or actually to correct the result. The fantasy of the bridge giving way under the boy who purloins apples lies somewhere in between, an excellent example of how Piaget's stages are not self-contained. Although scarcely a restorative punishment and most certainly impelled by animist thinking, the collapse is not entirely arbitrary either. To accept the punishment of parents constitutes the most "natural form of reparation" (322). Inflicted pain places the relationship of moral authority back on normal footing after the disruption of disobedience. An essentially materialist perception of punishment harmonizes with the more general worldview of the realist child.

In the third and fourth stages, children develop much greater sensitivity to the spirit of the law over its letter and a concomitant ability to apply it in diverse situations. They factor the intent of the perpetrator into judgments about the severity of punishments and consider the rationale behind rules: "The priority of intention over external rules implies an increasingly delicate differentiation between what is spiritual and what is material" (Piaget 1932: 190). Second-order moral laws are not immovable objects, and the crux of social interaction lies in interpreting and applying alternate points of view: negotiation and reciprocity become the glue of social relationships. As the child matures, the "subjection of his conscience to the mind of the adult seems to him less legitimate" (324). Piaget does allow, however, that the early relationship between parents and children is not entirely one of constraint. It contains the seeds of reciprocity: "There is a spontaneous mutual affection, which from the first prompts the child to acts of generosity, and even of self-sacrifice, to very touching demonstrations which are in no way prescribed. And here no doubt is the starting point for that morality of good which we shall see developing alongside of the morality of right or duty, and which in some persons completely replaces it" (195).

L'Enfant et les sortilèges is considerably removed from the games among working-class children in Geneva that Piaget (in a methodologically problematic move to many) used to extrapolate his theories about moral development. We might, however, apply his conclusions to the Mother: an omnipotent dispenser of rules which the Child accepts from "on high" as the inevitable way of the world. Piaget refers repeatedly to the quasi-divine nature of the child's perception of the adult, and Colette's impossible staging instructions—the giant apron and scissors again—communicate something of a transcendental character. With a "spirit of contradiction" the child explodes. Does his ensuing anarchic behavior reflect the "born criminal" in the child, as one British psychoanalyst held about childhood in 1922, a being "completely egocentric, greedy, dirty, violent in temper, destructive in habit" (Synnott 1988: 39–40)? One contemporaneous reviewer of the work (Lion 1925) referred to the Child "as the ordinary child of our day; badly raised, lazy and angry, and already inclined toward all the nefarious instincts of the human race" and Ravel (1989: 351) himself called his protagonist a "vilain enfant" (wicked child) in one interview, doubtless off the cuff. As we have seen, for Piaget the child's rage expresses the powerlessness in the condition of the preoperational stage much more than real malevolence. The Child's rampage ends with the declaration "Je suis libre, libre, méchant et libre!" that marks the frontier between his anger and the animation of the objects. This giddy assertion should be construed as fundamentally ironic: true autonomy can occur only in a more decentered subject who understands rules as contingent and negotiated.

The Mother's reaction to her child is ambivalent. On the one hand the punishment—sugarless tea and bread—has little to do with the material facts of the Child's disobedience. The relationship between deed and result is both arbitrary and syncretic, exactly the way preoperational children conceive of punishment. Yet, on the other hand, she also enjoins her son, "Et songez à votre faute . . . songez, songez surtout au chagrin de Maman!" (Think about your mistake . . . think, think especially of Maman's sorrow!). She underlines human consequences, perhaps somewhat self-indulgently, and encourages autonomous thinking. Maman offers little guidance here. Ultimately children must internalize a decentered subject-position through individual growth and effort within more-or-less helpful facilitating structures. Objects that spring to life with lessons about reciprocity seem imaginatively to articulate common ground between guidance and self-reliance in a child-centered approach to learning. They are "adult" actors, after all, who have something to say about consequences. Nevertheless, the furniture, clock, cup, fire, and wallpaper are not exactly human. They are the product of self-generated dream, hallucination, or fantasy and bear important lessons about reciprocity. The Child's offense lies not in "wounding" inanimate objects, but in the consequences of his violence that lead to deprivation for himself as well as for other *real* human beings. The Princess is more lifelike, and at the next stage the Child becomes caught up in the ebb and flow of an affective relationship and true engagement of his feelings. The fate of the Princess remains unknown because he has destroyed the last page of the story, thwarting narrative closure and suspending desire. But the Princess also experiences narrative and desire herself (perhaps even for the child) that suggest a more poignant human cost to his destructive act. The heightened lyricism, with glimmers of mortality and sexuality, seems to probe deeper than the surface pleasures alluded to by the earlier objects. As a mirror-opposite image, the wild polka arithmetic episode throws this articulation of a sensual world into high relief. And then, the animals appear, Colette-style. Desire plays out in "real" life as nature quivers with libidinal energy.

The child professes that he captured the squirrel out of aesthetic impulse in order to admire "tes beaux yeux" (your beautiful eyes). "Oui c'était pour mes beaux yeux! Sais-tu ce qu'ils reflétaient, mes beaux yeux? Le ciel libre, le vent libre, mes libres frères" comes the reply (Yes, it was for my beautiful eyes! Do you know what they mirrored, my beautiful eyes? The free sky, the free wind, my free brethren). Another threefold iteration of the word *libre,* eyes as windows to the soul, as the cliché has it. Now, the child peers in. Thus, articulation of the word *libre* prepares two of the most important moments in the opera, the first an ironic, self-indulgent proclamation uttered from the preoperational perspective, the second engaging more profound understanding. Call it a click, epiphany, intuition—the child altruistically binds the squirrel's wound to take an important step toward cooperation and reciprocity, autonomy and freedom. And he does so in the context of the violent eruption of the animals themselves, an eruption using the same harmonic vocabulary of seventh chords with raised fifths with which the Child himself had earlier egocentrically bristled, "Je suis libre." He casts away a bit of his preoperational self just as the savage and primitive intrude in paradise, one of the many parallels between animals and humans that Colette developed in her writing (Pavlovic 1970). The squirrels mete out a kind of justice that shows little sensitivity to the child. One might say the same of the spare-the-rod-spoil-the-child educational methods to which Piaget contrasted his empathetic approach, like punishments of sugarless tea and bread. Weaker moments—they happen in the lives of squirrels, and in the lives of adults.

Nevertheless, the return to mother offers the promise of a new plateau of development. The final fugue exudes a conventional religioso topos translated into secular spirituality. Extensive melismas and gentle hemiolas in slow tempo produce a sound world somewhat akin to sixteenth-century sacred polyphony. Yet unlike some of the music for the earlier animist phase, this music does not give the impression of pastiche. The spirit of the armchair lies in a costumed minuet, a kind of materiality where the border between the eighteenth century and the modern is as ineffable as the distinction between matter and spirit to the preoperational child (does the eighteenth century infuse Ravel's spirit; does Ravel's spirit infuse the eighteenth century?). The fugue has a more abstract quality, not only by long-standing convention but also because it does not represent anything tangible at the end of *L'Enfant:* "Il est bon,

Example 4.2 **L'enfant et Les Sortilèges**

Libretto by Gabrielle COLETTE   Music by Maurice RAVEL

il est sage." Spirit and matter: by this time in the work, the distinction has been forged and the spirit cherished. Ravel chooses a C major subdominant answer to his G major fugue subject to effect a particularly relaxed and comforting ambience. The fugue actually concludes with a long pedal in C major, over which float the E-minor fourths and fifths on the oboes (and now strings) from the beginning of the opera (see ex. 4.2). But there is no real regression here. The final harmony, a Ravelian major/major seventh chord, emerges from several measures where thirds unfold from the subdominant—c in the bass of measure 1, e–g–b–d in the sopranos (mm. 5–6), f-sharp the final pitch on the oboe (m. 7)—thirds that evaporate into the immaterial. The final decisive dip down to G in the bass voice seems undermined by a play of changing meters and pointed lack of a *ritardando*. The work comes to an abrupt halt, the end as a surprise. But perhaps there is no conclusion. Piaget's "spontaneous mutual affection [between parent and child], which from the first prompts the child to acts of generosity" has borne fruit and is now returned in the Child's final appeal to "Maman," an addition that Ravel himself appears to have made to Colette's text. The beginning of the opera will be replayed—it *is* replayed— but infused with a greater sense of independence and compassion, with spirit, soul, and thought. An end that is not an end: the openness radiates the promise of all children.

Notes

1. Half-diminished harmonies occur in the standard Durand piano-vocal score (plate number D and F, 10,699; 101 pages), 44/1, 45/2, 45/3, 47/1, 47/5, 48/4.

2. Also apropos is Langham Smith's observation that the perfect fourth strongly linked to the Mother features prominently in the music of the duet.

3. Marnat (1986, 575) is especially critical.

Music for a Postcolonial Child

Theorizing Malaysian Memories

ROE-MIN KOK

I am the native informant. I begin my story with an enduring childhood memory.

I am standing in an air-conditioned waiting area of an expensive hotel in Kuala Lumpur, the capital of Malaysia. My surroundings are meticulously Western in a city and climate unyieldingly tropical. I am seven years old. It is my first piano examination.

There he is. At a desk near the piano. Silver-haired, of regal carriage, replete with the self-confidence and authority of the colonial master. His skin is ruddy, fashionably suntanned—a genuine tan acquired in this exotic land. He is attired in white, because white refracts heat rays. It is the color traditionally favored by travelers to hot climes. I have been schooled in the gravity of the situation. I have been trained time and again in simulated settings to be meek and polite, to parrot, "Good morning, Sir!" Madams are rare. My piano teacher finds out in advance the gender of the examiner, so that we, her students, can practice the greeting until it is smooth on our young Malaysian tongues. The examiner is all-powerful. Not only can he administer a failing grade to you, thus wasting the previous year's work, time, and money; he can do so at his whim, because nobody else witnesses the examination, held behind closed doors in his hotel room. If this is only a suspicion, it is one born of a colonized mentality that constantly anticipates the white man's displeasure and its consequences—whether it happens in a *ladang getah* (rubber plantation) or in a Western-style hotel. I, the child, have to be respectful at all times and to be careful not to annoy him. My piano teacher's last-minute advice rings in my ears: "Remember to hand him your book of scales and to respond as soon as he asks you to play. Dog-ear the pages so that you can turn them easily. Don't repeat passages in which you make mistakes; cut your fingernails so they don't go 'clack' on the keys—that will irritate him."

In other words, her message to me is: be submissive, play the colonizer-colonized scenario, and you will be fine. Subconsciously I superimpose her instructions onto the pieces I play to make up the meaning of what I understand and physically execute as "music." When the time that has been allotted for the examination arrives, my fear has built up to such proportions that I refuse to enter the examiner's room. I cannot remember what to say; I cannot remember how to play. All I see is a towering white man who will speak to me with a strange accent and who will become angry if my fingers slip on the keyboard or my tongue slips in his language. I stand frozen. He comes out of the room, surprised at this disruption of his schedule, and the other waiting children scatter with whispered cries of "The examiner!" As his eyes focus on me, I feel my inadequacies even more and I cannot bridge that gap. I am, at that moment, in my mind, what I am sure he feels me to be: a disobedient little yellow child.

Today I am a scholar of Western classical music, a Malaysian Chinese academic active in North America and Europe.[1] Among other things, I am the product of a colonial music education—a set of policies formulated a world apart (literally and figuratively) from that in which it was delivered and received. The policies formed an arc of cultural power that extended from the Associated Board of the Royal Schools of Music in Great Britain to a child in Malaysia, a former British colony and currently an independent, multicultural Muslim nation in Southeast Asia. As a result of ideas about Western classical music transmitted from the former and received by the latter, my cultural identity was aligned over the course of my childhood and early adolescence to identify with colonial concepts for the colonized. In this essay I use postcolonial theory as a mode of cultural analysis wherein musical activity undertaken by a child in a specific time and place is shown to be the result of interconnections between issues of ethnicity, class, nation, and empire.[2] My story intersects with observations made about fictional children and imperialism: "There is obviously considerable slippage between constructions of 'the child' and of the native Other under imperialism" (J. Wallace 1994: 175; see Ashcroft, Griffiths, and Tiffin 1989: 16; Bhabha 1985: 74), but in this case, life events as I experienced them—seen from temporal and geographical distance—form my subject. Theorizing from my personal loci of enunciation,[3] I shall foreground and interrogate forces that have shaped this identity in order to facilitate reconciliation of the fragments created by the dominant discourse of my early musical education. On a broader level, the essay problematizes the process whereby Western classical music was transmitted to non-Western contexts under specific circumstances, addresses issues that underlay its transmission (including the imbalance of economic and political power, the role of national and family histories, and the complicated nature of the colonizer-colonized relationship), and analyzes their impact on the formation of cultural identity among young children in postcolonial settings.[4]

The self-evident is often the least examined: how did I come to study Western classical music? I was born to second-generation Chinese immigrants on Muslim soil in a corner of the Asian continent. From birth until my late teens, my existence was thick with Southeast Asian peoples, and Southeast Asian tastes, smells, and sounds. The British had been in Malaysia for more than a hundred years, but by the time I was born Malaysia had been independent for more than a decade.[5] *Independent*—such a deceptive word, for by the time they departed, the British had left their stamp on key aspects of Malaysian life. English was declared the nation's second official language after Malay; we became a parliamentary democracy with a symbolic monarchy; and our legal system and traffic and driving rules were based on British models. Malaysian high school students sat for British-style "O-" and "A-" level examinations (*Sijil Pelajaran Malaysia* and *Sijil Tinggi Pelajaran Malaysia* respectively). Perhaps more disturbingly, we also unconsciously and unquestioningly imbibed and duplicated colonial social practices, for example that of a social-hierarchical system based on ethnicity—an especially problematic legacy for a multiracial society.[6]

Malaysian "understanding" of British cultural practices occurred on a family-by-family basis, depending on ethnicity, income and educational levels, social aspirations, and amount of contact with colonials. My parents, born into large, improvident, Chinese-speaking families, had attended missionary schools in the 1950s and college in the 1960s. All had been staffed by British, or British-trained teachers, and offered British-based curriculums of study. In these settings, students (including my parents) laboriously polished their command of the English language, a prerequisite for membership in the educated middle classes to which they were taught to aspire. Away from home, in college, students also encountered British-style behavior, talk, and dress among peers, teachers, and college staff members.[7] Many of my parents' peers equated Britishness with power and economic and social success. Popular, confident students were not only fluent in the colonial tongue; notwithstanding their Southeast Asian heritages and physiques, they were "British" in as many ways as possible. Most directly copied their teachers' behaviors, thus unwittingly acquiring dated vocabulary, gestures, dress and tastes (as many of their teachers had left Britain before World War II), an "understanding" of English customs which they then transmitted to future generations of Malaysians.

To this day, my parents maintain habits learned as college students: they dunk, eat afternoon tea, enjoy Marmite, digestive biscuits, orange marmalade and lemon curd, and listen to BBC Radio broadcasts in Malaysia. They bought English children's literature for us: I became familiar with Enid Blyton, J. R. Barrie, and Beatrix Potter, and with quintessentially English tales such as *Robin Hood and the Sheriff of Nottingham,* and *King Arthur and the Knights of the Round Table.* My sister and I were dressed in Edwardian children's clothing: feminine white blouses with ruffled Peter Pan collars and short puffed sleeves, carefully matched with pleated skirts made of fine, floral-printed cotton— clothing that, as an adult living in North America, I reencountered with a nostalgic twinge in Laura Ashley stores. These practices were fully integrated into our Malaysian existence, seamlessly lived alongside Sunday morning dim sum meals, the ubiquitous Malay language, daily broadcasts of Muslim calls to prayer, strains of Canto-pop and Bollywood, roadside stalls peddling fresh durian and star fruits, sun-drenched beaches, and bustling, humid night markets filled with shiny trinkets from all over Asia. My family was not considered unusual in any way among the people with whom we socialized, as they, too, looked, behaved, thought, dressed, and talked as we did.

Middle-class Malaysians saw dazzling social potential in the piano, although after independence in 1957 the national government declared Western classical music a colonial legacy we could do without and dropped music altogether from the public school curriculum. However, in practice the situation was far from being clear-cut. As G. H. Heath-Gracie, a British musician visiting Malaysia, chronicled in 1960:

> Malayanisation is now proceeding apace. The process should be complete by 1962, after which all Ministries . . . will consist wholly of those whose race, outlook and aspirations are specifically Malayan. It must not be imagined however that there is the slightest anti-British feeling which might be stirred up either against Britons as persons or against their institutions. Nevertheless there is a tendency to look away from Britain towards other countries for whatever knowledge and experience Malaya lacks. . . . Of one thing [we] may be certain. Traditional Malayan music, although propagandized by radio all day and every day, is quite incapable of being rebuilt to serve as an element in social or intellectual evolution. Instead of Malayans buying their native instruments their fantastic and ever-continuing increase in individual wealth has boosted the sale of pianofortes on which purely Malayan music is unplayable. These sales

are largely to households of Chinese, Indian or Ceylonese extraction which are said to form more than half the population. [1]

Heath-Gracie's observations reflected a phenomenon rooted in colonial history and local cultural beliefs. In Malaysia, the piano had graced the homes of expatriates and the wealthy since the British arrived.[8] An unmistakable aura surrounded the instrument; it represented, to the Malaysian mind, qualities associated with the colonizers' lifestyles: "cultured," "wealthy," "powerful," "well-educated" and "refined." Privileged were those who played it. To the Malaysian Chinese community, Western classical music and the piano offered additional attractions. As the piano requires much discipline and time to master, the enterprise of learning the instrument is in line with Confucian teachings, which emphasizes among other things continuous, in-depth, and committed efforts in all educational undertakings.[9] Confucius had also taught that cultivation of music would lead to "goodness" of character.[10] Thus a Chinese child's successful mastery of music and the piano would engender satisfaction and guarantee respect for his or her family from within as well as outside of the Chinese community.

Middle-class Malaysians, especially the Chinese, welcomed the arrival of the Associated Board of the Royal Schools of Music (ABRSM) in 1948. Established in 1889 as an examining board by London's Royal Academy of Music and Royal College of Music (later joined by the Royal Northern College of Music and the Royal Scottish Academy of Music and Drama), the ABRSM offered to Malaysians by the 1970s and 1980s a system of evaluating skills in Western classical music, organized into eight levels or "grades" that progressed from elementary (Grade 1) to challenging (Grade 8).[11] Alongside practical skills, the ABRSM evaluated knowledge of music theory and ear-training at every grade, and music history at advanced grades. The system was supported by a range of materials produced by ABRSM Publishing: "examination books" or editions of music preselected by the Board for each grade, instructional manuals covering principles of theory, books of scales and arpeggios for each grade (complete with suitable fingerings), and previous examinations republished for students as practice material.

Quality control was achieved and uniform standards set by a trained corps of "examiners" who traveled to local and regional centers where they heard and judged each candidate's performance on an individual basis. After hearing the candidate's scales, arpeggios, and prepared examination pieces, the examiner administered a sight-reading test and an "aural examination" (ear-training test). The examiner wrote comments about, and assigned number grades to, each part of the examination and totaled them up to determine whether the candidate had passed (with "distinction," "merit" or plain "pass") or failed the grade. The results were announced and reports sent to candidates a few months after the examination. Each passing candidate also received a certificate announcing the achievement, printed on heavy paper embossed with the ABRSM seal and signed by its Board of Examiners.

As a concept, the ABRSM was brilliant: with a portable system for the certification of musical skills, it became in effect a putative music conservatory for students ranging from the beginner to the preprofessional.[12] Most of those who taught the system in Malaysia had themselves undergone ABRSM examinations. With the ABRSM's forays into the British colonies, beginning with Australia, Tasmania, Gibraltar, and New Zealand in 1897, it became one of the world's first music conservatories with a distance-learning program abroad.[13] In light of its subsequent activities in the British Empire, it seems significant that the ABRSM was founded only two years after Queen Victoria's Diamond Jubilee in 1887, a time "when imperial consciousness . . . was probably at its zenith" (Cannadine 2001: 181).

The ABRSM could hardly have chosen more fertile ground for its activities than Malaysia, where it arrived in 1948 amid the colony's negotiations for independence, eventually achieved in 1957.[14] Respect for British systems of education remained deeply ingrained among those in my parents' generation— privileged and brilliant Malaysians aspired to Rhodes Scholarships at Oxford University or to Cambridge University. The ABRSM's elaborate system and its Commonwealth-wide reputation gained unquestioning respect and approval from Her Majesty's Malaysian subjects from the very beginning. Here was European culture presented by educational experts in a systematic form, within reach of all who could afford to pay for instruments, lessons, books, and examinations. Successful completion of each grade would result in both "international" recognition (since the system was known throughout the Commonwealth) and local respect.[15] The high price tags of lessons and examination fees, the latter converted directly from British pounds, were prohibitive for all but the wealthy or the most committed.[16] Thus the enterprise of taking piano lessons became wreathed in an aura of pride and prestige for its middle-class adherents. For lower-middle-class families such as my own, the piano offered the additional attraction of a long-term investment: music could "round off" the children's education, strengthen their chances for admission to good universities, and provide an alternate means of future income if necessary (a belief held especially true for females in late-twentieth-century Hong

Kong, Japan, Korea, the People's Republic of China, Singapore, and Taiwan, as it had been for females in nineteenth-century Europe and North America). In other words, the piano both represented and provided an avenue to upward mobility.

At the age of six, I was aware neither of the historical and social forces described above nor of their imminent impact upon me. A stereotypically obedient Chinese child, I learned, practiced, and absorbed all that my parents and piano teacher taught me about music. My first piano teacher was a young Chinese woman who had decided to teach full-time after completing high school because of the lucrative salary and flexible hours. Her well-educated family included Oxbridge graduates, a fact that boosted her image as a piano teacher in Kuala Lumpur society, although she herself had studied piano for less than a decade before I came under her wing. As a six-year-old, however, I saw only a pretty lady who dressed exquisitely (in lace, frills, and ruffles as the young Lady Diana did), who spoke English and played piano with poise and elegance, and who treated me with affectionate discipline: a veritable fairy-tale princess. Enchanted, I immediately resolved to be just like her.[17]

From the beginning, my teacher emphasized that learning to play the piano was a "British" activity, something that children in faraway England did under the supervision of the very same ABRSM system I was learning. Such pronouncements were calculated to reinforce her authority, to reassure my parents that theirs was a wise investment, and to spur me to practice by presenting the piano-playing British child as a role model. To play piano was to be "British," and the better I played, the more "British" I became. I was taught that the mystical, beautiful sounds that could be produced with two hands had been born of "white" history and "white" people, not us. In multicultural Malaysian society, ethnicity has long been a quick, convenient tool of differentiation, so that all Caucasians, whether American, Russian, or British, are "white people" to Malaysian eyes—just as to the North American eye Koreans, Japanese, and Chinese are often taken to be "Asians" exactly like one another. Playing Western classical music, I could aspire to become "British" or "Caucasian." Eventually, surrounded though I was by general cultural impoverishment, I might become civilized. The ABRSM system promised to guide me toward this goal, examination grade by examination grade. To civilize: to "bring out of a barbarous or primitive stage of society; enlighten; refine and educate" (OED). The elaborate nature of the enterprise seemed to reinforce its quality. How could any mechanism as complicated as this not reflect cultural excellence? The wealth of signs and symbols both intimidated and impressed us; the entire process involved international travel, expensive hotels, embossed certificates and Her Majesty's patronage. Our minds registered the quantitative evaluations as reliable indications of each candidate's worth and degree of "Britishness" in activities ranging from beating time to playing pieces from the Western classical canon.

I was, in short, imbibing postcolonial values alongside note values, chord progressions, melodies, and rhythms prescribed by the ABRSM as suitable for my level of skill. In the wake of independence, as the multicultural population of Malaysia had struggled to define its cultural and political identity, established British models in all arenas beckoned our still-colonized mentalities. Just as the newly minted nation retained its use of British institutional frameworks, segments of its population subconsciously clung to and thus ultimately perpetuated the continuity and security they had experienced within British cultural frameworks and values.[18] Such people lived—I lived—in the grip of the colonized imagination, for the "Britain" and "Britishness" we espoused no longer existed. In the hands of institutions such as the ABRSM, however, the colonized imagination could be—and indeed was—transformed into monetary gain. As the ABRSM Honorary Secretary's report from the first foreign tour to Australia in 1897–98 reveals, artistic development and monetary gain were from the outset twin goals: "I recommend the Board to 'go forward' and to carry on this work energetically and without fear of its results. There is I am convinced, a large harvest of useful and artistic work, and also a substantial profit to be reaped therefrom" (Aitken 1897–98: 19–20).

In Malaysia in the 1970s and early 1980s, the ABRSM operated in an arena largely void of other resources for Western classical music: there were few concerts and opportunities for public exhibition of student skills, little airtime on radio and television programs, no music classes in public schools, few if any college-level music courses, and only a handful of music stores in Kuala Lumpur that carried merchandise related to Western classical music (practically all such items were for ABRSM examinations).[19] Undeterred, Malaysians subscribed to the ABRSM in numbers disproportionate to the country's population. Like other Southeast Asian ex-colonies such as Hong Kong and Singapore, Malaysia posted unusually high numbers of examination candidates annually.[20] I was a deeply loyal if equally deeply insecure participant in ABRSM examinations, a blend of the colonized native and compliant Chinese child. From the ages of six to thirteen, I absorbed and trusted wholly in the ABRSM—my only avenue to Western classical music. I believed in the system's infallibility and in its judgment of my skills. In my inexperience and the absence of evidence to the contrary, I thought that the pieces of music prescribed for each grade were the only ones that existed. I did not, indeed could not, have a repertoire other than those pieces, since hardly any other music was sold. I remember playing Bach, Bartok, Beethoven, Chopin, Clementi, Handel, MacDowell, and Mozart over a span of eight years. This limited repertory, hardly representative of music then available in Great Britain, was apparently deemed sufficient for the ABRSM's goals in the colonies and later provided me with the clue that the institution's purpose had been to generate financial gains as well as to educate about music.

Although the ABRSM marketed itself as a prestige-laden private educational enterprise, the depth to which its directors understood the complex cultural situation and music-educational needs of the Malaysian market remains unclear. Had the Board researched Malaysians' attitudes and needs with regard to Western classical music? Did the Board know about the lack of resources Malaysians faced? Was the Board concerned that the ears and brains of those who processed the music it prescribed had otherwise had little exposure to and experience with the cultures of which the music was inextricably part? The ABRSM seems to have been contented to transfer its methods, created and practiced in culturally, politically, and economically different Britain, directly into a postcolonial setting, instead of adapting the methods in ways that would have shown sensitivity to the Malaysian context. By selling Malaysians Western classical music under the expired aegis of empire, the Board joined the multitude of interpellating systems in the colonized imagination and propagated colonial narratives in ex-colonies with vulnerable identities.[21] Catherine Szego has found in her study of a Hawaiian missionary-type school that "colonial education that privileges the learning of a foreign music over indigenous music is an obvious site for exploring power relations" (2002: 716; see also Szego 1999).

As a child, I remember puzzling over the different cultural domains in which I functioned on an everyday basis, albeit at varying levels of immediacy: Chinese-British-Malay-Indian. When I engaged in Western classical music activities, however, I underwent what I have come to think of as consistent destabilization of my identity in the encounter between a cultural system perceived as established and hegemonic (European via the British) and one struggling to define itself (Malaysian-minority Chinese). Throughout childhood and into early adolescence, my absorbent mind retained messages sent and received in the encounters, and these messages then formed the basis for my later "understanding" of the West, its culture, and its music. My early musical education was a process that did not much foster intellectual curiosity and musical activity, but one in which I was taught to think in terms of cultural, national, ethnic, and economic hierarchies. It is a story of colonial "violence" wrought on young minds and psyches.[22] The "violence" was wrought with a cultural tool—Western classical music—whose much-touted universality supposedly invites and nurtures interaction across time and cultures, geographies, ethnicities, and genders. Yet these very boundaries and limits were constant and often painful components of my early musical education. Motivated by different reasons, all of us—the ABRSM, my parents, my piano teacher, and myself—participated willingly if unwittingly in an ideological process that ultimately reinforced the colonizers' cultural subjugation of the colonized.

Had I, like most of my Malaysian friends, been content to stop my music training at Grade 8, I suppose I would not have come to seek full understanding of the circumstances I have described. I derived so much pleasure from playing the piano that by the age of thirteen, as I completed the final grade offered by the ABRSM, I was sure I wanted to become a musician (albeit without knowing what that meant or entailed). Perhaps the decision, born of a colonized imagination, represented a continued yearning to become "British." At this point I began to wonder if one could become a musician simply by passing examinations: Where did the process end?

The ABRSM lured children and ambitious parents with certificates and promises of prestige. But when I, a native awkward with youth and an accent, approached ABRSM examiners informally to inquire about pursuing music, I met with discouraging responses: "I don't recommend that you study piano professionally" and "You could sit for our diploma examinations in performance or teaching, and teach piano in Malaysia." Such advice, at once cautionary, well meaning, and dismissive, may have been considered appropriate in Britain, where "second opinions" could be sought and/or further research conducted with information and opportunities available outside the context of the ABRSM. In postcolonial Malaysia, where the ABRSM was the most respected authority on Western classical music, the words served only to deepen the self-doubt in my colonized psyche. Already fearful and inferior, my adolescent self saw and heard: *We are willing to take you this far—as long as you pay Us—but don't you dare go any further into Our world and Our culture. If you are not one of Us by birth, there is no room for you here. You can dabble in music, yes. But that is Our limit for you, and therefore it should be the limit you set yourself.*

My reaction at that time—surprising as it sounds today—was in fact understandable or even logical in the context of my then-limited exposure and training, and my veneration of the ABRSM. Such veneration, the result of colonization processes I describe earlier, decisively colored my interactions and understanding of "white musicians" and "white culture." I began studying Western classical music because it had been held up by my parents, my teachers, my society, and the ABRSM as a way to better myself. I had believed in colonized and colonizer alike. Caught in the web of the colonized imagination, I alternately lost and modified my identity in response to the historical and social forces swirling around and shaping me. Why did that happen? Because I was young and lived in a society where conformity, consensus, and submission are prioritized over criticism and dissent; because at that time I assumed that things had always been that way and would always be so; because I had heard of others who had had similar experiences; because I hadn't been aware that we, colonized and colonizer, had in fact been creating and living together the minutiae and emotional realities of postcolonialism—and thus making postcolonial history.[23]

My early music education under the ABRSM system left lingering effects on my outlook on and approach to Western classical music up until my years of graduate study in the United States of America, when I immersed myself in critical approaches to knowledge. Before then I did not have the words to describe, or perhaps was not even fully aware of, the subaltern deep within. During my undergraduate studies, my American teachers wondered at my timidity in expressing myself musically and intellectually. I simply thought I was unworthy of judging and voicing my opinions about Western culture (how could I, when I didn't belong culturally?). I did not know what to think or say about music at all. I wanted only to imbibe all that Westerners were willing to teach me, a non-Westerner, and fell silent beside those who were bold, white-skinned, had grown up with abundant opportunities to listen to Western classical music, or who had traveled to Europe. I wondered at the casual, friendly terms on which Americans accepted me as a music student, when all Westerners I had come into contact with as a music student in Malaysia had seemed distant to my endeavors. I cringed inwardly at the sound of the British accent, instinctively associating it with unassailable authority and superior knowledge, states I felt I could never achieve. I worried about discussing Western music as a non-Westerner to a roomful of Western faces. I mistrusted my multicultural identity, irreconcilably hybridized and fragmented with relativistic planes of understanding and inferior, I thought, to what I saw as the "white" world's privileging of factory-like uniformity, linearity, and efficiency of feeling and thought. At every turn, my colonial-style early music education functioned as a cultural cue cum social reference point for the process I underwent: surprise and shock, followed by a growing awareness of its long-term effects on me, and finally a struggle to realign the parameters of my identity and understanding of "white people" and their music.[24]

I have submitted to analytical scrutiny here what I remember of the inevitably unstructured and subjective impressions and feelings that made up my private childhood experiences of learning Western classical piano music in Malaysia. Looking back on the experiences as an adult scholar, I realize that like much childhood knowledge they were at once opaque and perspicacious, limiting and broadening, fiction and fact, past and present. Unlike other types of childhood knowledge, however, the colonial presence I already sensed in my youth had been a constant and mysterious enough source of ambivalence that I eventually sought its identity and its name. In finding both, I have finally found part of myself.

Notes

I wish to thank Kofi Agawu, Susan Boynton, Amanda Minks, Sarah Morelli, Patricia Tang, and the anonymous readers at Wesleyan University Press for their helpful comments on earlier versions of this essay.

1. This essay explores the formation of my musical identity primarily from the ages of six to thirteen (late 1970s–mid-1980s). I left Malaysia to pursue undergraduate and graduate studies in music in the United States of America. The ideas in this essay were initially developed in a graduate seminar on literary theory at Duke University in spring 1995, team-taught by James Rolleston, Walter Mignolo, Fredric Jameson, and Barbara Herrnstein Smith.

2. On the history of the term *postcolonial,* see Mishra and Hodge 1991.

3. Mignolo argues for the importance of "postcolonial loci of enunciation as an emerging discursive formation and as a form of articulation of subaltern rationality" (2000: 88). By "subaltern forms of rationality," Mignolo means "not only that subalternity is a social class phenomenon and an object of study but that subalternity is characteristically theorized by those who are implicated in the very forms of subalternity they are theorizing" (86). Such work "attempt[s] to incorporate knowledge of the personal and social body, to restore the body to reason, and to reason from the subaltern (social and personal) body."

4. Few music scholars have explored the application of postcolonial theory in their work; a thought-provoking and valuable exception is Agawu 2003. Agawu begins by highlighting postcolonial theory's "potentially fruitful and ethical ways of making sense of the (musical) world" and identifies scholarship that is "postcolonial in spirit" (xviii). Like postcolonial theorists Gayatri Spivak, Edward Said, and Homi Bhabha, Agawu brings perspectives born of his status as both (African) native insider and (Western) scholar outsider to critique what he sees as problematic aspects of African music scholarship ranging from ideologies of representation to issues of notation and ethics. Perhaps in keeping with Agawu's goal to deexoticize contemporary Africa in the eyes of the West, he describes but does

not problematize Ghanaian students' participation in Western classical music activities at Achimota School (13–15). The activities seem to have been a well-established tradition by the time he attended the school in the 1970s. In this essay I problematize my experience of learning the Western classical piano tradition at a time when the tradition was still a novelty to Malaysians.

5. The British gained Penang Island in 1786, and by the final decades of the nineteenth century had established control over West Malaya and East Malaya. Independence was achieved in 1957. For a history of Malaysia, see Andaya and Andaya 1982. *Malaysia* was coined in 1961, before which the country was known as Malaya. For convenience, I use *Malaysia* throughout the essay.

6. On British-created class hierarchies in the colonies, see Cannadine 2001.

7. Edward Said (2000: 185–86) has described a comparable situation in a British-run educational institution in Cairo, Egypt, around 1949–51. At Victoria College, "the Eton of the Middle East," students were "schooled in the ways of a British imperialism that had already expired."

8. Richard Leppert (1995: 116–17) describes the cultural significance of the piano in eighteenth- and nineteenth-century India. The situation seems to have paralleled that in pre- and postindependence Malaysia. Leppert focuses on the musical activities of colonials ("Anglo-Indians") and does not deal with Indian reception of the piano and Western classical music.

9. As illustrated in, for example, Confucius's teaching of the Way and in Ssu-ma Ch'ien's account about Confucius tenaciously practicing a *ch'in* piece until he could sense the character of, and accurately identify, the composer. See Lin 1943: 67–68.

10. Confucius asks, "If a man is not good, what has he to do with the rules of propriety? If he is not good, what has he to do with music?" (1998: *Analects* 3:3).

11. I describe the Board's examination system as I remember it from the late 1970s to the mid-1980s. According to the Board's Web site (www.abrsm.ac.uk, accessed December 13, 2003), the system practiced today remains similar, with the addition of a "Prep Test" (pre–grade 1) and a "Performance Assessment for adults . . . who may wish to have their musical skills assessed without taking an exam."

12. Although the ABRSM is not a "music conservatory" in the traditional sense of the term (it is not a physically centralized institution, nor does it employ a stable corps of music teachers), it offers systematic music education via a standardized set of examinations that certify the accomplishment of certain musical skills. The music requirements appear to have been partially based upon Felix Mendelssohn's curriculum model at the Leipzig Conservatory (1843), popular in Europe since the nineteenth century, wherein training in harmony, theory, and musicianship was emphasized alongside applied skills. See Parakilas 1999: 154–55.

13. Agawu (2003: 14) mentions in passing the ABRSM's activities in Ghana, Sierra Leone, South Africa, and Nigeria in the 1970s. See also Kwami 1994 and 1989. The British-based Royal Academy of Dance (RAD), established in 1920, offers a similar worldwide system of evaluation for dance. In Canada, the Royal Conserva-

tory of Music (established 1886) began offering music examinations at the elementary and intermediate levels in 1935 and may have been adapted from the ABRSM system. The Canadian system of music examinations is available throughout North America (as compared to the international reach of its British counterpart). I thank Elizabeth Day for information about the RCM.

14. See *The Associated Board . . . Annual Report . . . 1948*. Also corroborated by agenda item "3. Malaya. Mr. Macklin reported that the Board had been in correspondence with the education authorities and it was hoped to hold Practical Examinations in Malaya in 1948" (*Draft Minutes . . . 1947*). I am especially grateful to Mr. Richard Morrison, Dr. Nigel Scaife, and Ms. Sarah Levin for allowing me access to primary sources in the Board's archives in London.

15. For example, by 1948 the ABRSM was conducting examinations in Australia, Canada, New Zealand, India, Ceylon (now Sri Lanka), Malta, Jamaica, Trinidad, Bermuda, Barbados, Antigua, British Guiana, Malaya (now Malaysia), and Singapore. See *The Associated Board . . . Annual Report . . . 1948*.

16. The exchange rate of the Malaysian ringgit (MR) to British pounds (BP) in the late 1970s and early 1980s fluctuated between seven and eight MR to one BP.

17. My reaction speaks of the esteem in which teachers are traditionally held in Asian societies, a theme that has been explored by ethnomusicologists with reference to indigenous musical traditions. See, for example, Wong 2001.

18. Historically, the minority Chinese and South Asian communities of Malaysia were more pro-British than were the native Malays. Most members of the Chinese and South Asian communities had immigrated to Malaysia at the end of the nineteenth century, fleeing economic difficulty and famine in their homelands. Welcomed by the British as much-needed labor for the rubber and tin mining industries in Malaya, both ethnic groups flourished economically and professionally under colonial rule. Postindependence, my Chinese parents may well have felt for their preindependence educational experiences in British-run institutions something Svetlana Boym (2001: xviii) describes as "restorative nostalgia . . . [which] attempts a transhistorical reconstruction of the lost home . . . [and] does not think of itself as nostalgia, but rather as truth and tradition."

19. James Chopyak (1987) has documented the Malaysian government's efforts, presumably in the 1980s, to establish a musical culture that would promote national unity. As he explains, however, "There is currently [i.e., in the 1980s] a shortage of qualified music teachers in Malaysia. . . . there is often a great disparity between what appears in the music syllabus and what is actually taught in the [public] schools. In a number of schools observed by this writer music classes were simply singing sessions in which everyone sang songs (in Malay or English) to a piano or guitar accompaniment. Efforts are being made to train more music teachers within Malaysia itself . . . a few potential teachers are also sent to the United States to study music education" (434). Chopyak does not specify the schools he visited, but they were probably located in urban areas; in addition,

the *Kurikulum Baru Sekolah Rendah: Buku Panduan Khas Muzik, Tahun Satu* (*The New Elementary School Curriculum: Special Guidebook for Music, First Year*) was published relatively late, in 1983 (453). In the late 1970s and early 1980s, I attended public elementary schools in rural areas (Sekolah Rendah Kebangsaan Kem Terendak in Malacca, and Sekolah Rendah Kebangsaan Our Lady's Convent in Sitiawan, Perak), both of which featured little music in their curriculums. Other than Western classical piano music, I sporadically came into contact with Canto-pop and Bollywood movie music on radio and television; American popular music of the 1940s through 1960s (through American television shows and my father's LP collection), and American popular music of the 1980s (through my sister's tape collection). In my mid- and late teens (a period that falls outside the years I discuss in this essay), I attended a high school that had originally been an Anglican missionary school. My headmistress organized a school choir (it was not part of the school curriculum) that performed Christian-inspired choral music at annual school concerts. I served as rehearsal pianist and accompanist of this choir for three years.

20. For example, out of a total of 78,317 candidates outside Great Britain in 1977, Singapore entered 15,159 candidates; Hong Kong, 11,850; and Malaysia (including East Malaysia, or Sabah and Sarawak), 17,806; as compared to New Zealand, 12,152; Trinidad, 882; Guyana, 627; India, 566 and Belgium, 186 (*The Associated Board . . . Annual Report . . . 1977*). In 1980, of a total of 104,150 entries outside Great Britain, Singapore entered 19,792 candidates; Hong Kong, 17,858 and Malaysia (including East Malaysia, or Sabah and Sarawak), 28,956. See *The Associated Board . . . Annual Report . . . 1980.*

21. I use "interpellating" in the Althusserian sense. In "Ideology and Ideologized State Apparatuses" (2001: 117–20), Althusser argues that subjects are ideologically produced to perform roles they are allocated in the social division of labor. Considered in this light, the ABRSM was one of several ideological systems that conditioned me into the role of the colonized. Reports from ABRSM examiners, for example that by Heath-Gracie quoted above, provide evidence that they often gained partial understanding of local economic, social and cultural conditions and limitations during their tours. Research on institutional response to these reports is part of my ongoing project on the history of the ABRSM's international activities. Historically, colonization has been attributed to diverse motivations, including capitalistic exploitation, the desire on the part of the colonizer to "civilize" native populations, and the desire to remake colonized societies outside of Britain in the image of British society. See, for example, Howe 2002: 76–87; Said 1978; and Cannadine 2001.

22. Amanda Minks discusses Pierre Bourdieu's notion of "symbolic violence" (2003: 122–28) in relation to this essay in her afterword. I thank Minks for the reference.

23. Readers have asked whether Malaysians considered setting up an alternative

system of musical education. I emphasize that as far as I could tell, all who subscribed to the ABRSM, including my family, did so out of a respect for and belief in the system. In other words, we were happy with the ABRSM and saw no reason (again, as far as I could tell) to think about devising an alternative. This attitude in itself speaks of many things, including the quality of the ABRSM system, Malaysian subscribers' judgment of the same, the deep inroads colonization had made on this aspect of Malaysian life—in short, the complicated and compromised nature of the colonizer-colonized relationship.

24. See Mueller 2002 for an overview of research on music and identity among youth.

Telling Histories

Memory, Childhood, and the
Construction of Modern Griot Identity

PATRICIA TANG

Ethnomusicologists, anthropologists, and historians have long been fascinated by the griots of West Africa. Known for their musical and verbal artistry, griots have served as musicians by blood lineage and keepers of oral history in many West African cultures from as early as the fourteenth century. An important part of the kings' courts, the griots were responsible for knowing the genealogies and histories of their patrons. Through their words and music, griots were able to uphold and reinforce the status of the kings and nobles, thus vitally supporting the social hierarchy. According to one famous saying, "A king is a king only if there is a griot to tell his story."

With the ancient kingdoms and empires now themselves a part of history, modern times in West Africa paint a very different picture for griots. French colonization brought about vast changes to the traditional Senegalese social structure, with the official caste system effectively dissolved by the time Senegal gained independence in 1960. In the face of this rapidly changing social environment, modern griots can no longer depend on their wealthy patrons of the past. Although singing and drumming used to be the exclusive hereditary occupation of griots, nongriots (those of noble descent or from other castes such as blacksmiths and weavers) are now participating in musical activities once forbidden to them.

As a result of these changes, griots need to find new and creative ways to maintain their role in modern society.[1] One way in which they are doing this is by telling their own stories—perpetuating their own histories, especially to Western researchers who continue to document them and preserve their memories on paper.

This essay examines the construction of modern griot identity through such personal narratives of the past, specifically of childhood. Drawing upon life histories of Wolof griot percussionists in Senegal (masters of the sabar drum), I will look at the ways in which adult griots talk about their childhood years as a way of validating their place in society. At a time of social and economic change in which griots feel the need to protect their hereditary occupation in Senegalese society, narratives of childhood separate griots from nongriots, allowing the former to maintain exclusive claim to their closely guarded traditions.

◆ Masters of the Sabar Drum

Reflecting the enormous diversity of West Africa, the music of griots varies greatly from one culture to another. Perhaps the best-known and most researched griot tradition is that of the Mande, for whom the kora (twenty-one-stringed harp lute) is a primary instrument. Among the Wolof people of Senegal, the sabar is the primary and exclusive instrument of Wolof griots, known as *géwël*. The sabar is a single-headed drum played with one hand and one stick.[2] The sabar ensemble consists of hourglass-shaped, open-bottom drums of varying heights, as well as several egg-shaped bass drums. Customarily played in an ensemble ranging in size from four to sixteen, the sabar is played by *géwël* family drum troupes.

Sabar drumming is prevalent in nearly all aspects of Senegalese culture. A week after birth, infants are baptized (given names) to the sounds of sabar; weddings are also celebrated with sabar drumming and dance.[3] Sabars support wrestlers in traditional Senegalese wrestling matches, and for recreation, sabars can be heard daily in the neighborhoods, providing the music for dance parties (also called *sabar*).[4] In recent decades, the sabar has also served as the rhythmic backbone for *mbalax*, the popular music genre made famous by Youssou N'Dour, and now an important export of Senegalese culture. Thus from life-cycle events to neighborhood dance parties and the modern music scene, the sabar is undisputedly the Senegalese instrument par excellence. Still played almost exclusively by Wolof griots (*géwël*), the sabar has helped Wolof griots to maintain an important role in Senegalese culture to this day.[5]

◆ Methodology

This essay is based on research carried out in Dakar, Senegal, over a period of seven years, from 1997 to 2004. In 1997–98, I lived in Dakar, conducting field research for my dissertation on Wolof griots (*géwël*), specialists in the sabar tradition. During this time, I studied sabar drumming with members of the Mbaye family, a prominent family of griot percussionists. My research involved private drum instruction with Lamine Touré, as well as attending and filming many sabar events at which the family sabar troupe performed. In addition, I conducted numerous interviews with members of the Mbaye family (of which Touré is part), representative of three different generations of sabar percussionists.

Although I did not set out to collect life histories, the open-ended nature of my interview questions, as well as my familiarity with the people whom I was interviewing, led them to discuss their lives in great detail.[6] As a result, over the course of several long interviews, I was able to record the life histories of various griot percussionists.[7]

In the course of my research, three common topics emerged from the telling of life stories: (1) family background/lineage, (2) accolades (prizes and competitions won), and (3) childhood. The stories of one's childhood were by far the most detailed and lengthy part of each life history. All the *géwël* I spoke with had shown talent in drumming as a child, and this early start was clearly very important to them at both an individual and social level.[8] To distinguish themselves from others, Wolof griot percussionists draw upon their childhood memories in recounting their histories as a way of constructing their identities and reinforcing their significance to Senegalese culture.

Although griots in Senegal are ultimately concerned with maintaining their status within Senegalese society, they have looked beyond Senegal for the means to do so. Because recognition by the Western world (and in particular, by Western researchers) can serve as a mode of empowerment, the decision to talk to researchers inevitably leads to positive gain, both financial and in public status.[9] For this reason, griots have generally been very open to talking to Western researchers.

In this essay, I analyze the construction of griot identity through the critical framework of the griots' words themselves, but as transmitted to a very particular source: the Western researcher. In a competitive world, the griots I interviewed were all more than happy and willing to talk to me.[10] They were proud to tell their stories, but more important, they wanted to make sure their stories would be told to others, or written down for posterity. Thus the griot, who traditionally has served as the keeper of oral history, is making use of Western researchers to make sure his own legacy continues through print and in distribution to the West.

◆ Interpreting Life Histories

The life history has often been used by anthropologists as a means for learning about African cultures, with notable examples including Mary Smith's classic *Baba of Karo* (1981), Patricia Romero's *Life Histories of African Women* (1988), Sarah Mirza and Margaret Strobel's *Three Swahili Women,* and Marjorie Shostak's *Nisa: The Life and Words of a !Kung Woman* (1981).[11] In all of these examples, the researcher has attempted to represent the tradition bearers as closely as possible "in their own words," so to speak, with "the richness of autobiography rather than the sketchiness of archival reconstruction" (Slobin 1989: 78).[12]

However, life histories inevitably involve a complex collaboration between researcher and tradition bearer, reflecting the selective agendas of both. Jeff Todd Titon (1980: 277) problematizes the life history, stressing the importance in "distinguishing story from history when the medium is talk." He distinguishes between biography, oral history, life history, and "life story," which he defines as a self-contained fiction that "simultaneously serves as an expression of personality and self-conception of the tradition bearer" (290). Although I prefer to use the term "life history" because I feel that history can be told through a story, I do so taking into consideration Titon's concept of the life story. We must keep in mind that when asked about their lives, griots must be selective in what they wish to include as part of their life histories. Memory is selective, and tradition bearers have reasons why they choose to emphasize some aspects of their lives while omitting others altogether. Thus, in analyzing Wolof griot narratives given for the purpose of recording by a Western researcher, one must conclude that their inclusion of and emphasis on childhood memories is one of the choice elements in constructing contemporary griot identity for the West.

◆ Learning Process and Environment

Sabar drumming is a skill that is passed down from one generation to another within a *géwël* family. Few *géwël* decide to take on drumming at a later age; instead the vast majority begin to drum as toddlers. Sabar drumming is never taught through formal lessons or apprenticeship, but rather is learned by observation and early exposure, a learning process J. H. Kwabena Nketia has called "slow absorption" (1973: 87). The years from childhood to puberty form the crucial period that fosters talent and allows *géwël* children to gain a high level of skill by their teens. In addition, the family network, inclusive of infants and children in all activities, clearly creates a positive learning environment and encourages children to absorb knowledge of sabar.

As sabars are an integral part of *géwël* lifestyle, children are exposed to sabar drums and drumming from infancy. In addition to their traditional purposes (as musical instruments), sabars have been cited for other formative purposes as well. For example, *géwël* Macheikh Mbaye reminisces that he learned to stand and walk by holding onto sabars for balance. In another example, *géwël* Lamine Touré remembers his mother giving him and his brothers toy drums to get them to stop crying.

In *géwël* families, children begin drumming at an early age, as young as two years old. As children from around the world "play" (*fo*) in the most general sense of the term, *géwël* children "play" sabar, fabricating makeshift drums and mimicking adult drumming activities that they observe. Small children (ages two to three) generally begin with empty plastic containers, beating them with a stick. Eventually (at age four or five), they graduate to large tomato paste cans; when emptied, a small leftover piece of goatskin can be fastened to the opening to create a small sabar-like drum. As they get older (ages six or seven), the tomato cans no longer suffice, and the children make drums out of broken or unwanted mortars (large mortars and pestles are a staple in every Senegalese kitchen). Made of wood, these mortars more closely resemble sabars and are larger than tomato cans. After playing with these various levels of makeshift drums, the children gain the skills to tackle a real, full-sized sabar drum. When an adult percussionist feels that the child is ready to perform on a real sabar, the child is invited to play with the family drum troupe.

However, before they ever play a real sabar, with their makeshift drums, children have a means to practice what they learn through observation and careful listening. Sabar dance parties are widespread and common, and griot percussionists are accustomed to bringing small children to their drumming events. *Géwël* children are both allowed and encouraged to attend "adult" activities from an early age.[13] Thus through repeated exposure, children learn the various rhythmic parts, as well as longer and more complicated musical phrases (*bàkks*).

The skills learned on the toy drums are of great significance. Even as toddlers, the ways in which *géwël* children drum closely mimic their elders. Through meticulous observation, children memorize, using vocables, the many *bàkks* (musical phrases) played at an event; the next morning, they rehearse them. Small children form sabar ensembles much like adult ensembles, assigning a certain part to each child and maintaining a high level of discipline. Sometimes young boys will even invite young girls to come dance at a sabar dance event; using rocks as chairs, forming a small circle, the boys will drum and the girls will dance.

Having provided some background regarding *géwël* childhood, I will now present four brief case studies of griot percussionists. The first three, Macheikh Mbaye, Sitapha "Thio" Mbaye, and Lamine Touré, are percussionists from the *géwël* family with whom I worked closely during my field research. The fourth case study, Amary Mbaye, is taken from a secondary source to serve as a comparative example, and to show that the phenomenon is not specific to my interviewees.

◆ Case Study: Macheikh Mbaye

Macheikh Mbaye was born on October 21, 1932, in Dakar. Born into a *géwël* family of sabar drummers, Macheikh Mbaye is fiercely proud of his family's long history of percussionists. He was at the height of his career during the end of the colonial era, and was even decorated by President Senghor for his accomplishments in 1969. Today, he is still considered one of the foremost *tambour-majors* of his generation, along with Doudou Ndiaye Rose and Vieux Sing Faye.

As a child, Macheikh Mbaye was raised by his maternal uncle, Modou Yacine Ndiaye, an accomplished drummer in his own right.[14] Macheikh Mbaye explains that when he was young, his relatives tried to make him go to school, but his mind was elsewhere:

> When I went to school, I was not good at all, because my entire mind was on the drums. I would live with the drums, all day; when I woke up I saw the drums; when I got back from school, I saw the drums; I was surrounded by them all of the time. So I would just play when I was a little kid. I would play and play, and as I grew up I found myself becoming a pretty good drummer. Nobody ever taught me how to play; I mean, nobody just took my hand and showed me the way to play. I was simply surrounded by the drums, and I learned how to walk by bumping into the drums. When I was three, four, five years old, I was able to play. When I was eight, my uncle used to watch me playing, and he would cry. People would ask him why he was crying, and then he would say, 'He is still a young boy, but what he is playing is beyond me! That's why I cry.' This is what explains [why I have the right to] talk about this topic, because I

inherited it. Drumming and singing is something you inherit; you don't study it. It's in the blood. (Tang 2001: 85)

In another interview, Macheikh Mbaye explains how he used to drum on his father's shoe.

When I was five, six, going on seven, my uncle and father would just take me wherever they had a drumming session or *tànnibéer* [night-time sabar dance event]. And once in the circle, I would sit in between the *ndënde* and the *gorong* [two sabar drums]; I would then take my father's shoe and using a stick, whatever they beat—you know, whatever rhythm that came out from their drums—I would play the same on my father's shoe. That's actually where I started to really play. . . . That's where it all started, and as time went on, you know, I learned how to play.[15]

These brief excerpts reveal much about Macheikh Mbaye's upbringing and the importance he places on childhood. First, he explains that he grew up in a sabar environment. For him, sabars were a part of his natural surroundings, both at home and at drumming events that he attended as a small child. The fact that he credits the sabars for aiding him to learn how to walk is also significant. In this case, an extremely important phase of human development, which is normally taught by a parent, is instead taught by drums.

Macheikh Mbaye also stresses his talent and proficiency at drumming at the age of eight years. He then immediately ties this into the fact that he is authorized to tell me about the sabar tradition. Drumming, he argues, is something that one inherits, and the fact that it can only be passed down through blood is only reinforced by emphasizing one's childhood years.

Now in his seventies, Macheikh Mbaye talks about his role in teaching succeeding generations of young percussionists in his extended family.

So the other people in my group, I taught them how to play. . . . When my children grew up, I decided to give them what I got from my parents. Now my son Khalifa is playing in the ensemble of the Théâtre National Daniel Sorano; Biran, my nephew, is playing; Moustapha Niass [my son] . . . I'm passing on to them everything I know. And now they are very good drummers. They take the drums that belong to me and play with them. . . . What I learned from my father, and what my uncle taught me, I passed it on to the next generation. (Tang 2001: 90)

◆ Case Study: Sitapha "Thio" Mbaye

Born to Massaer Mbaye and Agida Seck on September 18, 1959, in Kaolack, Sitapha Mbaye (known as "Thio") has been one of the most successful percussionists in the Senegalese modern music scene. After starting his professional career with the famous *Ballets d'Afrique noir,* Thio Mbaye began playing with singer Ismael Lô in 1984. Since then, he has played with Omar Pène and Super Diamono and recorded and performed with major West African artists such as Youssou N'Dour, Cheikh Lô, and Salif Keïta.

Thio Mbaye first explains that he was born into a family steeped in the griot drumming tradition: "Above all, I was born in a griot family. My father and his father were both drummers. So I inherited it from my father . . . You know, I already had rhythm in my blood. I was born into it, so it was part of me" (Tang 2001: 94). He then describes how he, like Macheikh Mbaye, was born into a sabar environment.

> When I was little, I saw my father playing, my mother dancing, and my mother playing too. So, I can say that I was born with a drumstick, so to speak. From a very young age, I was already familiar with the sabar, drumsticks, and my father even made me a little sabar, my size . . . but I didn't only play my little sabar, you know? Because I would see the big sabars too, I would go like this (grabbing on to them), until sometimes they would fall on top of me and I would cry. Voilà, that's the way it was; when I was very young, I truly had sabars at my disposal. I had sabars in the house, the bathroom, in the hallways, in the garden—everywhere there were sabars. So, I was very close to the sabars when I was young.[16]

When talking about his childhood, Thio Mbaye highlights the fact that he made his own toy instruments at an early age.

> There is something that is very important: when I was about three or four years old, I created my own instrument. With the mortars, I would take mortars and then put holes in them, then mount a skin on them, with the goatskin—I stole the goatskins during the nighttime, yes! [*laughing*] My father, when he was young, he created his own percussion instruments made out of bottles. He would break the bottle, then put a head on the open end, with goatskin. I have never seen anything like that since, but my father, when he was very little, he did this . . . he explained this to me. And me too, when I was very little, I would take the mortars, and

transform them into sabars. Yes. And up until the day I was circumcised, it was that day that I stopped playing the toy sabars—it was that day, that the little brother of my father, Iba Samb, he brought together all the sabars, the day I came back from the hospital, and he said, voilà! Today you will no longer play the toy sabars, because you are circumcised, so now you will play real sabars. I said no, because I was in pain; but this is the story of how I grew up with the sabars. . . . You know, when you are little, you must have something to inspire you before having real access to sabars, because long ago, we didn't have small drums.

In discussing his early training, Thio stresses the importance of memory and imitation as a child percussionist.

We had a lot of time on our hands to learn, to learn what we had seen, or learn what we had heard. You see, children have a good memory; that's why when I was a little kid, and I saw the grownups playing, everything would stay in my head. The next day, we would give ourselves names [of the grownups]. For example, I'll be Tamsir, you can be Iba Samb, you are so-and-so. You play like this, the accompaniment is like this, et cetera. We would play exactly like what we had seen the day before, in the big sabar; so though we were small, you would have the impression that it was grownups playing.

A number of Thio Mbaye's own children have shown promise in drumming from an early age. He explains that his four-year-old son, Khadim Mbaye (photo 6.1), has already shown great talent in drumming on his Nescafé can, relating it to his own childhood experience of makeshift drums.

When my children are very young, they are all interested in the sabar. . . . In Khadim's case, I think he's going to be a percussionist, because he really really loves the sabar. And when you are small, when you love the sabar, you can even create your own sabars. That's what's amazing. For example, the tomato cans, the coffee cans . . . like I said, my father began with large bottles which he would cut and then cover with a skin, in his own way. And me too, I created sabars out of mortars, when I was small, I was the one who was inspired in this way. I would take the mortars, and everyone would get mad at me and say, watch out! If he gets a hold of your mortars, he will turn them into sabars! So that is how I began.

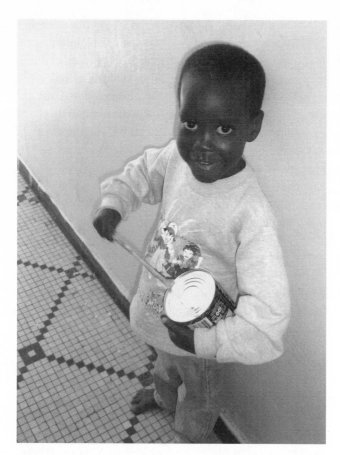

Photo 6.1 **Khadim Mbaye, son of Thio Mbaye, drumming on a Nescafé can, 2004.** Photo courtesy of Patricia Tang

◆ Case Study: Lamine Touré

Lamine Touré was born to Mari Sow and El Hadj Touré on September 13, 1973, in Kaolack. Now widely recognized as one of the leading percussionists of the younger generation, Touré has enjoyed a fruitful career with his family drum troupe, as well as with the *mbalax* band Nder et le Setsima Group.

Touré explains how he used to play in a sabar ensemble as a child.

When I was very small, I began to play when I was four years old, the pots, the little sabars. You know, the little sabars that we made . . . when the tomatoes were finished, we would take the big tomato can and mount it with a skin, and we would play on that. . . . We would play, me and Lendor; I was the oldest, he was a few months younger, and I was four;

we began playing in the doorway of the main household. We had an order
. . . do you know why we played well? We were well organized. We were
accustomed to going to big sabars to watch, so we saw how important
discipline was. We would say it's you who will lead today. The rest would
follow. Another day, somebody else would lead. . . . We played all the time,
in that big doorway. (Tang 2001: 101)

Lamine Touré's stories of his childhood are corroborated by his mother,
Mari Sow, who reminisces:

Lamine would play on the tomato cans. You know, whenever the drum
skins [of the real drums] popped, they, as little boys, would take the
broken skin and reuse them by putting them on the tomato cans. And
that's what they used to play. And what they played sounded very good!
    Lamine would run back home from school, simply so that he could
play the sabar. He used to play all the time. And I knew that he would become a drummer. That's all he wanted. It is normal for him to play the
sabar, because he inherited it from his grandfather. A grandson of Samba
Maissa Seck will always play drums.[17]

Meanwhile, Lamine continued playing sabar with his group of friends,
which included Lendor Mbaye, Karim Mbaye, Assane Niang, and Issa Sow. For
fun, they would organize sabars (neighborhood dance parties) for the young
girls in the neighborhood. This was how they practiced. One day, their hard
work earned them the opportunity to do what they had never done before:
play in a real sabar. Their luck came when their uncle, Ali Gueye Seck, needed
drummers for a program he had one evening. Lamine was eleven years old.

Ali Gueye Seck [Lamine's uncle] had his own group of percussionists.
One day, he had a program, but all of his percussionists were off playing
at other gigs. This was a big problem for Ali Gueye, because he had nobody to accompany him. So he came to our house, and saw Thio's mother,
Agida Seck. Agida said, well, take the kids—they're here! We had already
gone to sleep. But Agida convinced him that we played well and he should
take us. We were still young and had never played on real sabars—only
tomato cans and mortars. But Ali Gueye was desperate, so he agreed, and
came to get us. So Lendor, Assane Niang, and Issa Sow and I went with
him.
    We took a taxi. We were sooo excited—our first time really playing!
And we were going to play on real sabars! But he scared us, too. He said,
you better play well! But we said, yes, we are real percussionists, we won't

disappoint you. So during *saaji* [warm-up], we played. There were us four kids, one other older guy, and Ali Gueye—we were just six. When the women came, they said, Ali Gueye, but these are kids! How can they accompany you? He said, you'll see. And we showed them.

But the sabars were heavy. (We carried them standing up.) We got tired quickly. But Ali Gueye wouldn't let us give up; he would yell at us and hit us. We were scared and tired. Issa Sow even began to cry because he was so tired. But we played well. Afterward, they gave us each 300 CFA [Communauté financière d'Afrique]. We were so excited with 300 CFA![18] After walking home, I arrived around one o'clock in the morning. My mom was worried that I was home so late, but I told her we played well, and I gave her 100 CFA. I kept my 200, and in the morning, I went to the corner store and bought lots of things—peanuts, chewing gum, and mint candies. (Tang 2001: 103)

This was the beginning of Ali Gueye's "kiddie" sabar group. Because they all enjoyed working together, and the audiences enjoyed seeing the kids play, the group was a success. Although his memories of the children's group include some rough moments (due to Ali Gueye's strict disciplinarian style), Lamine gives Ali Gueye a lot of credit for helping them to become good percussionists.

We were very excited and happy to play with him. We liked his way of playing, and the way he dealt with us. He was very serious, and could be mean; we were afraid of him. But that's why we became such good percussionists. He wanted us to really play well, to use a good hand technique, and to play strongly . . . We got very tired. But because we were afraid of him, we played well.

. . . With Ali Gueye, we would even sleep over at his place . . . because by the time we finished playing, often it was nighttime, so we would just go to his place and crash. We were very young, but my mom didn't mind; we slept at his place, ate at his place . . . every day, we were at Ali Gueye's; we would even help him to shave skins and mount the sabars. We did a lot with him.

Ali Gueye even bought matching outfits for us because we were doing so well. We would play at soirées—in Kaolack—we did a competition, we even competed against Omar Thiam's group.[19] And we won—we blew them away! It was in a big hall at the Chamber of Commerce. (Tang 2001: 103)

As a teenager, Touré decided to move to Dakar to pursue a full-time career as a percussionist. By his twenties, Lamine Touré had become an established percussionist in the popular music scene, playing with such groups as Mapenda Seck, and most recently, Nder et le Setsima Group. He also holds a central role within the family sabar troupe, serving as the *dirigeur* (lead drummer). Although he is four decades younger than Macheikh Mbaye, he has already taken on the responsibility of teaching his younger brothers and cousins.

◆ Case Study: Amary Mbaye

This case study comes from the work of Cornelia Panzacchi. In her article "The Livelihoods of Traditional Griots in Modern Senegal" (1994), Panzacchi introduces Amary Mbaye as a drummer and a genealogist. Mbaye also trains the famous "dancing horses" of Péex, the city where he lived at the time of the interview (1991). A *géwël* from Kayor, the region north of Dakar, Mbaye told Panzacchi how, in his family half a century ago, the children's talents were discovered and encouraged:

> Usually the head of a *géwël* family would have many wives, and each one might have many children. Out of all these children, who were all males . . . my father was to discover the qualities with which every one of us was gifted.
>
> Out of paper and cans he made little drums for each of us and gave one to everyone. He was then able to see which of the children loved his instrument. The child who beat his toy drum and even managed to play tunes on it showed that he was certainly gifted, whereas the other children neglected their instruments and preferred to spend time singing, or discussing . . . In this way, by observing his children at play, my father was able to discern for which task each was gifted and the occupation he could master. And from this time onwards, he knew whose destiny lay in becoming a singer, a drummer, a dancer. (Panzacchi 1994: 199)

Mbaye explains that a child with a particular talent for drumming would then be trained by a male relative until he was allowed to accompany the elder to festivities, where he might take minor part. If a performance was well received, the young musician could attain a certain celebrity status and be asked to perform on other occasions, thus building up his reputation (Panzacchi 1994: 199).

◆ Conclusion

These case studies show a wide range of perspectives on griot childhood. In the case of Macheikh Mbaye, individual agency is emphasized. Rather than specifically attributing his drumming education to particular teachers in his family, he stresses the importance of growing up as a small child in a sabar environment. It is almost as if the drums themselves served as his teachers. However, now a part of the older generation, Mbaye is proud to discuss his own role in teaching the younger generation. He thus reinforces his griot identity through discussing his proficiency in drumming as a small child, as well as emphasizing his role later in life in educating other children in the family.

Like Macheikh Mbaye, Thio Mbaye also emphasizes the importance of growing up in an environment surrounded by sabars. He highlights the creativity of young *géwël* talent in making drums out of many different kinds of materials and hails the ability of *géwël* children to memorize and imitate with great adeptness.

Lamine Touré vividly remembers his early years and stresses the importance of the discipline and technique that was learned through close observation of his elders, practiced through child's play. He openly credits his teachers (such as Ali Gueye) and their role in his learning process. Sabar is once again an inherited tradition, one that is passed down from one generation to the next.

In Amary Mbaye's family, Mbaye's father consciously used child's play as a means to discover talent. Toy drums were given to children not just to occupy their time, but to serve as a talent scout. After seeing which children seemed to have a proficiency in drumming, the children would be apprenticed to an elder percussionist, attending as many drum events as possible until they learned the ropes. The experience is very similar to that of Lamine Touré.

Through examining these life histories, it is clear that the childhood years are the central part of a Wolof griot percussionist's training. However, it is the fact that adult griots choose to emphasize this part of their past while telling their life histories to Western researchers that shows the importance of childhood in constructing griot identity. Griots do not "just learn to play"; they are immersed in the tradition from an early age, and this is something that non-griots can never claim. In a day and age when Senegalese society is rapidly changing and Wolof griots feel the need to defend their claim to their musical professions, their stories of childhood enable them to validate their exclusive right to drum.

Notes

I would like to thank Susan Boynton, Roe-Min Kok, Sarah Morelli, and the anonymous reviewers for their helpful comments and suggestions.

1. On the modern role for griots, see Panzacchi 1994.

2. The use of one hand and one stick is somewhat uncommon, thus making the sabar technique unique. Most West African drums tend to be played either with two hands or with two sticks.

3. Naming ceremonies (*ngente*) are an important ritual for Senegalese Muslims, who make up 95 percent of the country's population.

4. *Sabar* refers both to the name of the drum and to the neighborhood dance event at which it is most commonly played. For the purposes of this essay, I will use the unitalicized term for the drum, and the italicized term (*sabar*) to refer to the event.

5. For further reading on Wolof griots and sabar drumming, see Tang 2001. Another hereditary group of West African drummers that would serve as an interesting comparative study is the Dagbamba *lunsi* of Ghana, although they are not considered "griots" (i.e., they are not part of a social caste system). See Oppong 1973, Chernoff 1979, Goody 1982, and Locke 1990.

6. I did not begin conducting formal, recorded interviews until I had already spent five months in Senegal and knew my interviewees quite well. I believe that as a result, they were very comfortable and open in talking about their lives.

7. Some interviews were conducted in Wolof with the assistance of my research assistant, Papa Abdou Diop. Translations were also done with Diop's assistance. Other interviews were conducted in French or in a mixture of French and Wolof. All interviews were transcribed verbatim in their native language before being translated into English.

8. This conclusion is based on formal interviews I conducted with eight members of the Mbaye family (Macheikh Mbaye, Lamine Touré, Alassane Djigo, Mari Sow, Sitapha "Thio" Mbaye, Massaer Daaro Mbaye, Macheikh Mbaye Jr., and Karim Mbaye), in addition to informal discussions with other griots in Dakar and Kaolack.

9. Cornelia Panzacchi (1994: 206) states that during her time in Senegal, the "current rate" a European or American scholar had to pay for a recorded sixty- to ninety-minute interview with a well-known griot was 10,000 CFA (the equivalent of US$20). In 1997, when I attempted to make contact with a famous griot who will remain anonymous, he told me he needed to see 50,000 CFA (US$100) before he would speak a word. On a relatively tight student budget, I did not feel comfortable with or able to oblige to the request. After this experience, I made a conscious decision not to "pay" for interviews per se, but to get to know the griots first and establish a more friendship-based (rather than financial) relation-

ship with them (see note 6). In this type of relationship, financial exchange still occurred, but more indirectly (for example, when someone in the family needed money to send a child to the hospital), rather than my explicitly "paying" for interviews. Through establishing this relationship from the beginning, I was able to align myself more with the griots themselves rather than being thrust into the role of patron.

10. For further reading on competition and conflict in the Mande griot context, see Hoffman 2001.

11. Notably, these life histories are all about women.

12. This is from an "interlude" in Slobin's book in which he introduces the life histories of three generations of immigrant *hazzanim*.

13. The practice of adults bringing children with them to all events and activities, as opposed to leaving them behind, is common practice in many African cultures; see Blacking 1967: 30 and Nketia 1973.

14. Macheikh Mbaye's father, Daouda Mbaye, was also an accomplished percussionist, but due to age and health was not as active as a drummer when Macheikh Mbaye was in his formative years.

15. Unpublished interview with Macheikh Mbaye, March 24, 2004, Dakar, Senegal.

16. Unpublished interview with Thio Mbaye, March 26, 2004, Dakar, Senegal.

17. Unpublished interview with Mari Sow, May 8, 1998, Kaolack, Senegal.

18. Currently, 300 CFA is about US$0.50.

19. Omar Thiam is a well-known and respected Serer griot in the Kaolack region.

Destined for Greatness
One Song at a Time

Coming of Age as a Korean *P'ansori* Performer

HEATHER A. WILLOUGHBY

This essay investigates the coming-of-age experiences of three Korean performers and the pervasive role that traditional music and traditional life has
played in their formative years. I have chosen the three female subjects, Kim
So-hŭi, Yi Chu-ŭn, and Song-hwa, because of their popularity, the amount of
critical information available about their lives, and their accessibility for interviews. I document and analyze direct and indirect influences of traditional
Korean music in the lives of these women and show how they balanced Confucian ethics and modern-day ideals in their daily choices. In particular, I focus on the three women's transitions from childhood into adulthood, when
they made important decisions that involved several issues: Korean ideals of
womanhood, cultural expectations, personal and social identities, and the role
of traditional music in Korea in the twentieth century.

Kim So-hŭi was born in 1917 in North Chŏlla Province, an area well known
for its many *p'ansori* singers, scholars, and critics. She was among the first
women to gain widespread recognition as a master singer and was designated
an Intangible Cultural Treasure by the Korean government in 1963. Yi Chu-ŭn
(b. 1972), who feels that she was fated to become a performer, had to learn to
balance personal and social expectations in fulfilling that destiny. She began
singing lessons at the age of eight and has dedicated her life and academic pursuits to the art of *p'ansori*. The third performer, Song-hwa, is a fictional character from the immensely popular film *Sŏp'yŏnje* (1993).[1] The characterization
of Song-hwa represents Korean cultural perceptions of a stereotypical *p'ansori*
performer's life. Thus, it is useful to compare and contrast the depiction of
Song-hwa's "experiences" with the actual experiences of Kim So-hŭi and Yi

Chu-ŭn, since all three women, whether by fate, choice, or coercion, devoted their lives to becoming professional performers.

I have designed this essay to allow the life stories of Kim So-hŭi, Yi Chu-ŭn, and Song-hwa to reveal issues pertinent to each individual's experiences. I do not claim that the three young women's lives represent those of the "average" Korean female adolescent, nor do they necessarily paint a stereotypical portrait of other *p'ansori* performers' experiences. However, by observing their lives and life choices, we can draw certain conclusions that are applicable to the coming-of-age experiences of many young women. For instance, all three overcame specific social boundaries in order to succeed in a male-dominated society and profession. In much the same way, many women today must make choices in their youth that will enable them to hurdle culturally sanctioned limitations and maintain a sense of social propriety simultaneously. Additionally, young Korean females are constantly bombarded with images of ideal "Koreanness" through the popular media, and each must choose, just as Kim, Yi, and Song-hwa did, to accept and conform to those expectations, or to forge their own paths. After chronicling specific aspects of each of the three performers' lives, I will outline the relevance of their experiences to today's youth. In order to understand better the cultural milieu in which these women live(d), however, I will begin with a description of *p'ansori,* including a brief history of the genre and its pedagogical techniques.

◆ Historical Perspectives

P'ansori is a solo narrative art form in which a singer (*kwangdae*), accompanied by a single drummer, relates a long and complex tale through song, spoken passages, and corresponding dramatic gestures. Throughout its inception and later development in the mid–eighteenth century, *p'ansori* singers were traditionally men, with only three women known to have been professionally trained before the twentieth century.[2] Beginning in the mid–twentieth century, however, the situation for female *p'ansori* singers changed drastically. Due to social, cultural, and economic factors, many women trained in the art of *p'ansori* singing, and today most performers are women. A brief history of *p'ansori* as a genre and description of the traditional training undergone by young performers will enable us to analyze how Kim, Yi, and Song-hwa's lives conform to or diverge from the norm, particularly from the point of view of pedagogical experiences.

P'ansori, as an independent art form, emerged in the mid–eighteenth century.[3] Originally it was performed by and for people of the lower classes and did not involve the literate aristocrats who penned the social histories of Korea. Thus little is known about the exact origins and early evolution of the *p'ansori* genre; however, two theories have been proposed by music scholars. The first speculates that the genre grew out of the performance practices of itinerant entertainers, and the second claims that *p'ansori* is closely related to the rituals and narrative songs of the southern-tradition shamans. Marshall Pihl has argued that *p'ansori* probably developed from a melding of the two traditions (1994).[4]

Because *p'ansori* was rooted in the folk culture of Korea, the tales often contained satirical passages lampooning the noble classes *(yangban)* and surreptitiously complained of the injustice suffered by the lower classes, including the *kwangdae* themselves, who often lived in poverty as itinerant musicians. Despite the social chasms created by the class system, by the mid–nineteenth century interactions between the *kwangdae* and *yangban* increased as the latter's interest in *p'ansori* grew. A symbiotic relationship developed between seemingly opposite elements: *kwangdae*, who sang about the *yangban*'s elitism and subjugation of the lower classes, and the *yangban*, who enjoyed, financially promoted, and documented *p'ansori*. *Kwangdae* performed regularly and frequently in the homes of *yangban*. The latter even occasionally endowed their favorite singers with modest political titles, thus affording *kwangdae* prestige and protection, as well as the right to demand higher fees for their services.

In the first half of the twentieth century, traditional Korean life and musical enterprises experienced far-reaching changes, the result of political and cultural suppression imposed during Japanese colonial rule,[5] and of turmoil caused by the Soviet-American conflict (1950–53) that eventually divided the Korean nation. Chan Park, a contemporary *p'ansori* singer and scholar, has noted that during the early 1900s many Korean musicians adopted nationalistic values and tried to revive interest in traditional music by resuscitating folk genres and "cleansing" music that had been "corrupted" by Japanese and other Western influences. "Weary of being knocked about by the current of modernity, they reoriented themselves, promoting fresh interpretations and a revival of *p'ansori*'s 'old style' *(koche)* aesthetics, described as genuine, traditional, unadorned, natural, straightforward, authentic, or dignified. . . . They aimed for a distillation of the 'Korean' voice and the purging of centuries of social stigmatization" (C. Park 2003: 100–101).

Another significant musical development of the 1900s was the creation of *ch'anggŭk* (National Theater). *Ch'anggŭk*, the staging of *p'ansori* tales, includes costumes, scenery, and instrumental accompaniment. The vocal timbres and songs used in *ch'anggŭk* are similar to those of *p'ansori*. However, instead of a single *kwangdae* portraying all of the characters in the *p'ansori* narratives, *ch'angguk* performers each enact the role of only one persona. By the 1940s, all-female *ch'angguk* troupes had emerged and rapidly surpassed in popularity the all-male or mixed-gender troupes. "The Yŏsŏng kugak tongho hoe (All-Female National Music Association) was organized by *p'ansori* giants, including . . . Kim So-hŭi. . . . By the end of the Korean War (1950–1953), all-female troupes were springing up 'like bamboo shoots after the rain.' For over a decade after their emergence in 1948, various female troupes received undivided admiration, especially among female audiences" (C. Park 2003: 105). In the 1970s, however, large-scale public curiosity in *yŏsŏng kugak* and *ch'angguk* abated, forcing many female singers trained in the style of *p'ansori* into the performance arena of the solo genre. Then as now, economic factors arising from the postmodernization of Korea may also have accounted for the low number of male singers. According to Kim So-hŭi, contemporary Korean economy prevents men, who must compete for financial resources in a capitalistic society, from undertaking rigorous and time-consuming training as well as the monetary sacrifices necessary to become a *kwangdae*.[6]

Since the inception of the Chosŏn dynasty (1392–1910), female performers or *kisaeng* have held an important and multifaceted role in Korean society. Like their male counterparts, *kisaeng* were born into the low- or slave-classes and stigmatized as outcasts. However, some gained considerable power from their association with the noble *yangban*. As entertainers for the elite *kisaeng* had opportunities to become literate—enabling them to create their own poetry— as well as become proficient in performing refined songs and dances. A few were even designated "medical *kisaeng*" and provided healthcare for women of the noble class (Chang 1986: 253). *Kisaeng* underwent rigorous training, but if successful they reaped the social and material benefits of the upper classes. The *kisaeng* were truly privileged, as not even noblewomen were formally educated or instructed in the arts. Korean society's strict adherence to Confucian mores meant that most women were not only illiterate, but were also discouraged from any pursuits that might distract them from their (male-dictated) goals— obedience and service to their fathers in childhood, to husbands during marriage, and to sons in old age (Kim Yung-Chung 1976: 44).

Although Confucianism is no longer the official governmental and cultural foundation of social mores, its influence is still predominant. According to Chungmoo Choi (1998: 2), during the Japanese occupation enlightened male intellectuals "preached about the importance of women's liberation and education to strengthening the nation. . . . However, the nationalist position of the male elite did not separate women from nation and emphasized enlightenment for women only as mothers." Drawing on the work of feminist critic bell hooks, Choi points out that the formerly "colonized males adopt the stance of the colonizer as a way of recuperating their masculinity" (14). Sasha Hampson explains that despite recent legislative changes such as the Equal Employment Act, Korean women's behavior and participation in society are still constrained by the resilient "axioms of Confucian thought: filial piety, family loyalty, conformity to group norms and chastity" (2000: 170–71).

Hampson's argument rings especially true for Korean society's treatment of, and social expectations for, young women. Certainly Korean male and female adolescents today commingle in public (which they were not permitted to do after the age of seven during the Chosŏn dynasty), enjoy popular media, or pursue advanced academic degrees; yet an aura of Confucian propriety seems to linger. For instance, when Chan Park began learning *p'ansori,* her master teacher Chŏng Kwan-jin said: "If you wish to be a good singer, you must first be a good human being. . . . [I require] that you fulfill your duty to your parents first. I'd rather you be a good daughter than a skilled singer" (C. Park 2003: ix). Conservative viewpoints such as Chŏng's have affected the life and coming-of-age decisions of each of the three performers in this study, as shall be seen in the following descriptions.

◆ *P'ansori* Performed

The typical performance setting of contemporary *p'ansori* is minimal; neither stage props nor special costumes are used. The singer sits or stands on a straw mat, wears traditional Korean clothing, and uses only a folding fan to represent objects (a sword, book, or saw, for instance), ideas (for example, power), or attributes (including bashfulness or sorrow). The fan may also be opened and closed to add to the soundscape, or to emphasize certain aspects of the text sung. In addition, the drummer and audience contribute to the atmosphere with their *ch'uimsae,* or words of encouragement: *Ŏlssigu!* ("Way to go, right on!"), *Chot'a!* ("Nice!"), or *Kŭlŏch'i!* ("So it is!").

In order to relate musical and dramatic nuances effectively, a *p'ansori* singer must learn to produce a large number of characteristic tone qualities. *P'ansori* favors a rough husky voice that conveys dramatic power and folklike qualities. A smooth vocal quality is said to lack dramatic expression (Yi Po-hyŏng 1973; Chŏng Pŏm-t'ae 2002). The harsh vocal quality called for is not easily obtained. A professional performer undergoes years of intensive training to develop a powerful voice capable of many dramatic colors; critics often claim that a singer reaches his or her prime only in his or her fifties. Singers will practice continuously for hours until they become hoarse, eventually developing calluses on their vocal chords. They may sing in the mountains or under waterfalls, attempting to match the sounds of nature, while strengthening their voices and obtaining the desired timbral qualities.

The act of sequestering oneself in a remote natural setting is one of many steps a dedicated performer will take. Chŏng No-sik (1940), biographer of many nineteenth- and early-twentieth-century *p'ansori* masters, noted that a singer typically began training in early youth under the tutelage of a family member or neighbor. In the first phase of study, the novice would concentrate on basic techniques of interpretation and performance, and also acquaint him or herself with the vast repertoire of *p'ansori* narratives. Until recently, the lengthy *p'ansori* libretti were not written down for pedagogical purposes; all repertoire lessons centered on rote learning with a master teacher, followed by individual practice. Although the texts are now available and distributed to students, the tradition of oral transmission remains prevalent today.

After initial training, a novice singer would leave home to apprentice him- or herself to a famous master singer. Marshall Pihl explains that this second phase of study was physically the most demanding and lasted two to seven years. For the novice, it was a period of deprivation and of punishing efforts to acquire the proper vocal qualities. At the end of the apprenticeship, the aspiring *kwangdae* would cloister him- or herself in the mountains to refine his or her *p'ansori* techniques. The idea of perfecting one's art in solitude in the mountains (traditionally associated with Shamanistic and Buddhist practices, rites, and beliefs) is not unique to *kwangdae;* rather, it is an East Asian cultural ideal whose ultimate goal is mental, physical, and spiritual transcendence of the mundane in the service of art.[7]

In the past, the *p'ansori* singer would lead the life of an itinerant performer after returning from seclusion, participate in various competitions and festivals, and attempt to establish both a reputation and a home base in order to attract students and continue the propagation of the genre.

We shall see that the experiences of three female performers adhere to, but also significantly diverge from, the traditional route described above. In addition, their dedication to *p'ansori* singing affected nearly all aspects of their youth.

◆ Kim So-hŭi: Famous "Baby Star"

When I first met Kim So-hŭi (1917–95) in 1986 at a concert to rally and inspire college students before an anti-American demonstration, I could not imagine that she had ever conformed to the stereotypical image of a demure, shy, and passive Korean woman. Then nearly seventy years old and barely five feet tall, Master Kim emanated a remarkable sense of strength and confidence. How did this woman, born of a humble family in the early twentieth century— a time of great political upheaval on the Korean peninsula—became one of the greatest and most highly esteemed performers of *p'ansori?*

According to Kim, she was approximately twelve years old when she was first introduced to the music that would dominate the remainder of her life. Born near the city of Koch'ang, North Chŏlla Province, in southwestern Korea (home to many nineteenth-century *p'ansori* singers, scholars, and critics), she paradoxically did not become acquainted with the genre until she moved north to the larger city of Kwangju to get a better education. She explains:

> One day as I was heading off for school I saw some people setting up a tent for some kind of musical performance, and during class, I heard a beautiful sound echoing through the neighborhood. On my way home, I realized it was a performance by Yi Hwajungsŏn, one of the most famous *p'ansori* singers of that era. . . . Yi Hwajungsŏn's voice was magnificent. . . . I was simply intoxicated by her voice. I couldn't move!
>
> After hearing her, I tried singing myself—imitating what I'd heard that day. Why, I was singing all the time. It made my sister [in whose home I was living] so angry. She was constantly scolding me. She wanted me to study, not sing songs, but my brother-in-law intervened on my behalf. He saw that I had talent. (Pickering 1994: 58)

Once Kim had decided to study *p'ansori,* she would not be deterred from her ambitions, even if she broke tradition by going against the wishes of her family. Not all of her family members opposed her dreams, however. Kim told a magazine interviewer that she was "given the name So-hŭi by her maternal aunt and that it was a matter of 'inevitable fate' that she follow the path of a 'So-hŭi' rather than that of a 'Sun-ok'" (Pihl 1994: 105). By this she meant that the name given to her at birth, Sun-ok, lacked the elegance and dramatic flare of So-hŭi.

Kim's brother-in-law introduced her to Song Man-gap, a direct descendant of one of the oldest and most highly respected lines of *p'ansori* masters. Even after Kim herself was viewed as a master singer by the public and designated an Intangible Cultural Treasure (1963), she lowered "her voice with respect when referring to her first master, whom she describes as having been 'the highest-ranked *p'ansori* singer in the country, the King of *P'ansori'*" (Pihl 1994: 105). She studied in group lessons of twenty to thirty students, and also privately for three hours or more per day, learning melodic passages not taught to the larger group. Several years were spent learning "The Tale of Shim Ch'ŏng"—a story of filial piety wherein a young woman sacrifices her own life so that her blind father might regain his sight. Master Song Man-gap believed that stories which deal with intimate relationships between men and women, such as "The Tale of Ch'un-hyang," were inappropriate for adolescents to learn. Thus Kim maintained the propriety required of a young girl even in matters of art. When she finally learned "The Tale of Ch'un-hyang," Kim says that she, like other female performers, was taught to omit passages in which physical relations between the main characters were poetically described. One of Kim's students, Ahn Suk-sŏn (b. 1948), described the difficulties of singing such passages with strength while maintaining a sense of femininity:

> It is so important to put strength in your abdomen and open your mouth really wide, even at the expense of showing the inside of your mouth, uvula and all. . . . When a woman opens her mouth so wide, to the point where a huge vein stands out on her neck . . . I used to be really ashamed, you know, but I conquered that. . . . And the sexual jokes? It is not considered a woman's place to say them before the audience, you know, like Hŭngbŏ's frequent intercourse with his wife. Skip it, or they'll consider you indecent. (C. Park 2003: 229)

Even after Kim reached her late teens, propriety played a role in her training at the Chosŏn Vocal Music Research Institute in Seoul. She says that Confucian civility and morality were emphasized to the coed student body: young men and women were allowed neither to interact, nor to speak with one another, on pain of expulsion.

Kim became a very accomplished singer and won an important competition at the age of thirteen (her nickname, she says, was "baby star"). Privately, however, she felt professionally inadequate until after she had completed ten years of study. This type of self-criticism is in line with the Confucian tradition wherein one's talent and potential for fame are sublimated to one's elders, the master singers. Kim moved to a Buddhist temple in 1934 and devoted two years to deepening and broadening her knowledge (Pihl 1994: 106). In 1936 at the age of nineteen, she gained national renown with the release of the "Victor Label Tale of Ch'un-hyang," a joint recording by five highly accomplished singers (including Yi Hwajungsŏn, whom Kim had first heard a mere seven years earlier). It was a singular honor for the young performer to appear on equal billing with great masters of the era, particularly the one partially responsible for her career choice.

Kim feels that her entry into *p'ansori* performing was relatively easy and gratifying in comparison with those who suffered contempt and ostracization. She has only one regret about her childhood: "I wish that I had started a little bit later. That is, I wish I had finished my schooling before I started my musical career. I used to be so envious of the schoolgirls I saw on the streets of Seoul. I did study each morning before I went to practice my music, but I wish I had received a formal education" (Pickering 1994: 59). In another interview, Kim explained: "Even today it's a matter of lasting regret that I really couldn't study. Even after achieving some success through *p'ansori,* I still continued to lament about my schooling while touring around giving my performances. Then, one day, an educator who heard me said I should look into correspondence lessons. And so, with those lessons, I finished my high school studies" (Pihl 1994: 249).

The learning, performing, and recording of *p'ansori* dominated Kim's adolescent years. She was clearly not a typical young Korean woman of the early twentieth century. Although she had sacrificed a formal education and experienced isolation from family and friends, she gained unusual advantages. Like the *kisaeng* of the Chosŏn dynasty, Kim had a certain amount of power in a male-dominated world. Already as a youth, she had been able to dictate the path of her own career while maintaining the requisite respect for her elders. Although she was restricted by moral codes and ethics of the day, her profession enabled her to travel throughout Korea and to parts of China—behavior not possible for most women of her generation. Later in life, she also traveled extensively in the United States and Europe, where she performed *p'ansori* for foreign audiences.

◆ Yi Chu-ŭn: Little Genius Singer

According to David Feldman (1986), a prodigy is a child who by the age of ten exhibits skills at the level of an adult professional in an intellectually demanding field. Although there are countless gifted children in the world, a true prodigy is a rarity. Feldman writes:

> It is the fortuitous convergence of highly specific individual proclivities with specific environmental receptivity that allows a prodigy to emerge. This is an infrequent and unlikely event. The convergence is not simply between two unitary, looming giants—an individual and an environment—but between a number of elements in a very delicate interplay: it includes a cultural milieu;

the presence of a particular domain which is itself at a particular level of development; the availability of master teachers; family recognition of extreme talent and commitment to support it; [and] large doses of encouragement and understanding. (12)

Yi Chu-ŭn (b. 1972) appears to be one of very few Korean children whose life would meet these criteria.

Like Kim, Yi believes that becoming a *p'ansori* singer is fulfillment of individual destiny (a point to which I will return later).[8] By the time she was four, Yi had displayed musical gifts which her family wanted to cultivate. Although Yi had a desire to study the *kayagŭm* (twelve-stringed zither), dance, and singing, fees for private arts school were prohibitively expensive, so she concentrated on *p'ansori* alone. Yi feels that she was born to sing, and her grandmother continuously told her she was talented. "So," she explained to me, "I lived as if I *was* talented."

She initially trained with Kim Hŭng-nam. Because of her youth, she was not taught entire passages but learned each song bit by bit. According to Yi, her teacher believed in her ability, young as she was, to become a wonderful singer. His constant encouragement strengthened her belief in herself and she worked diligently so she would not disappoint him. She won many awards and became a local child star. While in elementary school, she was already famous in her hometown, Mokp'o, because she often appeared on television programs. Her schoolteachers treated her differently, but, instead of being jealous, her friends were proud of her accomplishments and relished knowing someone famous. Yi was also proud, and at that age (perhaps unconsciously) deemed humility an unnecessary attribute. She often looked down on other children but now regrets having done so and makes efforts to get along with her peers. Her schoolteachers, who encouraged her to display her talents and profound knowledge of *p'ansori,* often unwittingly nurtured her self-indulgence and pride.

In 1980, a group of well-known *p'ansori* performers visited the traditional arts center in Yi's hometown of Mokp'o, on the southern coast of Korea. At the request of Yi's teacher, master singer Shin Yong-hŭi (a disciple of Kim So-Hŭi) listened to and was impressed by the young *p'ansori* prodigy. Shin discussed with Yi's family the possibility of moving the child to Seoul so Yi could become her student. Yi's father initially disapproved, but her grandmother, who always encouraged her talents and firmly believed that Yi would need a profession, persuaded the family to allow her to become Shin's disciple. The eight-year-old moved 195 miles from her family to study *p'ansori* with Shin and attend the Elementary School for the Gifted and Talented. With Shin, Yi studied in group classes as well as privately for an hour and a half every day. In just two years she had learned her entire repertoire: four *p'ansori* tales (out of the five extant) whose performance time totals nearly twenty-five hours. When asked how many hours she practiced each day, she replied, "Without rest. Always. Forever!" The child prodigy was mastering three-hundred-year-old songs at an age when other youths are only just beginning to become interested in music on the radio (Marks 1979).

Yi adopted unusual study habits while studying with Master Shin. She learned much from observing other students, including those who were far older than her and famous in their own right, such as Ahn Suk-sŏn and Pak Yang-dŏk. According to Yi, Shin considered the prodigy a "little genius singer," indulging her in many ways. Normally a young child is not permitted to speak to an adult in the middle of a lesson, let alone correct an older student, but that is exactly what Shin allowed Yi to do. Yi would not only boldly admonish older students, but would even demonstrate the correct way to sing a given passage. Even though she was young, she was not afraid to speak the truth—she knew her art well and did not hesitate to share her knowledge.

Shin further indulged Yi by favorably comparing her to others. For example, Shin would challenge another disciple: "Why does Chu-ŭn know this passage when she is so young, and you do not?" Looking back, Yi acknowledges that this was perhaps not the best pedagogical approach, but it gave her the confidence she needed to pursue her aspirations. When asked how others responded to her behavior, Yi readily admits, "They disliked me and told me I was too arrogant." Shin mentored the child beyond the world of *p'ansori* by emphasizing etiquette and proper deportment for a young lady. Yi reports that Shin would often reprimand her for the way she walked or carried herself in public, but when it came to music, Shin never dissuaded Yi from speaking her mind and pushing the limits of her abilities.

Through experiences such as this we see that throughout Yi's youth she existed in a liminal sphere between adulthood and childhood. In terms of music, Yi was treated as an adult; her talents were recognized as being mature, enabling her to assess the skills of others, and admonish them as if she herself were the master teacher. However, outside music and practice sessions, Yi was regarded as a child who needed to be nurtured and instructed in the rules of social decorum.

Yi's need for parental care can also be seen by the fact that after only two years in Seoul she returned to her hometown to attend junior high and to be near her mother, who likewise badly missed her daughter. Yi later returned to

Seoul (with her grandmother as chaperone) to attend the National Traditional
Music High School. She subsequently attended the prestigious Seoul National
University, where she earned a master of arts degree in traditional vocal music studies. She is currently a full-time musician and *p'ansori* singer at the National Center for Traditional Korean Performing Arts.

Overall, Yi Chu-ŭn's youth represented an interesting blend of conformity
and challenge to Korean tradition. For instance, out of respect for her teacher,
she mostly disregarded the popular fad of dyeing hair in unnatural colors;
however, in 1999, she rebelled slightly by highlighting her jet-black hair with
dark red. This practice seemed rather out-of-place for a traditional musician;
her newly dyed hair was a noticeably lighter color than the knotted black wig
typically worn at the nape of the neck during performances. Chan Park comments on the conflict between the female performer's desire to sustain the traditions of *p'ansori* and her need to express herself freely:

> Just as *p'ansori* unfolds on the modern stage a slice of the past in the
> form of a straw mat, women in singing religiously wear the *tchok*
> (women's traditional chignon), a stark contrast to male singers' early
> abandonment of the *sangt'u* (men's traditional topknot) and horsehair
> headband and hat. The fake *tchok* a female singer carries in her dressing
> equipage illustrates that women are not as free to move away from their
> role as an "exhibit" of tradition as men. While adhering to the physical
> image of the traditional *kisaeng* or female *kwangdae*, women in *p'ansori*
> also strive to cultivate the cultural image of their new identity as carriers
> of a revered tradition, as "artists" and *sŏnsaeng-nim* (revered teachers).
> (C. Park 2003: 231)

Asked about her hair-dyeing experience in 1999, Yi had replied, rather flip-
pantly, that her teacher had reprimanded her because such trends were deemed
inappropriate for a conveyor of tradition. In a more recent interview (2002), Yi
claims that she now believes it important to maintain traditional dress standards upheld by *p'ansori* performers, while seeking her own identity as a singer
and Korean woman.

Another example of how Yi Chu-ŭn negotiates the traditional values of
p'ansori in a rapidly changing world is her nostalgic desire for the ethical and
moral codes of Neo-Confucianism as described in the *p'ansori* tales she sings.
Yi believes that although the tales told in *p'ansori* are antiquated to some degree, they also teach valuable moral lessons of conduct. In a recorded interview, she explained:

There are five *p'ansori* tales, each of which teaches its own ethics—the values of our ancestors. It would be good if we could revive them in the modern world—where Ch'unhyang is loyal [to her husband] to the end or where Shim Chŏng is willing to throw herself as a sacrifice into the sea to show her filial devotion—those are values we should pursue. One cannot sing [the *p'ansori* tales] without really playing into the song in a similar way. One comes to think that, ah, I should be like them [the characters] too.

Yi concludes that her life reflects lessons learned from *p'ansori*:

I live with my grandmother. . . . Of course, I would not be able to compare my filial devotion to that of Shim Chŏng, but I really try to be good to her, to respect and serve her. So many bad things happen in relationships between the elderly and young, but I try to be different. I always try to sympathize with their feelings. I think that is the influence from doing *p'ansori*. It is the same with the teacher-pupil relationship. I believe the genre of *p'ansori* offers many [positive] instructions to those who learn it.

Yi's *p'ansori*-based choices and values may appear outdated to her twenty-first-century Korean social contemporaries, but her achievements in youth and beyond have also impressed them. Yi continually works to maintain the propriety of tradition, while demonstrating remarkable self-confidence in forging her own path as a woman of strength and determination.

◆ Song-hwa: Sacrificing Sight for a Song

Sŏp'yŏnje (literally, "western school") refers to a style of *p'ansori* originating in the southwestern province of Chŏlla. It is also the name of one of Korea's most popular films. Released in 1993, *Sŏp'yŏnje* grossed the highest earnings in seventy years of Korean filmmaking, and by the end of its first run had been viewed by two million people—an unprecedented number—in Korea.[9]

The movie depicts the lives of three people: Yu-bong, an itinerant *p'ansori* singer; Song-hwa, an orphan girl; and Tong-ho, her brother. Yu-bong had loved Tong-ho's mother, a widow who had died in childbirth. The story is set in South Chŏlla Province in the 1960s as Tong-ho attempts to find his long-lost "sister" and adoptive father, whom he had left years ago.[10] The film unfolds in a series of flashbacks: Tong-ho recalls his childhood days wandering from town to town as Yu-bong performed and imparted to his children the art of *p'ansori*. Yu-bong's story begins in the 1940s, a time when industrialization and Westernization were rapidly encroaching upon and marginalizing traditional Korean culture and arts. A particularly vivid scene depicts Yu-bong performing *p'ansori* on a traditional straw mat in an open marketplace. A small crowd gathers around him, but it is soon attracted to a loud Western-style marching band (with brass instruments, an accordion, and drums). As Western cultural forces began to supersede Korean traditions physically, aurally, and psychologically, traditional Korean artists became increasingly destitute. Tong-ho eventually ran away from his father and what he deemed the meaningless and unbearable apprenticeship to which he and Song-hwa had been subjected.

In the 1960s, Tong-ho begins to piece together the fate of his father and sister in the years since his departure. Immediately after he left, Song-hwa became lethargic and lost her will to live. Yu-bong nursed Song-hwa back to health, but also gave her a mild herbal poison that caused her to go blind gradually. Yu-bong believed that blindness would teach Song-hwa the depth of suffering necessary to become a great *p'ansori* artist (perhaps it would also ensure her dependence on him). Tong-ho hears that Yu-bong has died and that Song-hwa ekes out a living as a poor, blind, seminomadic singer. After a lengthy search, Tong-ho finds Song-hwa, and though their reunion is realized only through song, they overcome their deep grief through a cathartic *p'ansori* performance in which Tong-ho serves as Song-hwa's drum accompanist.

Many have analyzed the film's depiction of Korean society, gender roles and identity, national sentiments, and the genre of *p'ansori* itself (see Kim-Reynaud 1994; Cho 1998; Koh 1995; Willoughby 2003). In this part of my essay I shall focus on the young Song-hwa's profound devotion to both her father and the art of *p'ansori*, and her coming-of-age experiences, particularly with a sentiment indigenously known as *han* (resentment, suffering, lament).

Im Kwŏn-taek, the film's director, evokes a sense of *han* in the movie, an emotion some have claimed is not only unique, but essential to Korean culture and character. Cho Hae Joang has noted that one of the reasons for the film's popularity is, in fact, the pervasive theme of "searching for our culture," including an understanding of history, folklife, and sentiments such as *han*. As the translator of Cho's article further notes, "*Uri munhwa ch'atki* or 'Searching for our culture' was a movement that arose in the 1970s on college campuses as students began to reconstruct and reinterpret traditional Korean cultural forms. The movement was a response to cultural colonialism and an effort to strengthen Korean identity. It focused not on the 'highbrow' culture of court music and dance but on the 'lowbrow' culture of agricultural peasants" (Cho

2002: 138n). In the case of *Sŏp'yŏnje,* Im Kwŏn-taek attempts to portray Song-hwa as an ideal Korean female from the "searching for our culture" movement —a member of the lower class who not only experiences the depths of *han* but also sublimates it in order to transcend mediocrity and become a master of *p'ansori.*

As will be demonstrated, Song-hwa's experiences and sacrifices are excessive, even for *p'ansori* singers who dedicate their childhoods and lives to the promulgation of the art. Nonetheless, the character is meant to be realistic, or at least plausible—the archetypical *p'ansori* performer willing to sacrifice everything for the fulfillment of her destiny. Thus an analysis of her adolescent experiences and choices, contrasted with those of Kim So-hŭi and Yi Chu-ŭn, will enable better comprehension of *p'ansori'*s role in the coming-of-age process.

Early in the film, we see ten-year-old Song-hwa and her younger brother, Tong-ho, practicing *Chindo Arirang,* a popular southern-style folk song, under Yu-bong's tutelage. Yu-bong abruptly expels Tong-ho from the lesson when the boy is unable to replicate the song's sounds accurately. We see Yu-bong completing household chores in a relatively decent rural house as the children practice *p'ansori* in another room. The scene closes with Tong-ho, who has now been relegated to the role of a drummer, accompanying Song-hwa as she practices difficult *p'ansori* passages while Yu-bong instructs her in correct singing posture. Clearly *p'ansori* is a daily exercise as well as a way of life for the family, with the children learning everything by rote from their father.

The adolescents Song-hwa and Tong-ho are not typical children playing games or enjoying the camaraderie of their peers but function in the myopic world of an adult *p'ansori* performer. While Yu-bong chats with a friend in a village restaurant, the children sit alone in a corner. When their father performs in a marketplace, they remain immobile by his side. When he gathers in a bar with other *kwangdae,* they wait outside, peering through the windows. They are young only in the sense that they have not yet mastered the music that permeates their existence. Song-hwa's coming-of-age is atypical of Korean youths in the 1940s and 1950s. She lives and breathes the insular world of *p'ansori,* the only lens through which she perceives and experiences the world. Like Yi Chu-ŭn, the children are empowered with maturity through the mastery of music. However, even Yi, who began to study *p'ansori* at about the same age as Song-hwa did and dedicated her adolescent years to diligent study, had friends among her peers and led a relatively normal childhood. Song-hwa had neither leisure activities nor friends.

In another scene a teenaged Song-hwa performs *p'ansori* at a party for aris-

tocrats. While she sings, a male patron dances and gestures suggestively toward her. He then asks Song-hwa to become his mistress: "I can sell my land
for you. I can sell the trees for you." Flaunting his wealth and status, he simultaneously implies that Song-hwa herself may be easily discarded, like firewood.
Another man then commands Song-hwa to serve him alcohol, but Yu-bong
protests that she is too young. The nobles see Song-hwa not just as a talented
p'ansori singer, but also as a female paid to entertain their every desire (including sexual). Song-hwa serves the drink but is then made to drink with the
men. Yu-bong and the noblemen argue until the performers are ousted with a
warning to remember their place; they are simply peasants and may never be
invited back (thus limiting their already meager income).

This scene reminds us of the period in *p'ansori*'s history when the nobility
considered the performers outcasts. The male aristocrats view Song-hwa and
her youth as an expendable commodity; her singing and body exist only for
their pleasure. For her father, on the other hand, *p'ansori* is an elevated tradition, not a socially dictated act of etiquette. As Song-hwa matures, she must
learn to negotiate her identity as a low-class female *p'ansori* performer who
perpetuates her father's idealized notions of her art.

The movie portrays Song-hwa's hardships: losing her birth parents at an
early age, living the life of an itinerant musician, and being abandoned by her
beloved brother, in addition to her struggles in learning *p'ansori*. To deepen
her sorrows and force her to focus on vocal production, her father poisons
her with a Chinese herbal tea until she becomes blind.[11] In a climactic scene
near the end of his life, Yu-bong finally admits to causing Song-hwa's blindness and explains what he sees as the integral relation between *han* (profound
grief) and *p'ansori* timbres: "The *p'ansori* of Sŏp'yŏnje must upset and break
one's heart. Your *p'ansori* is too smooth to carry such grief. Grief is accumulated through one's life. Life is to accumulate grief and grief cannot be separated from life. You lost your parents and you lost your sight. You had more
than enough pain, but your *p'ansori* doesn't express such grief."[12]

The next scenes show Song-hwa practicing outdoors in the dead of winter,
surrounded by snow-covered trees and formidable mountain peaks. Her home
is an abandoned hovel secluded by mountains. In this setting Song-hwa's songs
reverberate among the hills and she finally masters her own voice and achieves
transcendence. Life remains difficult as the aging father and daughter sub-
sist on meager meals of gruel. When Yu-bong is beaten by a neighbor whose
chicken he is caught stealing, Song-hwa intervenes, crying in desperation. As
the daughter tends her father's wounds, he says:

What a terrific voice. Did you hear? That is the voice you need to express rage in *p'ansori*. At last, I feel the grief from your *p'ansori*. . . . I made you blind. You knew that didn't you? You forgave me. Otherwise, I would feel the grudge against me from your *p'ansori*. But I didn't. From now on, overcome your grief and aim at the perfection in your *p'ansori*. Tongp'yŏnje [eastern school of learning] is heavy and vigorous. Sŏp'yŏnje is sorrowful and tender. If you overcome your grief there is no Tongp'yŏnje or Sŏp'yŏnje, but only a mastery of sound.

This profound statement highlights one way Korean artists discuss and portray important correlations between sound and suffering. Yu-bong insists that experiences of grief are intimately linked to *p'ansori* singing, but in the end he explains that it is actually the *process* of overcoming or sublimating the pain that will lead to the perfection of sound.

Yi Chu-ŭn had several important things to say about the film. First, she does not believe that most mid-twentieth-century *p'ansori* singers lived the type of itinerant existence portrayed in the film. Certainly musicians traveled for competitions or performances, but by the time depicted in the film few were ostracized or subsisted as wandering musicians. Yi finds Song-hwa's training process realistic: daily practice and rote learning from a master singer are analogous to Yi's own experiences. Yi also says that musicians continue to experience emotions similar to Song-hwa's when the latter falls down screaming in frustration at the difficulty of mastering *p'ansori* sounds among the mountains. "In the process of training, I think every musician will be the same. When one's goal is 100%, but you can only reach 50%, there is a sense of despair."[13] Yi finds suffering overemphasized in the film. The filmmakers "exaggerate to an extreme degree that artists have to be different from ordinary people, and that at the time the social status [of the musicians] was really low. Today, musicians are looked up to—things have changed."

Despite Yi's critique of the film's unrealistic aspects, its portrayal of characters can teach us something about adolescence and the coming-of-age process as a *p'ansori* performer. Like her real-life counterparts, Song-hwa is completely dedicated to *p'ansori*. Her art is the prism through which she forges her entire identity as a female, and performer, in Korean society.

◆ Final Observations

Adolescents listen to, consume, and use music for a variety of reasons. Music may be entertainment, or may in fact help the young cope with the turbulences and challenges of maturing into adulthood. Korean youth have a complex relationship with their social-cultural circumstances. They must strike a balance between accepting or rejecting highly respected but insular traditions and currents in contemporary globalization. In traditional Korean society, where a silent form of filial piety associated with social disempowerment was esteemed above nearly all else, adolescents of the past had little power to effect changes. Today they are beginning to create their own, new youth culture, where, as in the past, music plays a significant role in the formation of ideals and social mores.

Like today's adolescents attempting to find their own voice in Korean society through music, Kim So-hŭi, Yi Chu-ŭn, and Song-hwa each faced the challenge of maintaining tradition while at the same time negotiating social boundaries that have existed for centuries. As demonstrated in their life choices, tradition does not have to be simply discarded but can be woven into the fabric of contemporary society.

In youth and adulthood, Kim So-hŭi exhibited remarkable strength of will and even defiance against societal norms to achieve success in a male-dominated society and musical field. Her adolescent respect for her master teachers, but also her fierce unremitting pursuit of her destiny, are inspirations for today's young students of *p'ansori*. According to Kim's daughter, Park Yun-cho, herself a highly accomplished musician, *p'ansori* singers must sacrifice many of the normal pleasures of life—dedicating their time and talents to the pursuit of excellence. She noted that while her mother was in her midseventies, she spent at least four to five hours per day practicing for what would be her final concert. It is this willingness to devote her life to *p'ansori* (even at an age at which others might have been enjoying the leisure of retirement) that enabled Kim So-hŭi to be designated one of the truly great masters of the art. Park adds that what *p'ansori* musicians gain, not in terms of renown, but rather in terms of understanding the depths of human experience and emotion, is well worth any sacrifice.[14]

Yi Chu-ŭn, trained in the pedagogical lineage of Kim So-hŭi, reflects the elder performer's tenacity in fulfilling her destiny as a *p'ansori* performer. Although Yi did not make the same type of sacrifices as Kim, she, too, simultaneously embraced and flouted tradition from an early age for the sake of *p'ansori*. She claims that fate led her to become a singer although she may have had other life and career choices:

Since becoming a *p'ansori* singer I have had difficulties, but even though it is hard at times, I enjoy being a singer. That is why I feel being a *p'ansori* performer is my destiny. I try to imagine myself quitting this profession and getting married. If I did that I presume I would have to support my husband [emotionally], but I want to dedicate myself to my work. If I could do it both ways, it would be great, but I cannot give up my profession because I have already invested too much. When I envision giving up this career, I feel as if I might be sick. Again, it is for this reason I believe *p'ansori* is my destiny.

On the one hand, Yi lives for and in a traditional world where conformance to rigid Confucian mores remains paramount. However, her strength of character enables her to defy an unwritten rule of Korean life which dictates that women should be married and bear children by a certain age in order to be deemed acceptable in Korean society—ancient or contemporary.

According to anthropologist Laurel Kendall (1996: 4),

A scan of travelers' accounts and of ethnography suggests that marriage has been an abiding Korean preoccupation. Cornelius Osgood offers the wry comment that "Marriage under the old Korean system was almost as certain as death" (Osgood 1951: 103). . . . Kim Eun-Shil, conducting fieldwork in Korea as a native anthropologist and unmarried woman notes, "When I asked women why they got married, they laughed at my absurd question and said that they wanted to live a normal life."

Traditional Korean women were uneducated and obliged to obey various male authority figures in their lives. They had few opportunities to participate in social affairs or exert power outside the home, and had few legal rights with regards to marriage, divorce, or inheritance. In fact, a Korean female was not considered a woman by society until she was married *and* had had a child, preferably a son. "She could obtain social recognition, but only in her capacity as wife of a prominent man or mother of a successful son. When she was given an award, it was not for her own merit, but for her contribution to her son's successful career or to her husband's promotion in his official rank" (Kim Yung-Chung 1976: 50–51). It is not surprising that most Korean women (or more typically, their families) actively sought wealthy matches. Today, Korean women have more agency and power both legally and culturally. However, Korean female adolescents continue to desire and plan for marriage in their late twenties at the latest. Careers are regarded as temporary diversions until the "real" goal of marriage can be fulfilled. It is fascinating then, that although Yi Chu-ŭn conforms readily to the traditional values prescribed in *p'ansori* as compared to her contemporaries, she remains single for the sake of *p'ansori*.

Song-hwa, although perhaps not always by her own choosing, sacrificed sight and a normal childhood for her art. Although she was ultimately unsuccessful, financially speaking, her dedication led to artistic self-mastery, a highly respected trait in Korean society. Some may view Song-hwa as weak or passive, but I believe that she asserted her own sense of power, determination and confidence. In a scene near the end of the film, we observe that the innkeeper of an inn where she had been living offered to provide her with a stable home, as well as dedicating himself to her, and by extension, to her art. In the end, however, she chooses to continue her life alone as an itinerant performer. We can thus conclude that despite her relative poverty in material terms, she is rich in remaining a keeper of a profound tradition.

The *p'ansori* performers I have described fall into a highly specialized category: daily consumption and creation of music is vital to these women, as is constant, total immersion in the world of *p'ansori*, including the traditional lifestyles expected of performers of the genre. Music defines their lives in every way. Kim So-hŭi, Yi Chu-ŭn, and Song-hwa each sought and found contentment with her place in the world of Korean life, values, culture, and history via her destined profession.

Notes

I am indebted to the assistance, editor efforts, and patience offered to me by Susan Boynton and Roe-Min Kok, as well as the other readers of this article for their most helpful suggestions. I also express my gratitude to the musicians, both those who are living and those who have passed on, for their dedication to an art that has greatly enriched my life. Although I only met her once, I dedicate this work to Yi Chu-ŭn's grandmother—for without the inspiration and continual encouragement she provided my teacher, I may have never found my own voice. *P'alja kŭrae . . .*

1. No last name is provided for Song-hwa in the film, so I will refer to her by her given name. In the case of the other performers, I will adhere to the Korean tradition of writing surnames first, and will generally refer to Kim So-hŭi as Kim or Master Kim, and Yi Chu-ŭn as Yi, whereas with other Korean performers and scholars I discuss, I will always refer to them by their last and first names. In all cases I will use the McCune-Reischauer method of Romanization.

2. Although it is possible that women had studied *p'ansori* informally before the late 1800s, there is no written record of their existence. Shin Chae-hyo (1812–84),

a petty government official, was not a professional singer himself but contributed greatly to the development and promulgation of *p'ansori* and trained the first female singers, including, most notably, Chin Chae-sŏn (b. ca. 1847). Following in Chin's footsteps were Kang So-ch'un and Hŏ Kŭm-p'a (dates unknown). The first famous female master singer and inspiration to Kim So-hŭi, Yi Hwajungsŏn, lived from 1899 to 1943.

3. Portions of this paper, including the majority of the information regarding the history and training processes of *p'ansori* performers, are taken from Willoughby 2002.

4. Marshall Pihl (1994: 8) describes the historical development of *p'ansori* in this manner: "From shaman narrative songs [*p'ansori* performers] gained rhythmic patterns of drumming and singing, techniques of vocalization, interweaving of sung and spoken passages, and interpolation of songs from other traditions. From solo actors of farce and storytellers they inherited skills of characterization, improvisation, narrative development, and audience management. And the folk culture around them was an abundant source of such materials as myths, legends, stories, ballads, laments, and work songs."

5. The official dates for the Japanese occupation of Korea are 1910–19. Japanese influences on the Korean government, however, began in the late nineteenth century, and political power and cultural control were retained until the end of World War II in 1945.

6. For example, as of 1999 the total number of members of the National Center for Korean Traditional Performing Art's Folk Music Troupe was forty-four, including six *p'ansori* singers, five of whom are women. The only male *p'ansori* singer, Chŏng Hoe-sŏk, is a fourth-generation *kwangdae*.

7. In Korean, for instance, the words *torŭl dakkda* mean to improve or master one's sense of morality or ethics. In idiomatic use it denotes a person who has mastered his or her talent by ascending the mountains.

8. In 1999 and 2000 I spent many hours with Yi Chu-ŭn, taking *p'ansori* voice lessons with her and enjoying various adventures in Seoul. Although we spoke on many occasions about her life and work, she was reluctant to grant a formal interview—she respectfully deferred to her master teacher, Shin Yŏng-hŭi. I am indebted to Kim Jin-woo, a friend and colleague who interviewed Yi Chu-ŭn in October 2002, when I myself could not return to Korea to do so. Jin-woo interviewed Yi for this essay with questions I prepared.

9. See Choi 1998; Kim-Renaud 1994; and Koh 1995 for further statistics.

10. Although Yu-bong, Song-hwa, and Tong-ho are not blood relatives, I will refer to them by their "adoptive" names or titles: father, sister, and brother. These are the Korean titles by which they address one another, and it was not uncommon for a *p'ansori* singer to leave his or her birth parents and become an apprentice to a master teacher, thus creating new familial bonds.

11. The idea of blindness has various implications. First, an interconnected-

ness between blindness and performance is conducive to a "popular belief that if the eyes of a person are shut, the natural energy (*ki*) of that person will go to the mouth and ears, rendering him or her a better singer" (Kim-Reynaud 1994: 15). Second, the *p'ansori* tale that Song-hwa is attempting to learn in the scenes after she becomes blind describe Shim Chŏng—a dutiful and filial daughter who willingly sacrifices her very life in order that her blind father can regain his sight and resolve much of the *han* that has accumulated throughout their lives.

12. The text is taken from the English subtitles. Although they do not replicate precisely the Korean dialogue, I have chosen to use them in order that English-speaking viewers can easily find the portion of the movie from which I am quoting. It is important to note, that in this particular scene, the word *han* is used exclusively, although translated into English as "grief" or "pain."

13. Yi Chu-ŭn, personal interview with Kim Jin-woo, Seoul, October 2002.

14. Park Yun-cho, personal interview, Seoul, March 3, 2005.

Part III

Musical Socialization

How do the young relate to, or become part of, the social fabric? Part 3 maintains focus on issues of the self already highlighted in part 2 but shifts the context from the individual to the collective, looking at group practices and behaviors. In addition to "making sense" of their own lives, individuals also "make sense" of or are inducted into their places in society. Studies of the latter process have occupied a dominant position in ethnomusicological scholarship on children's music under the term "music enculturation" (Minks 2002: 385). One should also keep in mind that musical socialization "is a paradigm of difference, of socialization into particular music-cultural norms, and so there is an emphasis on the imitative . . . capacity of [children]" (385).

Imitative in act and practice, music may lead to social inclusion and acceptance or, equally possible, exclusion and nonacceptance. The first two essays in part 3 (by Calico and by Gottschewski and Gottschewski) reveal that adults have formulated music-educational policies for the young that were heavily predicated upon the act of imitation, in the hopes that the act would teach the young worldviews, shape their system of values, and reinforce their understanding of their social-political status and roles, whether real, imagined, or projected (see Waterman 1956: 41).

The self-contained culture formed by youths in Cohen's study provides rich evidence for a process of musical self-socialization where young people autodidactically appropriate cultural capital and thereby gain both social appreciation and definitions of boundaries that separate them from others (Fiske 1992: 34). We are reminded that the process involves youthful initiative: "Young people choose socializing environments and cultural codes that ascribe social meaning to aesthetic objects . . . they socialize themselves by their choice of membership in cultures, by their efforts to become familiar with the chosen cultural codes, and by shaping these cultures and contributing to their cultural production" (Mueller 2002: 596).

—*Roe-Min Kok*

"We Are Changing the World!"

New German Folk Songs for the
Free German Youth (1950)

JOY H. CALICO

In 1949 the Soviet-Occupied Zone in eastern Germany officially became the German Democratic Republic, and the ruling Socialist Unity Party (SED) established antifascism as a primary theme of the GDR foundation narrative (Hell 1992). The SED also initiated a cultural reclamation project, laying claim to cultural products that predated the Nazis and their misappropriation of Germany's heritage in order to construct a suitable past for the new state. The rehabilitation of *Volkslieder* (folk song) played a substantial role in that agenda, since GDR national identity required a distinction between the new *Volk* of the workers' state and the old *Volk* of the Third Reich, but because the adult citizens of postwar Germanys were of course the very same *Volk* who had populated the Reich, the future lay with the youth. The inculcation of appropriate antifascist socialist values was vital for raising good citizens, and many intellectuals dedicated themselves to that cause. Hanns Eisler and Johannes R. Becher wrote the collection *Neue deutsche Volkslieder* (*New German Folk Songs*) for the *Freie deutsche Jugend* (FDJ, Free German Youth) in 1950. It combined antifascist socialist ideals with rehabilitated folk song in order to reinvent the *Volk* by shaping the first generation of German youth in a postwar society, the demographic Becher himself described as "the best part of our population" (1952: 115). Original songs designed for the new generation of German citizens and yet self-consciously referential to the storied German folk song tradition, they are uniquely positioned to create an appropriate past and link the antifascist socialist present to it. This essay examines the genesis of Eisler and Becher's *New German Folk Songs* as invented tradition, traces their reception history, and probes the significance of song for East German youth in the nascent GDR. The historical perspective is augmented by correspondence with people who grew up in East Germany and were willing to reflect upon their memories of *New German Folk Songs* and other songs for youth. Their responses are not intended to represent a comprehensive study of songs for youth in the GDR; rather, their personal accounts enrich our understanding of the role such songs played in the lives of East Germany's youngest citizens.[1]

◆ The Necessity of Invented Tradition in Postwar Germany(s)

As the SED would discover on multiple fronts, the difficulties inherent in the founding of any nation-state were exacerbated by the Nazi legacy. Further complicated by chilly international relations that would soon give rise to the Cold War, the need to legitimize the existence of the GDR was urgent. Conditions were ripe for the phenomenon Eric Hobsbawm calls "the invention of tradition." Invented traditions arise when a rapid transformation of society weakens or destroys the social patterns for which old traditions have been designed, as was the case in East Germany in 1950. Wherever possible, invented traditions attempt to establish continuity with a suitable historic past; they represent a process of formalization and ritualization, characterized by references to the past; and they are responses to novel situations that take the form of references to older situations (Hobsbawm and Ranger 1992). Each feature represents a means of negotiating a particular relationship with a desired version of the past in order to serve a present-day agenda—in this case, to legitimize the GDR as a bona fide socialist nation on German soil. This is apparent even in the title *New German Folk Songs,* an intriguingly paradoxical moniker that boldly asserted the collection's identity as invented tradition. The first two words modify the last in provocative ways, as one may question whether folk songs can be newly composed, whether something composed and notated by professional artists qualifies as folk song, whether new folk songs can be added to that venerable and presumably finite body of German cultural heritage. These questions reveal common assumptions about the origins and nature of folk song that are essential to the success of Hobsbawm's model, facilitating the creation and promotion of new cultural products as traditional. The adjective *new* establishes a particular relationship to the heritage of "German folk song," distancing this collection from its evocations of the past even while trading on that symbolism. Taken in its entirety, the title suggests new culture built upon an existing foundation of tradition, and yet somehow different from it. In this case, the new, or reinvented, tradition promoted values like antifascism and peace in response to the most recent historical layer of that foundation.

German is a powerful signifier of a specific geography, culture, history, and nation. The modifier *new* neutralizes some aspects of those associations while capitalizing on others in a selective process typical of invented traditions. Furthermore, because Eisler and Becher did not refer to these songs as East German, but rather as simply German, the word becomes tantalizingly inclusive. It alludes to aspects of German-ness shared by East and West Germany, preceding and permeating the imposed political division. Becher specified as much in his prefatory remarks to the first edition of the collection: "We want to learn to sing again, and we shall sing a song of freedom and peace. We hope that this new song of the people will transcend the boundary in the middle of our Fatherland and rise above it to become one song for all Germans" (Eisler 1975: foreword). The FDJ, the youth organization for which the collection was written, is most often associated with the GDR, but in fact the first postwar chapter was founded in Hamburg, West Germany, in 1945; the Soviet Military Administration in the Soviet-Occupied Zone followed suit on March 7, 1946. The FDJ had taken shape in the 1930s, when Germans representing various parties dedicated to antifascism gathered in exile and agreed to merge resources. Generally speaking, the earliest chapters of the FDJ founded in Paris (1936), Prague (1938), and Great Britain (1939) represented the combination of members and agendas from the Communist Youth Association (KJVD) and the Social Democrats Workers Youth (SAJ) under one rubric.[2] A pipeline developed whereby children became Young Pioneers (more or less the equivalent of Cub Scouts and Brownies, without gender distinction) at age six, Thälmann Pioneers (roughly equivalent to Boy and Girl Scouts) at age ten, and were then guided into the FDJ at age fourteen. West German chapters of the FDJ survived legally until June 1951, at which point the FRG banned the organization,[3] but in 1950 Eisler and Becher still had reason to expect their songs to reach young citizens committed to antifascism and peace in both Germanys. Certainly youth represented the best hope for the [re]invention of antifascist, socialist German *Volk*.

Use of *German* rather than *East German* also reflects a larger trend in GDR cultural politics of the 1950s in which a single, unified German cultural nation was thought to transcend the division imposed by arbitrarily drawn political boundaries. The culturally unified German nation was ostensibly apolitical and considerably less threatening than its previous physical incarnation, but no less coherent or powerful for its lack of explicitly political or military definition.[4] Becher had waited out the war in Moscow and returned to the Soviet-Occupied Zone in 1945 as the handpicked leader of the *Kulturbund zur Demokratischen Erneuerung Deutschlands* (Cultural League for the Democratic

Renewal of Germany). His vision for that organization from its inception had been antifascist, nonpartisan, and pan-German (Dwars 1998, Mayer 1991). As director of the Kommunistische Partei Deutschlands (KPD) Commission on Culture in Moscow, Becher had drafted "suggestions for action in the cultural sphere to assist the antifascist/democratic reeducation of the German people," and these served as a blueprint for his work in the GDR (Stephan 1974: 76). The Cultural League also had a presence in West Germany until 1952. When the FRG rejected the so-called Stalin Note that year, the GDR was then able to portray itself as the Germany genuinely committed to reunification.[5] Given that the chances of unification on terms satisfactory to the SED—meaning a single Germany under a socialist government—were virtually nonexistent, the GDR dedicated itself to preserving a common heritage and promoting artistic collaboration between the two Germanys.[6] In 1954, SED Chairman Otto Grotewohl described German culture as "the unbreakable bond between East and West Germany. This bond must be connected, preserved and secured" (quoted in "Musik muß hinaus ins Volk" 1954: 1). Thus the *German* of the title acknowledged shared contemporary German-ness common to East and West—antifascism in the form of the young *Volk*, represented by the FDJ, and the theory of a single German cultural nation—as well as the inevitable historic one.

The word that most conspicuously marks the collection as an invented tradition is *Volkslieder* (folk songs). The term itself was coined by Johann Gottfried Herder in the 1770s; his two landmark publications (*Stimmen der Völker in Liedern* of 1778 and *Volkslieder* of 1779) and the heritage of German folk song collection and publication he inspired comprise an invented tradition on a grand scale. With one new word, Herder "consciously engaged in an act of naming a previously unnamed quality of German-ness," and since then the notion of folk songs has both represented and contributed to the formation of German national identity (Bohlman 2002: 108). In the popular imagination, the term evokes powerful links with the past, authenticity, oral transmission, a common language, romanticized notions of pure and simple *Volk*, and rural and/or amateur cultures, connotations that were contrived to some degree from the outset. The success of the invented tradition of German folk song is dependent upon the associations of authenticity that have accrued to it, although many of the songs published by Herder and later collectors were composed, foreign in origin, or otherwise did not fit the popular criteria.[7] Their "true" origin was irrelevant; Herder's claim that German folk songs afforded one a glimpse of the German soul was persuasive, and the nomenclature alone seemed to imbue the songs that bore it with the well-nigh mythical symbolism of German national identity and unity. Perhaps no one exploited the power of this invented tradition for defining national identity more effectively than the Nazis. Considerable time and energy were devoted to both the theoretical study and the practical uses of German folk song under the Third Reich. The theorists refined definitions and classification systems, while those concerned with its applied use lobbied for incorporation into "education and in the everyday music making of state, party, public, and private institutions" (Potter 1998: 195). That appropriate songs were crucial for the education and motivation of the young citizen, both in school and in other organizations, was a basic tenet of the Nazi's opponents on the Left as well; witness the proliferation of *Kampflieder* and *Massenlieder* (protest songs and mass songs) during that period, many of which were composed by Eisler.

This is the invented tradition in which Eisler's and Becher's *New German Folk Songs* participated, reinventing that venerable heritage once again for purposes of establishing a new German national identity and, by extension, a new German *Volk* to inhabit it. They drew selectively upon several associations from both older and then-recent German history. They exploited the time-honored symbolism of authenticity, tradition, nation, and German identity that had accrued to folk song since Herder, and then they applied the name and all its attendant symbolism to newly composed songs by two professional artists. It is clear from Eisler's private notes that he recognized the contrived nature of this heritage, and also its importance: "To the Romantics, the *Volk* appeared in contrast to the educated layers as the undermost stratum of the Nation, the vulgar people who persisted in simple life forms and in naïve emotion not yet destroyed. The old German folk song, by which the folk means the nation, in which all classes of the nation participate because art song is lacking" (1982: 86).[8] Additional notes indicate that Eisler was quite preoccupied with the nature of folk song in 1950. The sketch "A Few Things about Stupidity in Music" dates from the second half of that year and briefly recounts a history of German folk song dating from the Thirty Years' War to Brahms, outlining different phases in its development. Eisler defended Brahms's arrangements because the art of folk song "is broad and diverse," so it is possible for a nineteenth-century master to rework a sixteenth-century song. He did not explicitly place himself in this lineage, but he appears to have been establishing antecedents for his own foray into folk song, using the example of Brahms to legitimize his presence as a trained composer within that tradition. He concluded this section as follows: "Folk songs can be good or bad. But they are never stupid. One finds stupidity only in so-called art songs, in so-called concert songs" (87–88). The implication that there is a connection between stupidity and the artifice of art song, as opposed to the intelligence and authenticity of folk song—even folk song arranged or composed by art music composers—makes it clear that he is consciously availing himself of the cluster of connotations cited above.

Eisler and Becher were ultimately driven by the conviction that leftist intellectuals were obligated to contribute whatever they could to the workers' movement. Their collection undermined the myth that authenticity must come from below, while marking Eisler and Becher as two mandarins who used their privileged status and education to promote the cause of the *Volk* and the workers' state. Each had established his credibility during the Weimar Republic[9] and now attempted to trade on it in the GDR (although the intervening war years would affect their reception, as will be shown below). The incorporation of such songs into education and social organizations was a hallmark of mass movements in the twentieth century and also tied them to the halcyon days of the Weimar Republic and the earlier antifascist efforts of the 1930s. Thus their reinvention of the German folk song tradition, which had itself been an invented tradition, is a classic example of the phenomenon. *New German Folk Songs* established continuity with a desirable version of the past (a unified German nation without fascism), and it represented a process of formalization and ritualization (incorporation into education and/or formal organizations). Finally, Becher and Eisler's response to a novel situation took a form that was familiar and had historic precedent (using folk song to develop and reinforce German national identity in times of disunity). The task of these *New German Folk Songs* was more daunting than the work previously expected of German folk songs, however. Eisler and Becher needed to reinvent more than German national identity; they needed to reinvent the *Volk* who had inhabited the most recent incarnation of a German nation as antifascist socialist *Volk*. Because the latter consisted by and large of survivors from the former, youth were their best prospect as agents for change.

◆ *New German Folk Songs* for the Enculturation of Youth

The FDJ commissioned the prominent pair to write a song in February 1950, and they responded with "Song of the Blue Flag" ("Lied von der blauen Fahne"). It was to become the first work in *New German Folk Songs*. The collaborative process went so well that the two men continued to work together, producing fifteen songs in a short period.[10] Becher documented this period in his diary, and entries reveal what appears to be genuine enthusiasm for the work and affection for his collaborator. The entry for February 5 reads:

The flag of the Free German Youth.
Image reproduced with permission
from http://flagspot.net.

"Eisler found the melody [for Song of the Blue Flag] straight away, and later completed it with an interlude that is magically cheerful and joyful. Together we will edit a songbook. His setting of 'Song of the German Homeland' [Lied von der deutschen Heimat,' later known as 'Homeland Song'] is also wonderful, and even a bit more beautiful is the music for 'The Old Ways' ['Es sind die alten Weisen']." On February 7, Becher described the frenetic pace of their work: "Eisler set the first ["In the Spring"— "Im Frühling"] immediately, we are now both in a total creative frenzy. Eisler is like a fountain, like a steady rain of sounds" (Becher 1952: 117, 122). Eisler gave a similar account in an interview on February 26, 1950:

> When we had finished ["Song of the Blue Flag"], we found we had a
> taste for this kind of work and wrote 15 songs in a very short period of
> time, often two in one day. Becher and I had a contest, so to speak. We
> worked cheerfully, fresh and fast, and it was truly fun because it appeared
> to us to be useful and urgently necessary work. Therefore it happened that
> we finished a song [text] at my house, Becher went home, where I had al-
> ready called to tell him that I had in the meantime composed the setting,
> whereupon he returned to my house and we continued our work. (Grabs
> 1976: 190)

Each spoke about his motivation for writing the collection as well. Becher described his daily commute into the city, during which he saw hundreds of youth clearing rubble under the blue flag of the FDJ, and concluded that "as the best part of our population, the youth are legitimately entitled to such a song" (1951: 115). The poet was ever mindful of what would be appropriate for his target audience and their current situation: "For the amateurs this kind of poetry is singable and easy to repeat, not salon-like or a horror. Easily understandable, because the singable, easily repeated poetry, the simple, plain folk tunes, are—in the final effect—directed toward all foreign and enemy elements that should be forced upon the people" (121). Eisler concurred that they were "marked by an easy comprehensibility. One can learn them without difficulty, and that is why they are called folk songs" (Grabs 1976: 191). He was careful to explain that these were purely folk songs and did not mix features of that tradition with those of other genres. "If I did that, it would be interesting, but it would be a new genre and not folk song." Here his remarks and those of Becher contradict one another, as Becher had written that "from the old folk song and from protest songs we have formed a new folk song, to touch the hearts of all people of good will" (Becher 1951: 254). They were in agreement, however, that the songs were not art songs for concert use, and Eisler specified that the accompaniment was meant to support the singer rather than to illustrate the psychological aspects of the text as was typical of the lied. Finally, "In our republic, art and culture are taken very seriously. One has a high level of responsibility for what one writes. This responsibility doesn't make artistic work easy, but it does make a successful performance of that task even more valuable" (Grabs 1976: 191).

Some scholars claim that Eisler developed an entirely new song genre through a fusion of elements from a variety of song types: mass, protest, art, and old German folk song (Betz 1976: 188). It is true that "In the Spring," for example, is noticeably indebted to Franz Schubert's "Morning Greeting" ("Morgengruß") from the cycle *Die schöne Müllerin* (Csipák 1975a) but certainly no accident that the model is a lied in a self-consciously folk song style. Nevertheless, Eisler explicitly stated that he was attempting to remain true to the folk song genre and to reintroduce a new simplicity to the music, and I would argue that this was done to draw upon the accumulated meanings of the invented folk song tradition. Any other generic title would have diminished the power of those associations. The simple folk elements he appropriated for those purposes are obvious: strophic forms, syllabic settings, regular meter and periodic phrasing, memorable melodies set within a small range, simple accompaniments, and diatonic harmonic language. Becher's poems are the literary equivalent: strophic, rhymed, and regularly metered, with hopeful, inspirational messages expressed in plain language.

Examples from three songs illustrate these points. "The Old Ways" exemplifies the lyrical style. Its text refers to old traditions and songs that are now manifested in new behaviors and songs. This negotiation between past and present, and the evocation of familiar imagery such as nature and group singing, make the work of the collection clear: to link itself to aspects of the past and the folk song tradition that are positive, simple, natural, and peaceful. The past is still essential, but it must come forth in ways appropriate for the present.

It is the old ways that arise anew in us
And blow in on the quiet wind from afar.
When the treetops bow in the evening wind

Then those who have fallen pass through our silence.
It is the old songs that sing out of me as new
And as in the old days we sing again in the evening.
There is a murmur in us that becomes a great choir,
And amazed, we look up to the stars![11] (Eisler 1975: 6)

Eisler set the text strophically in the form AABA, a form favored throughout the collection, and it has no introduction or postlude. It lends itself easily to amateur performance—there are just two melodic phrases for the entire song. Likewise, the key of D is easily accessible for amateur pianists, and the octave D–D range of the melody is manageable for most singers. The piano accompaniment consists of a constant quarter-note pulse in the left hand and eighth notes in the right; the right thumb reiterates the tonic or the root of the chord in the inner voice while the other fingers double the melody line. The admonition to sing the beautiful melody "very lightly, without sentimentality" and to keep the tempo "moderate with motion" should correct any tendency to perform the song in an affected manner.

Becher's text for "When Workers and Farmers" is optimistic about the future in the German socialist state. Note the use of nature imagery again, and the encouragement for people to improve their lot by taking control of their own lives and cooperating with others for the greater good of all. It was intended to empower citizens in a time of great uncertainty and despair—after all, even five years after the end of the war there was still much rebuilding to be done in Berlin.

It won't be much longer until there is peace,
And the sun will return as after rain showers.
Like a fearful stage set the rubble stands around us.
Soon the uncertainty shall frighten us no more.
There will be an end to the need, when you, the people, determine the
    time
And take your fate into your own hands.
When workers and farmers are in agreement,
It won't be much longer until there is peace.[12]

Once again, Eisler used a variation of the AABA form, and it is framed by a delightfully catchy syncopated introduction and postlude. The piano part frequently doubles the vocal line and consists almost entirely of an eighth-note pulse separated by rests against the singers' quarter notes. This accompani-

ment figure encourages crisp, march-like movement and does not allow singers to get bogged down in sustained note values. There are sustained quarter
notes in only one measure of the piano part, at the end of phrase B in measure
17. It adds weight to the cadence and reinforces the only instance of chromatic
inflection accompanying the vocal line: III within a sequence of root-position
chords (IV–III–vi–ii, leading to V in measure 18 and I in measure 19). The song
is in "march tempo" with a metronome marking of *ca* 128.

"The World Is Changing" has a similarly inspirational text, in which one
person recognizes that the darkness cannot last forever if all come together
and work to change the world. In almost Biblical language it acknowledges the
"shadow" that lay upon the earth, a darkness that could symbolize the then-
contemporary imperial capitalist threat to the west, the past weight of Nazi
atrocities, or both.

> As a shadow lay once again upon the earth
> And it appeared inevitable that it would become ever darker
> One man spoke: "The world is changing.
>
> "Take heart, the darkness must recede and light shine upon you and me
>   again,
> If we reach out our hands to one another,
> because we are changing the world."
>
> [REFRAIN] Was it not an ideal, or dreams, a beautiful implausible belief?
> The strength of a giant is needed to clear away the rubble of time.
>
> "Who is this giant?" came the question, and the man said:
> "All of us, you and I, when we dream and dare to speak this sentence:
> The world is changing."
>
> [REFRAIN]
>
> Sing a song of changes that will make us a free brotherhood!
> See, it is already light again on the earth, and the world is changing![13]

As suggested by the text, a soloist sings the verses ("one man spoke," "the
man said") and the full choir enters for the refrains. Eisler used simple but
effective musical means to create the essential contrast between the soloist
singing a slow verse in minor mode, and the full chorus singing a rousing call
to action in a major key.

Yet simple does not mean simplistic. Even within the narrow folk song parameters Eisler set for himself, his distinctive imprint is apparent in two features typical of his entire oeuvre: the inclusion of performance instructions that preclude sentimentality, even in the lyrical settings, and the tendency to avoid conclusive endings. Markings include "lightly, without pathos," "don't drag," "strongly," "fresh march tempo," and numerous admonitions of "lightly, without sentimentality." He subverts listeners' expectations variously at the ends of songs through rhythm, unresolved melody, and/or dissonance (Csipák 1975a and b). See example 8.1, which demonstrates this pattern with excerpts from the endings of four representative songs: "The World Is Changing," "Lenin," "Deutschland," and "In the Spring." At the end of "The World Is Changing," the tempo broadens a bit, but the vocal line ends on D rather than the anticipated tonic C. The resolution provided in the accompaniment is off the beat, extremely brief, and abrupt, so that it feels rhythmically unfinished or interrupted. The melody line in "Lenin" ends securely enough on the fifth scale degree, but the chord, which should be a second-inversion tonic on E-flat, is voiced with an A-flat instead of a G. The final measure consists of unison E-flats in marcato triplets so that the tonic is firmly reasserted, but then the rhythm feels incomplete because the momentum does not carry over to the next downbeat. "Deutschland" provides the desired rhythmic and melodic closure because the voice part ends on the first scale degree and the measure is marked with a fermata that allows it to be held for a satisfying duration, but the tonic G chord in the accompaniment is colored by a dissonant C instead of the expected D, and the song thus ends with a suspension that stubbornly refuses to resolve.

The conclusion of "In the Spring" features the voice on a rousing, sustained high E-flat—the fifth scale degree—while the root-position tonic chord underneath reiterates marcato A-flats in three octaves but assiduously avoids the requisite C. Instead, the chord is colored with both B-flat and D-flat, the two pitches on either side of the expected C. Such inconclusive endings can have several effects. One is to encourage repetition; if the song never feels quite done, the tendency is to sing yet another verse. (Eisler had certainly used that strategy to good effect in his famous protest songs intended for mass sing-along performance, such as "Solidarity Song" and "Song of the United Front.") Unresolved lingering dissonances can lend an edge to the otherwise heavily diatonic settings of the *Folk Songs*, discouraging overly sentimental performance in the lyrical songs and suggesting a serious undertone in the perky marches. Those that give the impression of being unresolved rhythmically keep performers and listeners alike on their toes, preventing them from being lulled into complacency by the otherwise familiar musical patterns and

Example 8.1 Excerpts from Becher/Eisler's *New German Folk Songs*

Excerpt 1: Ending of "The World Is Changing"

Excerpt 2: Ending of "Lenin"

Excerpt 3: Ending of "Germany"

Excerpt 4: Ending of "In the Spring"

lyrics. The premise that songs should be provocative harkens back to Eisler's epic theater experiments with Brecht, although one of their favorite devices, music that contradicts the lyrics in order to provide an additional layer of commentary, would not have been appropriate in this case. Unlike the sophisticated audiences of Weimar-era Berlin, members of the FDJ in the postwar period could not be expected to recognize and interpret multiple layers of contradictory cues. By and large, the works in *New German Folk Songs* were musically and poetically what they appeared, even if Eisler's settings were more interesting than they had to be merely to serve as vehicles for the antifascist socialist messages in Becher's poems. He communicates these messages in images and language consistent with the folk song tradition and appropriate for the enculturation of the values of peace, cooperation, hard work, optimism, confidence, and respect for tradition in youth (Minks 2002). Such values are promoted in songs for children and youth in order to train good citizens in societies around the world—capitalist, communist, tribal, religious, secular, and so on. The distinction in this case is that "good citizens" in postwar Germany would also by definition be explicitly antifascist and socialist. With the notable exception of the song "Lenin," Becher did not refer overtly to any of the figures or "isms" that defined the world in this period (fascism, antifascism, capitalism, imperialism, communism, socialism, etc.). Such explicit references are more appropriate for protest and mass songs than folk song, although he did employ common poetic euphemisms for generalized representations of good (sun, the light) and evil (the darkness).

The songs were a hit with the FDJ and the general public. Becher described a performance of February 8, 1950, at which "'Song of the Blue Flag' was enthusiastically received by a youth group. The singer caught a (political) cold, and so Eisler had to sing it himself. Those present could quickly sing along and together we formed a happy, joyful choir" (Becher 1952: 124). The songs were tremendously successful at their formal premiere on May 22, which occurred at the House for Soviet-German Friendship in Berlin. *Neues Deutschland* reported that the audience stood to join in a repeat performance of "Song of the Blue Flag" and "all in attendance . . . felt the fortune of this hour, which marked the birth of new German folk song" (Grabs preface to Eisler 1975). Finally, Becher's account of the performance on June 9 confirmed their popularity: "We received the greatest applause of our lives. People sprang from their seats, stomping and clapping, and some of the songs had to be repeated five times" (Becher 1952: 302). Musicologist Jürgen Schebera (1998: 228) has written that the songs made a strong impression on him as a child and were sung throughout the GDR, not so much for indoctrination but because they were accessible and represented a "very simple expression of the new time."

One of the most enduring of the collection would prove to be the song the FDJ had originally commissioned, "Song of the Blue Flag." Perhaps its longevity is due in part to the fact that it bears more than a passing resemblance to the East German national anthem Eisler and Becher had composed only a month before, "Risen from the Ruins."[14] See example 8.2, which shows the scores for each as they were published in the 1954 edition of the FDJ songbook, *Leben Singen Kämpfen: Liederbuch der Deutschen Jugend (Live, Sing, Fight: Songbook for the German Youth)* (Ott 1954). A certain similarity in musical setting might be expected, since the two poems are composed in the same poetic meter, but the resemblance goes far beyond that required for text setting. Musically, both are in the key of G major, although that is not an unusual choice for a song that should be easy to sing and play (there is only one sharp in the key signature). The characteristics historically attributed to G major have made it a favorite key for children's music since at least the late eighteenth century.[15] They also share a distinctive cadential pattern. In "Song of the Blue Flag," the figure from the third beat of measure 6 to the second beat of measure 8 is repeated in measures 14–16, and is melodically identical to measures 13–16 in "Risen from the Ruins." (The discrepancy in the number of beats comes because the first is notated in 4/4 and the second in 2/4.) The rhythmic settings are different, but the penultimate event in each phrase is dotted. Finally, their harmonic progressions are identical, and in both cases the next phrase is harmonized with a root-position IV chord. The form also contributes to the sense of familiarity, as this four-measure phrase provides a bridge to the return of the opening phrase that then concludes each song.

◆ The Legacy of *New German Folk Songs*

Eisler's characteristic synthesis of accessibility with sophistication and familiarity with novelty was especially well suited to songs for young citizens; some would permeate the consciousness of East German youth and remain with them well into adulthood. Correspondence with several people born in the GDR between 1952 and 1973 reveals that a handful of the works in *New German Folk Songs* remained in the repertoire or in the collective memory as much as thirty years later (the songs would have been age-appropriate for these respondents between approximately 1967 and 1985). "Song of Learning" ("Gesang vom Lernen") and "Lenin" proved particularly memorable, although

Example 8.2 **Melodies from Becher/Eisler's
"Risen from the Ruins" and "Song of the Blue Flag"**

as published in the FDJ songbook, *Live, Sing, Fight:
Songbook for the German Youth* (1954)

"Risen from the Ruins"

"Song of the Blue Flag"

some remember having learned the lyrics as poetry only, without music. Several learned "Song of the Blue Flag," while songs such as "The Old Ways," "In the Spring," "Germany," "Time for Wandering," and "Homeland Song" triggered memories in only one or two of the older respondents. One (b. 1960, Laucha) noted that "Homeland Song" appeared in the songbook published in 1968 but was omitted from editions published in the 1970s because the text was no longer consistent with the beliefs being taught. Similarly, another (b. 1967, Laucha) noted that by the time he or she was old enough to learn such songs, those with the word *Germany* in the lyrics were no longer sung. Almost everyone recalled having learned two by Eisler that predated the GDR, "Song of the United Front" and "Solidarity Song," and several cited those as songs they liked at that time. When asked about songs they remembered from childhood and youth regardless of composer or grade in school, several titles recurred repeatedly: "The Moor Soldiers," "I Carry a Flag," "The Little Trumpeter," "Be Happy and Sing," "The Thälmann Column," "You Have a Goal in Sight," "The Sky over Spain Spreads Its Stars," "The International," "Build," "Carpe Diem," "World Youth Song," "The Sun Lives Forever," "Through the Mountains," and "In the Snowy Mountains." These run the gamut from songs for very small children (Young Pioneers or even earlier) to those for young adults, but all seem to have been significant at the time and demonstrated staying power many years later in people's memories. It was also observed that the songs became more explicitly political in orientation as one got older. One respondent distinguished between Pioneer songs and those with a more heavy-handed political message: "I liked a lot of the songs for their music. Most of the lyrics had some Pioneer theme or another. I guess we could relate to those a lot more because they were written especially for kids. (Although some of the songs I always knew were putting it on too thick, for instance the love for the people from Soviet Union as in "Good Friends." We knew very well what reality looked like)" (b. 1973, Weimar).

English-language songs such as "The Ink Is Black," which was introduced in conjunction with a discussion of Paul Robeson, and "Black and White," described as an anonymous Negro protest song, were taught in seventh or eighth grade and in conjunction with regular lessons in English, and several respondents cited these songs among those they remembered and liked. Many recall singing Christmas songs seasonally with friends and family (but not in school), and two described having learned sacred songs in religious instruction classes.[16] Children learned songs primarily through music instruction at school, and some also referred to songbooks that they owned aside from formal textbooks. They were taught to read music but learned mostly by listening to the teacher sing something and then repeating it. Songs were performed a cappella or with guitar, piano, or accordion.

The music instruction textbook in use in 1979 lists the repertoire appropriate for grades five through ten and indicates that students learned ten songs by Eisler, only three of which are from *New German Folk Songs*. Of those ten, five were composed in the 1930s, and all of those have texts by Brecht; three are excerpted from plays, and the other two are mass songs. Of the five composed in the postwar period, four have lyrics by Becher ("Risen from the Ruins" and "Lenin," "Song of the Blue Flag," and "In the Spring" from the *New German Folk Songs*), while "Peace on Our Earth" has a text by Brecht. One might assume that the works in *New German Folk Songs* simply fell out of the repertoire gradually so as to be virtually absent by 1979, but in fact they scarcely survived the first year. Neither the songs nor their collaborators were prominently featured in the Third Festival for the World's Youth and Students in East Berlin in August 1951 (Koch and Mückenberger 1952). Only one piece, "Song of the Blue Flag," appears in the 1954 edition of the FDJ songbook.[17] A scant four years after their highly successful debut, the songs had already been virtually eliminated from the official songbook of the commissioning body. Yet the collaborators had been very optimistic about the fate of their folk songs in 1950 and had had ambitious plans for a much larger project. According to Eisler, this was supposed to have been the first volume in a new series from Aufbau, the publishing house of the Cultural League. "Additional volumes of folk song books, on which we are already working, will follow. The whole collection will have a sizeable scope and contain songs of many different kinds" (Grabs 1976: 190). Yet no additional books came forth, and the series ended even as it began.

Despite Eisler's and Becher's established records as allies of the workers' movement and their international status as prominent intellectuals, the reception history of *New German Folk Songs* was negatively influenced by factors that had little to do with the songs themselves or the collaborators' commitment to the cause. Decisions made in exile and missteps negotiating the landmines of cultural politics in the early GDR cost both men dearly, and the songs, which had been so popular initially, all but disappeared from the landscape of the youth movement. Becher's dogged devotion to a unified German culture earned the Cultural League frequent reprimands in the late 1940s because his vision did not brook sufficient Soviet influence (Naimark 1995: 401–8; Pike 1992: 200–245). On June 10, 1950, the morning after the second successful performance of *New German Folk Songs*, Becher was attacked in an anonymous (and thus official) letter published in *Neues Deutschland*, the or-

gan of the SED. It accused Becher's journal *Sonntag* of insufficient support for
the campaign against formalism and of portraying Western culture uncritically. As a result, he and the Cultural League found their influence and lati-
tude in cultural politics severely curbed. Efforts to curry favor with the SED
by criticizing the West only undermined his pan-German efforts, and he became the target of harsh criticism in the FRG as well. The cultural political
waters in the early GDR were treacherous, and despite their immediate success, some believed the lyrics in *New German Folk Songs* presented a confusing
political message. His political position became increasingly precarious, and
the premiere of *New German Folk Songs* would indeed turn out to have been
the highlight of his life; he died on October 11, 1958 (Dwars 1998: 593–94). As
for Eisler, the SED exploited his presence in the GDR for purposes of international public relations, but in fact his relationship with the party was continually strained. The SED leadership was comprised of former KPD members who had been in exile in Moscow and did not trust those who had gone
into exile in the West, particularly a composer who had earned a comfortable living in Hollywood. Eisler's own cultural political show trial commenced
in 1952, when the libretto he had written for a projected opera titled *Johann
Faustus* drew tremendous critical fire (Calico 1999 and 2002). His productiv-
ity slowed dramatically, and the opera remained incomplete at the time of his
death in 1962.

But in the heady days of early 1950, before Becher and Eisler became fatally
entangled in the machinations of cold war cultural politics, they captured a
historic moment of genuine optimism about the antifascist socialist future
of postwar Germany in their *New German Folk Songs*. When correspondents
were asked if they still sing any GDR songs for children and youth today, no
one singled out the Becher/Eisler collection. However, respondents did say
that they sing or have sung other East German songs for youth, either with
children, in response to requests from West Germans who are curious, or for
fun, when reminiscing with childhood friends. One was disappointed when
she reflected upon the apparent irrelevance of song and choral singing in contemporary German life: "It is a shame to observe that Germans in general—
on both sides—are no longer people who love to sing. Surely there are still a
few regions in the German states where more people sing than in others, traditions live and thereby also the songs. I find it regrettable that in this country
there is so little joy for singing in choirs everywhere . . . and therefore little opportunity to sing together" (b. 1955, Saalburg).

Another respondent expressed some surprise upon discovering the songs
still latent in her memory: "I do find it fascinating that the texts and melodies

are stored in my unconscious. I just can't get there but I could sing them if someone started . . . reminds me of Christa Wolf's protagonist of 'Kindheits-muster' who cannot get rid of the fascist songs after 1945" (b. 1966, Leipzig). Responses indicate that the role of song in the evocation of nostalgia is very powerful. That nostalgia may be for childhood and youth, for the GDR ("Os-talgie"), or for the unique experience of the two combined.[18]

> The songs are often just the triggers for memories. (b. 1969, Schwerin)

> Just as each poem, picture, and book corresponds to a particular Zeitgeist these songs correspond to the time and the feelings of those who wrote them. After I read through a couple of texts today I found that they moved me just as I had been touched by them as a 14-year old. (b. 1960, Laucha)

> I still find some of the songs beautiful today (nature, folk and workers' songs) and I still sing them. The Pioneer and FDJ songs are bound to the memories of my childhood and youth. (b. 1964, Löbnitz)

> I am not annoyed by them because they were/are part of my childhood, and I like thinking about that. (b. 1967, Laucha)

> Children's songs are important for well being. Some songs have thoughtful lyrics/human emotion/love of homeland. Others are ideologically over-loaded. (b. 1952, Caputh)

> I still like some of the songs because of the political ideals expressed in them, such as solidarity and antifascism. (b. 1966, East Berlin)

> Partly it seems to me that they come out of an older time, and are truly nostalgic. The songs are incarnations of past times. (b. 1966, Weimar)

The use of the FDJ song "Build" in the film *Good Bye Lenin!* echoes these respondents' experiences, and that film's popular success suggests that chil-dren's songs are an effective means of evoking the past. In fact, "Build," the song that eventually replaced "Song of the Blue Flag" as the FDJ anthem, is the most frequently performed song in the history of German film.[19] That a song of youth is so familiar, and its powers of evocation so potent, that it has come to represent an entire society in its idealized form suggests that the founding fathers of the GDR were right: enculturation through song makes an indelible, lifelong impression on young citizens.

Notes

Earlier incarnations of this essay were presented at meetings of the International Musicological Society in Budapest (2000), the national meeting of the American Musicological Society in Atlanta (2001), and the national meeting of the German Studies Association in New Orleans (2003). I am particularly indebted to the following people for research assistance: Sonja Fritzsche, Hiltrud Schulz, Ursula Oehme, Kirstin Westphal, Anke Pinkert, Göran Westphal, Anett Winkler, Rene Jagnow, Anna L. Coch, Gerald Brennan, Katrin Bothe, Jennifer William, Nadine Wolf, Shannon Okey, Susan Widmer, and Tamara Levitz. I am grateful to Daniel Shirley for assistance with the musical examples, and to Claudia Schlee for consulting with me about my translations of Becher's poetry. Thanks are due to the following for permission to reprint examples in this article: Rob Raeside, Director, Flags of the World, for permission to reprint the FDJ flag from http://flagspot.net/flags/de%7Dfdj.html; Breitkopf & Härtel, for permission to print the examples from *Neue deutsche Volkslieder* edition DV 9086 in fig. 8.1; Aufbau Verlag, for permission to cite excerpts from Becher's poetry; Hofmeister Musik Verlag, for permission to reprint "Lied der blauen Fahne" in fig. 8.2; and Peters Edition, for permission to reprint "Auferstanden aus Ruinen" in fig. 8.2. Publication of this research was made possible by a generous subvention from Mark Wait, Dean of the Blair School of Music at Vanderbilt University.

1. I am grateful to these correspondents for their time and attention, and for permission to quote their responses. They are identified by birthplace and birth date only. Several alluded to song and choir movements and the popularity of singing clubs, but as these phenomena emerged in the 1960s, I did not pursue them here.

2. See Mählert and Stephan 1996 and Walter 1997. The FDJ still exists as part of a network of youth organizations unified under the World Federation of Democratic Youth; see their Web site at http://www.fdj.de. For an overview of the cultural work of children and youth in the GDR, see Bauer, Bockhorst, Prautzsch, and Rimbach 1993. For the early history of the Pioneers, see Ansorg 1997.

3. For a brief overview and statistics about West German membership, see Zilch 1994: 17–21. For a history of its inception, see Herms 1996.

4. The concept of a single German cultural nation regained currency following (re)unification. See de Bruyn 1991: 62: "[The concept of the German cultural nation] forms the counterweight . . . to a kind of thinking that sees a unified nation-state as a precondition for the continuation of German culture. When I say that culture is the stable basis, impervious even to four decades of division, this does not necessarily mean that culture must become a reason to work for political unity if there are other reasons to work against it. The German cultural nation is thus sovereign, not subordinate to the sovereignty of states."

5. The legitimacy of Stalin's offer to surrender the GDR so that Germany could

be reunified has not been determined. It seems likely that the note was only a tactic intended to impede "West German rearmament and consolidation as a state." The SED would have had no way of knowing how sincere Stalin was, but once the FRG rejected the deal, the SED seized upon the opportunity to depict itself as the protector of German sovereignty. See Maier 1997: 16.

6. Minutes from meetings of the Composers' Union (Verband der Komponisten) in the 1950s reveal that much energy was expended in the name of "gesamtdeutsche Arbeit" (combined German work). See the Verband der Komponisten Archiv, Stiftung Archiv der Akademie der Künste in Berlin.

7. Seminal collections that followed in the nineteenth century included Anton Wilhelm Zuccalmaglio and E. Baumstark, *Bardale: Sammlung auserlesener Volkslieder* (1829); August Kretzschmer and Zuccalmaglio, *Deutsche Volkslieder mit Ihren Original-Weisen* (1838); August Heinrich Hoffmann von Fallersleben and E. Richter, *Schlesische Volkslieder mit Melodien* (1842); Zuccalmaglio, *Deutsche Volkslieder und Volksweisen* (1856); Ludwig Erk, *Deutscher Liederhort*, originally published in 1856 and then greatly expanded by F. M. Böhme in 1893–94 to include popular and national songs; and several other famous collections that did not include the word *Volkslieder* in the title but were enormously influential in the same vein, such as Arnim and Brentano's *Das Knaben Wunderhorn: Alte deutsche Lieder* (1805–8).

8. Günter Mayer traces this undated note, "Notiz über die ältere und neuere Volkslied," to 1950. For more on folk song in the GDR, see Steinitz 1972.

9. Becher and Eisler represented two factions of the German Left as it was reconstituted in eastern Germany after the war: those who had spent the war in Moscow, and those who had gone west. The return of Eisler from exile in the United States was an international public relations coup for the SED, as it could boast the renowned composer as one of its original citizens. Eisler had studied composition with Arnold Schoenberg but broke with him in 1926 when the incompatibility of his sophisticated atonal training and his commitment to the workers' movement became too great. He achieved prominence through his politicized collaborations with Bertolt Brecht, and then spent most of the decade between 1938 and 1948 in the United States, where he enjoyed success in Hollywood. Scrutiny from the House Un-American Activities Committee drove him back to Europe in 1948 and by 1949 he had returned to Berlin.

10. The total number is described variously as 15, 17, 18, and 19, depending on the source and date of the edition. The initial publication contained fifteen songs, and it is these to which Eisler refers in his interview of February 26, 1950. Others also wrote songs for the FDJ at this time; see for example Thilman and Zimmering 1951.

11. The text for the song "The Old Ways" had been previously published as the poem "Es sind die alten Weisen" ("It Is the Old Ways") in a volume titled *Heimkehr (Homecoming)* in 1946. As with other poems set as songs, Eisler made minor

adjustments to the title and text. The words Eisler changed appear in brackets after the word as it appeared in the published poem. "Es sind die alten Weisen / Die neu in mir [uns] erstehn / Und die im Wind, dem leisen, / Von fern herüberwehn. / Wenn sich die Wipfel neigen / Allabendlich im Wind, / Dann gehn durch unser Schweigen / Sie, die gefallen sind. / Es sind die alten Lieder, / Die singen neu aus mir. / Und wie vorzeiten wieder / Abends singen wir. / Es ist in uns ein Raunen / Und wird zum großen Chor, / Und zu den Sternen staunen / Andächtig [staunen] wir empor.[!]" (Becher 1966–81: 5:478; Eisler 1975: 6). All poems appear courtesy of Aufbau Verlag. Translations are my own.

12. "When Workers and Farmers" was first published as the final section of a three-part poem titled "Volkes Eigen" ("People's Own") in Becher's collection *Dichtung* (1949). "Es wird nicht lang[e] mehr dauern, / Und es wird Friede sein, / Und wie nach Regenschauern / Kehrt wider sonne ein. / Wie eine Angstkulisse / Stehn Trümmer um uns her. / Es soll das ungewisse / Uns schrecken bald nicht mehr. / Es hat die Not ein Ende, / Wenn IHR [ihr] die Zeit bestimmt / Und in die eignen Hände / Das Volk sein Schicksal nimmt. / Wenn Arbeiter und Bauern / Kommen überein— / Wird es nicht lang mehr dauern, / Und es wird Friede sein" (Becher 1966–81: 6:52; Eisler 1975: 10–11).

13. This text originally appeared as the second section of the three-part poem "Volkes Eigen (People's Own)" in the collection *Dichtung* (1949). Eisler omitted verses 5–7 in his setting. "Als ein Dunkel wieder lag auf Erden / Und es schien wie unabänderlich, / Daß es müsse immer dunkler werden, / Sprach ein Mann: 'Die Welt verändert sich! / Seid getrost! Es muß das Dunkel weichen, / Und ein Licht scheint wieder dir und mir, / Wenn einander wir die Hände reichen, / Denn die Welt verändern WIR! [wir.]' / War es nicht ein Wunschbild und ein Träumen / Und ein schöner Glaube, unglaubhaft—/ Um den Schutt der Zeit hinwegzuräumen, / Dazu braucht es eines Riesen Kraft. / 'Wer ist dieser Riese?'—war ein Fragen. / Sprach der Mann: 'Wir alle, du und ich, / Wenn wir träumen und zu sagen wagen / Diesen Satz: 'Die Welt verändert sich![.]' / [omit verses 5, 6, and 7] Darum singt ein Lied vom Anderswerden![,] / Macht euch frei und werden brüderlich! / Seht, es wird schon wieder licht auf Erden! [,] / Und die Welt, die Welt verändert sich!" (Becher 1966–81: 6:50–51; Eisler 1975: 7–9).

14. Settings by Otto Gerster and Eisler were presented to the Politburo on November 5, 1949, and the membership selected the Eisler version as the national anthem. For more on the anthem, see Amos 1997. West German popular songwriter Peter Kreuder subsequently brought suit against Eisler for plagiarism, claiming that Eisler had stolen material from his 1939 song "Goodby Jonny." Sally Bick (2003) traces the same controversial musical material in the Hollywood film score Eisler had composed for *Hangmen Also Die* in 1942. One respondent (b. 1960, Laucha) recalled learning all three verses of "Risen from the Ruins" in the seventh grade, but then being told to sing only the first verse a couple of years later because united Germany was no longer the goal of the socialist state. Another (b. 1966, East

Berlin) noted that he liked the national anthem but remembered singing it only rarely for the same reason.

15. According to C. F. Schubart (in his 1806 work *Ideen zu einer Ästhetik der Tonkunst*), G major is associated with "everything rustic, idyllic and lyrical, every calm and satisfied passion, every tender gratitude for true friendship and faithful love. In a word, every gentle and peaceful emotion of the heart is correctly expressed by this key." See translation and commentary in Steblin 1983: 124.

16. *New German Folk Songs* included two Christmas songs, "Christmas Song" ("Weihnachtslied") and "Children's Song of Christmas" ("Kinderlied zu Weihnachten"), proof that the tension between religious and secular observation of holidays was far from resolved in the GDR in 1950.

17. The songs are divided into four categories in *Leben Singen Kämpfen,* although the criteria for categorization are not entirely clear, particularly in the first two groups: Contemporary Youth Songs, Protest Songs, Folk Songs, and Hiking Songs. "Risen from the Ruins" and "Song of the Blue Flag" appear in the first group, while "Red Wedding" (text by Erich Weinert about the Wedding district in Berlin) and "Solidarity Song" appear in the second.

18. The most rudimentary Web search confirms that "Ostalgie" is rampant; for example, see http://www.ddr-im-www.de/ and the aptly titled http://www.auferstanden-aus-ruinen.de/. German eBay, Gowen Militaria, and Brandenburg Historica do a brisk business in GDR military memorabilia. For music, see http://www.musik-der-ddr.de. Children's songs are particularly popular; see, for example, http://www.blueplane.de/DDRLieder/ or http://www.andreasferl.de/Lieder. The Stadtgeschichtliches Museum in Leipzig had planned an exhibition about childhood in East Germany named for the popular song and magazine "Fröhlich sein und singen" for 2002–3, but it was postponed and retitled to incorporate material from the FRG. The nostalgia for GDR children's songs is even commercially viable, as several collections are now available on CD: *Sing mit, Pionier: Lieder der Jungpioniere, Blaue Wimpel im Sommerwind: Lieder der Jungen Pioniere, Fröhlich sein und singen: die Schönsten Pionierlieder,* and *Wenn Mutti früh zur Arbeit geht.*

19. *Good Bye Lenin!* was directed by Wolfgang Becker and released in 2003. It was a box office smash in Germany and won Best European Film at the Berlin Film Festival. With the conspicuous exception of "Build," written by Reinhold Limberg, songs of the FDJ appear to have inspired less nostalgia than songs for the Pioneers, probably because they tended to be more overtly political and are associated with a more mature, less innocent phase of youth. See the CD *Bau auf, Bau auf: Leben, singen, kämpfen.* Maren Köster (2002) refers to the prevalence of "Build" in German film in her introduction.

Defining the "Children of the Nation"

Three Stages of Children's Music in Modern Japan

HERMANN GOTTSCHEWSKI

AND MACHIKO GOTTSCHEWSKI

In the global history of Western music, Japan plays a distinguished role. Although neither a part of the European cultural network nor dominated by European immigrants, Japan was perhaps the first nation to accept European classical music on a broad basis and to produce a significant number of professional musicians able to compete with their Western counterparts. Furthermore, the countries that followed Japan, such as Korea, Taiwan, and China, seem to have done so in part due to Japanese influence, whether as a result of the educational policy enforced by the Japanese government in the colonial period, because of feelings of rivalry after the Second World War, or because Japan was a model for the successful modernization of a traditional Asian country. It is open to argument whether the great success of Western music in Japan was worth the sacrifices it entailed, particularly in traditional music culture, but it is undeniable that Japan occupies a key position in the globalization of Western music.

Why did the Japanese undertake such an adventure as the adoption of music from a totally different culture? It was certainly not that they were fascinated by that music. (Even if there are many Japanese who are fascinated by Western music, it is a historical fact that the decision to adopt Western music came first and the fascination second.) Rather, it was the belief that Western music reflected the Western spirit and that, conversely, Western music would make a nation resemble the West, consequently rendering it strong enough to remain in the modern world.

In an era when the national economy was not yet developed, it was, of course, not easy to persuade politicians that the introduction of Western music was useful and worth the sacrifice of public resources. It helped, however, that the belief just mentioned—the notion that the character of a nation was necessarily connected with their national music—was rooted not only in Chinese but also in ancient Greek philosophy and could thus easily be propagated as a "sufficiently proven truth" for conservative as well as for West-oriented politicians. Thus instruction in singing (for elementary schools) and in playing music (for middle schools) was introduced along with compulsory school education, officially in 1872 but in practice only a few years later.

There was a strong conviction in the ruling class that real social change could be achieved only through children's education. Changing the nation meant changing education, and creating a new people meant creating new children. The history of Western music in Japan is not least a history of children's music. And the history of children's music in Japan—as far as the music provided by adults for children is concerned—is not least a history of the struggle for "true national" Japanese childhood. The stages of children's music since the Meiji era (1868–1912) thus reflect the stages of finding national identity as well as of constructing childhood in modern Japanese society.

◆ Shôka—New Music for the Young Nation

Only fifteen years after the United States of America had forced the opening of the Japanese harbors for their ships in 1853, the exhausted regime of the shogun collapsed, and political power was returned to the emperor. Thereafter Japan took the bull by the horns, moved past the feudal system and its obsolete social barriers within a few years, and began to build a new nation that could compete with the Western world powers.

There was no doubt that a new nation could be formed only with new people. So the educational reform was one of the first measures the new government carried out. In 1872, a new school system was enacted, which introduced compulsory education for all children in the country. Children were among the first who experienced the spirit of the new era.

The new age had two faces, both looking far beyond the realities of daily life. One was the face of restoration, looking to the distant past of ancient Japan when, according to mythology, the Emperor had a godlike position and exerted spiritual power over his people. The other was the face of modernization, looking to the Far West, from which one could learn to build a prosperous economy and a strong military. These two faces were not considered antagonistic opposites, but rather two aspects, sometimes conflicting, of the new age.

This ideological constellation was also reflected in ideas about music education around 1880. The leading music pedagogue of the time, Isawa (or Izawa) Shûji (1851–1917), wrote in a programmatic text of 1879:[1]

Let me take the liberty . . . of briefly stating the prevailing opinions as to the matter [i.e., teaching of singing in schools], which can be summed up essentially into three. The first says that, as music is the chief means which excites and stimulates our emotions, and as human passions are naturally expressed by musical tones, the same music might be universally used by all mankind, in spite of the differences of country or of race; and that European music has almost reached perfection by means of the contemplations and experience of the last thousand years, since the time of the Greek sage, Pythagoras, and it surpasses very greatly oriental music in perfection and beauty. It will, therefore, be far better to adopt European music in our schools than to undertake the awkward task of improving the imperfect oriental music.

The second says that there are in every country and nation their own languages, customs, and usages, which being the natural outgrowth of the character of the people and the conditions of the land cannot be changed by human efforts. So the same is true with music which had its first origin in the inclinations of the human mind, and has since been preserved by each nation. We have never heard of any country in which the native music has been entirely supplanted by foreign music, and consequently to introduce European music into our country must, at least, be as useless an attempt as to adopt English as our language; therefore it will be a far wiser plan to take measures towards the cultivation and improvement of our own music.

The third says that the two former opinions are not entirely unreasonable, but they seem to run to the two opposite extremities of the matter, and hence, taking a middle course, the proper measure would be to secure new and suitable music for our country, by selecting the best from both European and oriental music.[2]

That the second approach was meant to be a restorationist one is not clear from these sentences alone, but in 1879 the only music instruction that already had begun at public schools in Tokyo was a project initiated by the Tokyo Women's Normal School together with the imperial *gagaku* (court music) department, where a song collection called *hoiku shôka* was in progress (see ex. 9.1). These songs were clearly restorationist in character. Their words were mainly taken from millennium-old collections of classical poetry; the melodies were newly composed in a style derived from the oldest Shinto ceremonial pieces and historical sources of music theory; and the instruments used for accompaniment were mainly those that had supposedly already existed

Example 9.1 **Shirogane (Silver)**

From *Hoiku shôka*, transcribed by Hermann Gottschewski

Words by Yamanoue no Okura (660–733)
Composed in 1878 by Shiba Fujitsune (1849–1918)

The repetition signs in the *wagon* part indicate the end of the repeated pattern. The first two bars of the *wagon* part are notated but probably not performed through perfomance practice tradition.

in Japan before the advent of Chinese influence.[3] Obviously the aim of these songs was a purification of young people, and the achievement of a true Japanese heart, although in a very theoretical and refined way.

In contrast, Isawa himself had just returned from his studies in Massachusetts, where he had learned—among other things—Western music education in schools, and he had his music teacher from Boston, L. W. Mason, invited to Japan. Although Isawa propagated the third opinion of "selecting the best from both European and oriental music," in effect only a small part of the restorationist approach found its way into his teaching material. The first printed songbooks for Japanese schools, published by Isawa's institute[4] in cooperation with Mason between 1881 and 1884, are almost a pure embodiment of the first opinion.[5]

A typical example is the song *Oboro* (おぼろ) from the first songbook[6] (no. 28), which uses a melody by Friedrich Silcher (see ex. 9.2).[7] The rhythm of the German original version is slightly changed (two half notes in bar 1 are split

Example 9.2 **Oboro (Faintly Smelling)**

From (*Shôgaku*) *Shôkashû shohen*

Words by Institute of Music, Tokyo
Melody by Friedrich Silcher

into quarter notes, quarter rests at the end of bars 2 and 6 are filled out with quarter notes), because in Japanese poems lines with five or seven syllables are favored. The songbook that contains this song was used in public schools throughout the country beginning in the 1880s and 1890s. The performance practice was essentially the same as that which had been introduced by Christian missionaries into Japanese churches and mission schools since 1873. The most widely used instrument for accompaniment was the reed organ.

Although song collections for schools from the 1890s—especially the influential official collection of eight songs for school ceremonies at public holidays, published in 1893[8]—contain a few more songs using *hoiku shôka* scales (including the current Japanese national anthem), all in all Isawa's "first opinion" prevailed, and after 1900 singing in school was almost exclusively based on Western music. Non-Western instruments and non-Western notational systems disappeared entirely from the schools. When a new set of songbooks called *Jinjô shôgaku shôka* (Shôka *for Common Schools*) was published by the Ministry of Cultural Affairs in 1911–14, only Japanese compositions were included—mainly because it was difficult to adapt Japanese words to Western melodies (Gottschewski 2003: 561)—but all songs that were new in these six volumes were composed in Western style.[9] Today the word *shôka* primarily signifies prewar school songs using Western melodies or melodies composed in Western style. Most *shôka* are written in major scales, and many of them are pentatonic (omitting the fourth and seventh note of the major scale).

For Isawa, the effect of singing for health and moral education was more important than whether Japanese or Western scales were used. His proposal of "selecting the best from both European and Oriental music" was perhaps carried out mainly to satisfy both the modernist and restorationist camps. His aim was to show that the differences between Western and Japanese music were learned and did not depend on the nature of the people:

> Comparing Japanese *Hauta* (short vulgar songs) and European fashionable songs, we find hardly any point of similarity between the two, so widely do they differ from each other. But in the comparison of Japanese *kotouta* (Koto song) with some of the European Hymns, some common ideas can be detected. Finally, the comparison of Japanese infant songs with those of European origin shows that almost entirely similar characteristics exist between them. This accounts for the fact that European and Japanese music consist of similar elements, differing only in the manner of their combinations. For the above reason, there is only a little difference in the pieces which are simple in construction as in the case

of infant songs, but the differences increase as the construction becomes complicated, as in the case of fashionable songs. (Isawa, translation revised by Cox, cited after Eppstein 1982: 65; see note 2)

The obvious conclusion, from this point of view, is that the most effective way of establishing a new music culture is to begin with children's songs, gradually developing the more advanced levels. The degree of attention the Japanese have paid to children's songs continually from that time up to the present is a sign that Isawa's view, though modified in detail, became one of the foundations of modern thinking about music in Japan.

However, as described above, both the modernist and the restorationist approaches were completely removed from daily life and from the music of the people, and, more important, Isawa's songs as well as the *hoiku shôka* used highbrow lyrics, in the language of ancient poetry, that were almost a foreign language for schoolchildren. Although some of the songs from the first schoolbooks became popular and are still popular today, the traditional songs used by children in playgrounds remained almost unchanged, and the new *shôka* did not pass beyond the school gates for a long time.[10]

◆ *Dôyô*—Childhood and Modern Poetry

In the first twenty years after the initial introduction of singing lessons in Japanese schools (1880–1900), the discrepancy between claim and reality in school music education was enormous. While Japanese educators studied modern theories and methods of education such as those of Johann Heinrich Pestalozzi (1746–1827), Johann Friedrich Herbart (1776–1841), Friedrich Froebel (1782–1852), and others, the teaching materials failed to serve their purpose because the words of the songs were simply incomprehensible to Japanese children. A step toward improvement was taken around 1900, when some songwriters and composers developed the "colloquial *shôka*" (*gen-bun-itchi shôka*).[11] An early and important example of this new style appeared in a songbook for nursery schools, written in 1901. Most of the songs in this book were written by Higashi Kume (1877–1969, words) and Taki Rentarô (1879–1903, music).[12] These songs employ the simple words that a mother would say when playing with her child. The rhythmic short sentences are enriched with onomatopoetic words (ex. 9.3).

Although the writers of these songs were scarcely taken seriously as "poets" at the time, the "colloquial *shôka*" gradually became popular in succeeding years and were widely used in the schools. A truly new kind of children's

Example 9.3 **Hato poppo (Pigeon poppo)**

From *Yôchien shôka*

Words by Higashi Kume (1877–1969)
Composed in 1901 by Taki Rentarô (1879–1903)

song, however, appeared only around 1920, when leading poets felt the need for more artistic songs for the modern age. In 1918, the children's journal *Akai Tori (Red Bird)*[13] was founded, which marks the beginning of the so-called children's song movement (*dôyô undô*). In the journal, poems and tales for and by children were published, and the great success of the journal led to the foundation of many other journals with a similar aim.

At the first stage, *dôyô undô* was a literary movement. As a counterreaction against the *shôka* that dominated all school music education, it had a twofold mission. First, it criticized the *shôka* for being of aesthetically inferior quality, because their words were written by teachers and scholars rather than by poets; second, it criticized the exclusively Western orientation of the *shôka* for not being based on traditional (national) children's songs (Kojima 1972: 59). In contrast to the authoritarian teaching style of the previous era and in line with a general political tendency around 1920,[14] liberal education and free development of children's individual talents were propagated.

While the first volumes of the new children's journals contained only words, they soon included new compositions for children as well, mostly solo songs with piano accompaniment in Western style, called *dôyô*.[15] Almost all famous Japanese composers of the time contributed to the journals.[16] The songs varied considerably in style from simple songs in the *shôka* style, appropriate for use in schools, to more artistic compositions that were intended to be sung by adults for children, or even songs for adults that had childhood or childish thinking as their subject. *Dôyô* typically have a more elaborate piano accompaniment, including a short prelude, and thus occupy a place between simple nursery rhymes and the proper Japanese *Kunstlied*, which reached its first heights at about the same time.[17] Since the piano was not common in Japanese households at that time, it may be assumed that recordings and, beginning in 1926, broadcasting were decisive for the acceptance of *dôyô* by the general public.

A comparison of examples 9.3 and 9.4 shows the difference between a *shôka* and a *dôyô*: The melody of the *dôyô* (ex. 9.4) uses a traditional scale with nuclear tones[18] surrounded by major seconds (D – F-G-A – B-flat-C-D). In contrast, the *shôka* (ex. 9.3) uses a pentatonic major scale. The accompaniment of the *dôyô*, however, is based on Western harmonic rules and closes in F major. (The use of Western harmony with a melody in a traditional Japanese mode occurs frequently in *dôyô*.)[19] While in the *shôka* the accompaniment is only filling the acoustic space, in the *dôyô* it is essential for the musical form; it has its own motifs and polyphonic imitation (in measure 4). In the *shôka*, there are no expression marks at all, but in the *dôyô* there are many. The expression *hato poppo* in the *dôyô* is presumably a conscious citation from the *shôka* above, because the use of the onomatopoetic *poppo* for pigeons—although common today—is said to be an invention of Higashi Kume (Kindaichi and Anzai 1977: 169). The words of the song combine two disparate impressions with each other, as is typical of small children's reminiscences. This connection seems to be innocuous, but it may contain a moral mission: it gives the "castle of Chiyoda," the seat of the Japanese emperor, a positive image.

The claim of the *dôyô*, as formulated by Kitahara Hakushû (1885–1942, one of the leading poets of this movement), was to activate the creativity and aesthetic abilities of children. The school songs (*shôka*), he stated critically, were almost unsuitable for this purpose (Gottschewski and Gottschewski 2004: 373). But did the *dôyô* serve it better? From the standpoint of literature, the

Example 9.4 **Chiyoda no oshiro (The Castle of Chiyoda)**

Words by Noguchi Ujô (1882–1945)
Composed by Fujii Kiyomi (1889–1944)

children's song movement may have been a big step in the right direction. But with regard to the music (which Hakushû[20] avoided discussing), the situation is less clear. There were composers who studied traditional nursery rhymes to find more childlike forms of musical expression,[21] but as a whole the pieces were musically either not very different from the school songs (for example, in the songs by Narita Tamezô, 1893–1945) or not very suitable for children (as Konoe Hidemaro, 1898–1973, said about his own songs).[22] Although a vast number of *dôyô* were composed, only a few of them remained popular among the Japanese people—in contrast to some *shôka*. However, *dôyô* were rarely used in schools, because they were not official teaching material,[23] and thus it may not be the character of the music alone that is responsible for its comparatively limited dissemination.

◆ *Warabe-uta*—The World of Children as Home

Examples 9.1 and 9.2 not only use the language of highly educated adults but also are written from the standpoint of adults looking at children as objects of education. A child who is taught these songs would in the best case accept the words as expressions of a beloved person (the teacher) but not experience them a part of his or her childish world. *Shirogane* (ex. 9.1) is a paradigmatic sentence *about* children rather than a poem *for* children. (Regardless of the original meaning of the ancient poem, it may have been chosen because it can be interpreted as meaning that good education is the most important thing people can do for their nation.) In *Oboro* (ex. 9.2) the children are taught to speak for themselves, but from the standpoint of the human beings the children have to develop into, not from the standpoint of the childish heart. The target of early singing pedagogy in Japan is the citizen of the Japanese Empire, not the child as such.

In contrast, the words of examples 9.3 and 9.4 make the child part of an imagined communication. Example 9.3 takes the viewpoint of a mother playing with her child, and example 9.4 goes a step further into the childish world by taking the viewpoint of the child himself telling an adult his experiences. (There are other examples in *dôyô* where children speak to each other.)[24] The four examples thus show an increasing awareness of childhood as a stage of development that not only precedes adulthood but also has specific expressions and feelings and is a world in its own right.

As mentioned above, however, this awareness was not developed in music as early as in poetry. Japanese children had their own musical world of nursery rhymes and play songs. These songs, transmitted from mothers to their children and from child to child, are now called *warabe-uta* to distinguish them from educational songs like *shôka* and artistic compositions like *dôyô*. For music education, to enter the world of children would have entailed taking the *warabe-uta* as a point of departure.

Although the idea that the development of a new national music had to start from the songs of the children had already been expressed in the earliest writings on music education, the indigenous nursery rhymes had been almost ignored entirely by the compilers of schoolbooks until the early 1930s. Paradoxically, the opinion that there was no essential difference between Western and Japanese nursery rhymes resulted in less instead of more attention to *warabe-uta:* Because there was no difference, there was no obstacle to using Western songs instead of *warabe-uta*. Sometimes Isawa Shûji mixed in one or two *warabe-uta* melodies with the Western folk songs that constituted the vast majority of pieces in his songbooks.

In the Taishô era (1912–26), however, a great change of attitude occurred. Not that there was any disagreement with Isawa that *warabe-uta* were the very foundation from which a music culture unfolds. But in contrast to Isawa's opinion that they were the *common basis* of all mankind (or at least of the East Asian people as well as the European),[25] later writers considered them a specifically national property, the basis of the national character of a people. The same differences between, for example, English and Japanese nursery rhymes, which were seen as mere coincidences by Isawa, were seen now as the paradigmatic manifestation of the contrasting characters of Western and Japanese people. The study of *warabe-uta* and other folk songs of their nation became a measure for composers to find their national identity and to achieve a true national style. This tendency was already strong during the children's song movement, but it came to be reflected in school song collections only in the 1930s. At that time, *warabe-uta* were propagated by some leading educators as "national songs" that were able to "educate national-minded people" (Gondô 2003: 42).

The view that *warabe-uta* convey something like "the nature of the Japanese people" is even present in some recent writings, as in Gondô 2003: 42, when Gondô Atsuko says that the esteem for *warabe-uta* may be interpreted as a "natural" counterreaction against the partly "coercive" and partly "accidental" penetration of traditional society with *shôka* education and Western music. It is a simplification, however, to view the esteem for *warabe-uta* only as a counterreaction to Western influence. On the contrary, it was learned from Western national movements and therefore no more than a conversion of Western ideas into the Japanese environment, just another kind of Westernization. Bôta (or Bôda) Kazuma (1902–42), for example, who was the first to publish a song collection exclusively devoted to *warabe-uta* in 1932, refers to other countries in the preface:

> No matter how excellent the Western school songs are, since they are Western music, we cannot expect them to give true satisfaction to school-children who are Japanese. In Japan there exist genuine Japanese nursery rhymes, born in the Japanese earth and raised by children. These are the true songs of Japanese children, and only with these songs can be achieved true satisfaction of their musical instinct, a sensation and understanding of musical beauty, and a cultivation of musical sentiment. It is already accepted in every country that the national folk music is a necessary and indispensable thing for national music education and the constitution of national performing arts. There is no need for long explanations if we state that those children's songs that have existed in Japan since ancient times have a most important position in the musical education of Japanese children and in the establishment of a music for the children of modern Japan.[26]

There is a problem, however, with the national character of nursery rhymes. If it is true that Japanese children can have the "true satisfaction of their musical instinct" only with the songs that are "born in their earth and raised by themselves," it would be a great mistake to educate children in west Japan with the songs of the children of east Japan or vice versa. The musical traditions of the Japanese regions were so different that politicians of the early Meiji era (1868–1912) had realized that the music of one region could never serve as the national music for all Japanese people.

The final consequence of Bôta's ideology would have been to regionalize all music education. This, however, was an unthinkable undertaking in a centralized state like Japan. Since the Meiji era, "the establishment of a music for the nation"—meaning one music for the whole nation—had been the unquestioned aim of music education policy. The oft-cited concept of "national music" had meant rather "an undivided music for all people" than "a distinct music only for Japanese people." Therefore, the centralized introduction of certain *warabe-uta* was necessarily the introduction of a new foreign music for most Japanese children. Rather than making the real musical experiences of children the foundation of music education, it created a romantic rural image of "true Japanese childhood," an imaginary home that was the nation. The predominance of Western-style songs in the schoolbooks was not fundamentally changed. Even in the last set of songbooks for public schools in the imperial era, published in 1941–42, more than 80 percent of the pieces remained in Western scales (i.e., mostly in major keys). But the traditional children's songs were given a new place among the teaching materials, and their number was greater than in any previous official publication.

Songs in *warabe-uta* style are found primarily in the first volume (for the first school year),[27] where five out of twenty pieces belong to that genre. Two other pieces in this volume are in a strange mixture of Western and Japanese scales, and the remaining thirteen songs are in major keys, almost exclusively pentatonic.[28] Table 9.1 shows the themes of the songs and their tonalities. The probable pedagogical aim of the song is indicated in parentheses. With one exception, songs about war, the military, modern life, school and so on are written in major keys, while the songs in *warabe-uta* style concern traditional children's games, nature, and traditional ceremonies. Far from clearing the path for further music education, the *warabe-uta* form a closed group that represents a backward-looking identity of the home in opposition to the forward-looking identity represented by Western-style songs.

Example 9.5 **Kakurenbo (Hide-and-Seek)**

From *The Book of Songs I* (1941)

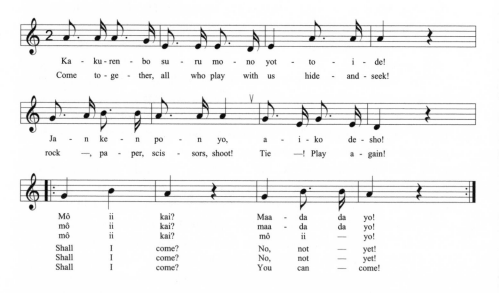

Table 9.1

I. Songs in *Warabe-uta* Style

3   Sunset (love for the hometown)
5   Hide-and-seek (ex. 5)
6   Catching glowworms
15 Waiting for the New Year's celebration
17 Ravens, fire brigade (defense of the hometown)

II. Songs in Mixed Modes

13 Lullaby
14 Doll (care for small children)

III. Songs in Major Keys

1   School, physical education (diligence, discipline)
2   National flag (feeling of awe, bravery)
4   School hike
7   Ocean, faraway places (imperialism?)
8   Horses (parental love)
9   Moon
10 Tale of Momotarô (allusion to naval warfare?)
11 Sowing (working for the welfare of the country)
12 Pigeons (social behavior)
16 Railroad game
18 Soldiers' game
19 Airplane (aerial warfare)
20 Nightingale (love for the hometown)

After *shôka* and *dôyô*, it was a logical development that the *warabe-uta* attracted the attention of music educators. But instead of encouraging the teachers to pick up the thread of the children's own rich regional traditions, the educators prescribed a centralized and restricted repertory of a few melodies. In this way they failed to close the gap between the old and the modern Japan. While *shôka* had introduced Western music culture to Japan, and *dôyô* was an important step in the development of modern composition there, the esteem for *warabe-uta* had relatively few consequences for Japanese music culture as a whole.

Notes

1. This article uses the modified Hepburn system for romanizing Japanese words; Japanese names are rendered according to Japanese convention, with the family name first.

2. The Japanese text was written in 1879, the English translation (by Isawa himself, revised by M. D. Cox, 1884) is preserved in the Tokyo National University of Fine Arts and Music Library, doc. no. F/16/11. Cited after Eppstein 1982: 63–64.

3. The *hoiku shôka* were composed between 1877 and 1882, and the collection contained in its final form about one hundred pieces for children from the first kindergarten class up to the higher grades. In 1883, they were prepared for publication, but eventually the publication failed, and the songs went out of use during the 1880s.

4. The Institute of Music (音楽取調掛) was founded in 1879 as a department of the Ministry of Cultural Affairs. In 1887 it became the Tokyo Academy of Music (東京音楽学校) and later the music department of the Tokyo National University of Fine Arts and Music.

5. Full coverage of Mason's role is outside the scope of this essay.

6. 『唱歌集』初編, *Shôkashû shohen* (*Shôka Collection*, vol. 1), edited by the Institute of Music, cited after Geidai 1987: appendix, page 18.

7. *Gebet* ("Lehr' mich beten") from Silcher n.d.: no. 1, words by Ernst Moritz Arndt. It is possible, however, that the immediate source of the Japanese song was an English song ("Murmur, Gentle Lyre") that uses the same melody. The words of *Oboro* are newly written and thus neither a translation of the German nor of the English version.

8. 『祝祭日唱歌樂譜』, *Shukusaijitsu shôka gakufu* (*Scores of Shôka for Public Holidays*), Tokyo 1893 (facsimile in Geidai 1987: 502–3) and many later editions.

9. Only one song in these volumes is in a traditional mode (a counting song taken over from an earlier schoolbook); six songs are in a minor key, one song is in a major key with modulation, and the remaining 110 songs are in a major key without any modulation, fifty-seven of them pentatonic, without the fourth and seventh scale degrees. See Kojima 1972: 55–56.

10. The sentence "The national *shôka* do not pass beyond the school gate" (国定唱歌校門を出でず) is so ubiquitous that we have not been able to determine its origins, but it states precisely the problem of early music education in Japan. Even in the 1930s, this sentence was used to criticize the current *shôka* textbooks (Sawasaki 1993: 171). According to Kindaichi 1995: 7, however, the statement was not really true after 1911, when the books of the *Shôka* for Common Schools series appeared and were made the basis of all music teaching material for public schools.

11. See, for example, Eppstein 1982: 98–115.

12. The works are published as 『幼稚園唱歌』, *Yôchien shôka* (*Kindergarten*

Shôka) (Tokyo: Kyôeki Shôsha Shoten, 共益商社書店 (editor and publisher), 1901).

13. See, for example, Woldering 1998.

14. This historical episode is often called "Taishô democracy," although a democracy as a political system was not installed.

15. The word *dôyô* is used for the composed pieces as well as for the poems themselves.

16. The participation of the leading poets and composers in the children's song movement is the decisive factor that makes the difference for the *shôka*. Kindaichi Haruhiko writes: "The Japanese *dôyô*, I am convinced, are made for children by a collaboration of the first-rank poets and first-rank composers of the middle Taishô era [1912–26]. It is a cultural heritage which should be held in honor throughout the world" (1995: 5).

17. On the Japanese lied and its relation to the *dôyô*, see Gottschewski and Gottschewski 2004: 367–82, esp. 372.

18. In songs based on Japanese traditional scales, phrases usually end with an ascending major second on a nuclear tone. If the nuclear tones are a fourth apart from each other, the upper neighbor of the lower nuclear tone and the lower neighbor of the upper tone (A and B-flat, in this example) are never used in succession. For the theory of Japanese scales and the concept of nuclear tones see, for example, Komoda and Nogawa 2002: 568–70.

19. However, while many of the *dôyô* use traditional elements in some way, it cannot be said that the use of a traditional scale in the melody is the norm. On the other hand, there are also a few *dôyô* that do not use Western tonality even in the accompaniment. See, for example, the song "Ano machi kono machi" by Nakayama Shinpei, cited in Gottschewski and Gottschewski 2004: 375–77.

20. Hakushû is the pen name of Kitahara, thus it is usual to cite him as Hakushû and not as Kitahara.

21. For example, Motoori Nagayo (1885–1945); see Gottschewski and Gottschewski 2004: 374.

22. See Gottschewski and Gottschewski 2004: 373.

23. At that time, a certification system for teaching materials was in force, which means that apart from the teaching materials edited by the Ministry of Cultural Affairs, only materials that had an official certificate from the Ministry were authorized. Among innumerable *dôyô*, only ten pieces made this hurdle (Koizumi 1969: 503).

24. See, for example, the song *Nanatsu no ko* by Noguchi Ujô (composed by Motoori Nagayo), cited in Gottschewski and Gottschewski 2004: 374.

25. It is not quite clear from Isawa's writings (and this was perhaps a question of lesser importance to him) whether he believed that the common basis of Western and Asian music arose from anthropological constants, historical connections, or mere coincidence. In the research report of his institute from 1884 are found some

speculations about a common source of Western and Eastern music in India. See, for example, Eppstein 1982: 89–90.

26. Bôta Kazuma, 坊田壽眞『日本郷土童謡名曲集』, *Nihon kyôdo dôyô mei-kyokushû* (*The Best Children's Songs from the Japanese Home*) (1932), cited after Gondô 2003: 43.

27. 『ウタノホン 上』, *Uta no hon jô* (*The Book of Songs I*), edited and published by the Ministry of Cultural Affairs (Tokyo, 1941).

28. In the school music of the first half of the twentieth century, the songs for the first school years are almost exclusively pentatonic. They gradually become heptatonic for the higher classes. See Kojima 1972: 56.

"And the Youth Shall See Visions"

Songleading, Summer Camps, and Identity among Reform Jewish Teenagers

JUDAH M. COHEN

And the old shall dream dreams, and the youth shall see visions
And our hopes shall rise up to the sky.
We must live for today, we must build for tomorrow.
Give us time, give us strength, give us life.

—*Debbie Friedman, Reform Jewish songleader*
and songwriter, and former songleading instructor
at the Kutz Camp Institute, 1981. Based on Joel 2:28.

August 10, 2000, at the Kutz Camp Leadership Institute, a Reform Jewish summer camp in the small Hudson Valley town of Warwick, New York. After a
standard communal dinner in the camp's dining hall, the over 150 high-school-
aged campers were treated to a special presentation. Normally, two college-
aged songleaders with guitars in hand would take their places on a central
raised platform and lead a "song session," comprising several selections from a
common repertoire. On this particular evening, however, the hired songleaders
receded to the back of the room and provided support to a class of fourteen
campers they had trained over the previous three weeks. Two or three campers at a time came to the platform, each group leading a song using techniques
they had acquired and rehearsed during their brief training period. The rest
of the campers rose from their seats to sing, dance, and clap along, welcoming
their peers into a new station within the camp's social fabric. After each group
left the stage, cheers of approbation confirmed the campers' achievements. Yet
for the feted new songleaders, such recognition was only a start: upon leav-

ing camp, many intended to assume positions of musical leadership within their local religious youth groups, or at other Reform Jewish camps, serving as anointed arbiters of a repertoire and art form particularly associated with young people.

In this essay, I will explore Reform Jewish songleading—the practice of leading a group in liturgical and paraliturgical Jewish singing, often using a folk rock–based idiom—as a phenomenon both propagated and mediated by young people.[1] Although initially established by adults as a way to educate youth, songleading has come to embody an organic voice and deep culture that the Reform youth movement claims as its own. I argue here that this songleading example provides important insights into the wider context of music associated with children: in particular, that such music may be associated more with social constructions than with actual perceptions of human development. Following ideas introduced by Patricia Shehan Campbell, Lawrence Hirschfeld, and Nancy Lesko, I will suggest that songleading, despite being associated with a limited age range by many, holds a crucial stake in helping young people create a musical value system that can serve as a basis for their musical culture as they enter the adult world.

I will use both "youth" and "childhood" to denote the first several years of a person's life, typically characterized by a socially sanctioned financial dependence upon older providers (such as parents or relatives). In the United States, an individual's eighteenth birthday is often denoted as a time when childhood ends and adult responsibilities start, including the right to vote and (theoretical) eligibility for the military draft. Yet the border between youth and adulthood tends to be far more porous, as other age-based legislation and practice tends to exhibit: the right to operate most motor vehicles in the United States is granted to those who have reached the ages of between fifteen to eighteen, depending on the state; an individual must be twenty-one to purchase alcoholic beverages; many families who send their children to college support them through graduation, at which point they are expected to make their own livelihood; and in Europe, youth discounts and identity cards often are valid through age twenty-five. A recent study conducted by the University of Chicago's National Opinion Research Center, meanwhile, has reported that Americans on average considered adulthood to begin around age twenty-six ([Harms] 2003).[2] Thus, in this essay, "youth" and "childhood" will represent a condition rather than an age span, during which individuals are not expected to provide for themselves.

◆ Theorizing Youth as Youth

Although children were considered an important group for song collectors from the end of the nineteenth century (see, for example, Fletcher 1888 and Yoffie 1947 as well as the broad bibliography compiled in Minks 2002), musical studies within the past several decades seem to maintain a decidedly adult-centric bias. Young people are remarkably overlooked as practitioners and purveyors of musical traditions; and if mentioned at all, they tend to receive either passing inclusion as part of a larger project (Finnegan 1989: 163–64, 224–26) or anecdotal reference (Feld 1992: 20–43). This lack of attention seems to be accompanied by an unstated perception of youth as denizens of a transitory "phase" in their lives that is less stable, less powerful, and to some extent less legitimate than the "arrival" of adulthood. Although implied only through exclusion in most studies, such perceptions come through clearly in those ethnomusicology works devoting any significant space to discussing youth: young people are typically portrayed less as individuals with individual ideas than as developing "preadults" striving to conform to a hegemonic "adult" culture.

Paul Berliner, for example, devotes the first chapter of *Thinking in Jazz* (1994: 21–35) to childhood experiences of established jazz musicians. His portrayal of how his interviewees became interested in the jazz idiom, presented by stringing together several musicians' childhood memories, is effective in creating a smooth group narrative of the "life in jazz." As expressions of the youth themselves, however, they make weak evidence. The anecdotes are removed by decades, are colored by the subsequent layering of many years of experience, and may better represent the interviewees' needs to portray their lives as logical trajectories. Berliner's interest in the hindsight narrative—rather than the actual experience—is underlined by his lack of critical comment on the content of his anecdotes. Following in the tradition of innumerable musician biographies and autobiographies, "youth" thus becomes more a reflection of adult memory than of youth activity itself.

Another approach outlined in the literature involves portraying children as proto-adults, who are analyzed to gain an understanding of how people form ideologies commonly discussed within the "adult" world. Such is the case in Kyra Gaunt's illuminating dissertation studying black girls' songs (1997). The girls' sound worlds to her are portals into understanding how the young girls formulate a sense of "blackness" through their play; yet "blackness" (and even "femaleness"), in Gaunt's view, appears to be a teleological, unitary concept

undifferentiated by age. She notes: "[Girls' games] represent a gendered female expression in black culture at the same time as they reflect the essences
of black music making as a whole" (xi). Gaunt's project thus focuses less on
the phenomenon of children *as* music makers than on the notion that music
making *informs* important general concepts of difference. Whether a child or
an adult addresses these concepts differs mainly in content, not culture.

John Blacking's 1967 study of Venda children's song, finally, shows more
clearly an unconscious bias against the legitimacy of children's musical practices in the literature. Blacking openly admits he entered the field with the ex-
pectation that he would find Venda children's song to be merely a simplified
version of adult song. Through careful observation and analysis, however, he
discovered that just the opposite was true: the repertoire of Venda children
actually had little overlap with the common adult repertoire, and it involved
what he saw as different musical styles. More remarkably, Blacking observed
that the musical content of the children's songs seemed to be just as complex
as that of the adults. Blacking's conclusion, however, was curious. Despite ac-
knowledging that children and adults appear to exist in their own musical
worlds, he concluded that, "although the songs are apparently unrelated to
adult music, and they do not represent a musical *gradus ad Parnassum,* their
structure is in fact related to the adult music which the conditions of their social life enable them to hear on many occasions" (Blacking [1967] 1995: 29). De-
prived of a direct and documentable link between children and adult music
in terms of the material itself, Blacking appears to have taken a more abstract
route in championing the adult world as the primary arbiter of musical value,
framing childhood as a time for testing out musical norms imposed by a stable
(and static) adult world.

The model of an adult hegemony imposing itself on youth is also used
as a prime motivating factor in the Birmingham School's literature on musical subcultures. Spearheaded in musical terms by Dick Hebdige's *Subculture* (1979), these sociological studies tend to focus on the youth that rebel
against what they perceive as an adult hegemonic power. Subculture became
an important concept in the emerging field of popular music studies; and its
sociological background has since been supplemented and critiqued by eloquent fieldwork-based explorations of youth expression in the rap scene (Rose
1994) and dance clubs (Thornton 1996), among others. Yet while this important body of work effectively examines the voices of "youth," it also portrays
young people as most expressive when they enter into a politically charged,
often anti-Establishment atmosphere. The forms of social deviance displayed
within the dance club scene, just to cite one example, represent only a nar-

row focus on young peoples' lives and highlight a somewhat constructed politics of identity and power. To remedy this, I coincide with Sarah Thornton in her assertion that "a shift away from the search for 'resistance' actually gives fuller representation to the complex and rarely straightforward politics of contemporary culture" (1996: 168). Even more, however, I wish to suggest that a study of youth-associated politics and identity exhibits fundamental differences from the project of understanding a system of youth expression *as* youth expression.

Patricia Shehan Campbell's 1998 book *Songs in Their Heads* is one of the most prominent scholarly works to date that focuses on the process of children making music *as* children.[3] "Music may be [children's] own expansive and expressive thinking at work, a means through which to develop thoughtful reflections of their experiences," she notes. "But we have seldom taken the time to tap either the musical thoughts or the natural behaviors of children or to seek systematically the function of music in their daily lives" (5). Campbell splits her fieldwork into two main approaches: observations of children's musicality during times of play, and personal interviews with several young research subjects. From these differing forms of research, she formulates a model of childhood music making that is generative, deeply internalized (thus her title), and strongly based in the sounds children encounter everyday. Children, Campbell shows, have the power to hear and interpret the world on their own terms, often holding little regard for the value systems extant in the adult world. By studying the music children make from a child's perspective, therefore, it becomes possible to recognize them within their own vibrant and original culture area. Such an approach is highly significant, for as the anthropologist Lawrence Hirschfeld (2002: 624) has noted, it overturns the notion that childhood is merely reverse-engineered adulthood. By empowering the role of children as learners and creators of their own cultural norms, the equation can be viewed in reverse: might adulthood in fact be created anew by each successive generation of children?

It is this model that I wish to explore. The population I studied consisted of high school students who gathered more or less voluntarily in a specialized religious summer camp devoted to developing stronger ties with their religious movement and heritage.[4] Campers were for the most part under the immediate supervision of staff members only slightly older than they were, and they were encouraged to form a coherent and responsible community of peers during their monthlong stay together.[5] Notably, the use of music—and songleading in particular—was especially prominent in creating this community. On display in times of "play" (such as spontaneous sound making or after-dinner song sessions), the songleading repertoire also extended to formally or-ganized events such as daily religious services and evening programs, creating a sort of musical language that campers used to express themselves in a variety of religious and nonreligious group and individual settings.

Yet the creation of meaning at a summer camp in one given session pre-sents only an ahistorical snapshot of childhood, frozen in time and deceptive in significance (or lack thereof). Following Hirschfeld's lead, I will attempt to investigate songleading not only as a musical discourse of a particular age group at a particular time, but—through historical research, interviews with former campers, and observations of current debates in the Reform Jewish musical scene—as a foundational part of a musical life trajectory. My inter-est in doing so is to put "youth music" into a more deeply qualitative context, thereby surmounting the artificial (perhaps culturally imposed) boundaries of the childhood/adult dichotomy. Such an approach, I suggest, will provide additional insight into understanding the formation and propagation of chil-dren's culture; but even more than that, I hope it will challenge basic assump-tions in the literature linking chronological and cultural maturity.

◆ Summer Camp: A Place to Cultivate Youth

Songleading is a particularly useful foil for the investigation of childhood culture, primarily due to its association with a prime location for youth expres-sion: the overnight summer camp. As anthropologist Randal Tillery (1992) has suggested, the inherent nature of youth summer camps is one of heightened reality, fostered, interestingly enough, by the participants' removal from their respective home environments. Typically taking place in a pastoral setting, summer camps gather young people into temporary, homogeneous, closed communities, frequently for several weeks at a stretch. During this time, away from the standard social, power, and technological structures of their home communities, campers often have the opportunity to reflect upon and trans-form themselves. Notes Tillery, "for some[, summer camp is] a place at a dis-tance from their home life where they actually do get the chance to think criti-cally about that life and . . . make different choices for themselves based on their new understanding" (1992: 386). At the same time, the summer camp en-vironment emphasizes interaction and cooperation among the young attend-ees, who, while supervised by older individuals, become the center and focus of camp life. Campers often feel the freedom to express themselves with par-ticular vigor as a result; more broadly, this leads camp units to cultivate their own collective cultural identities and value systems over the course of the camp session. In this manner, the group experience becomes a dominant discourse throughout the campers' times together and often continues to operate as an entity of particular emotional value once camp itself has ended. Many camps, for example, have helped campers retain their sense of community well beyond the camp session itself by distributing yearbooks, holding reunions, selling T-shirts, and sending out promotional videotapes.[6]

Reform Jewish camps also aim to foster a sense of group identity among its attendees, albeit with an added agenda. Started in earnest in 1948 by several of the movement's young rabbis,[7] Reform Jewish camping programs (initially called Youth Leadership Institutes) aimed to instill young Reform Jews with a knowledge of and passion for an idealized Reform Jewish lifestyle; the founders hoped young people who attended the programs could eventually incorporate the practices and knowledge they learned at camp into their lives at home. Camps would additionally encourage community and participation in other realms of Reform Jewish life over the rest of the year: campers could meet and form friendships with other Jewish young people from their local geographical region, thus leading to strengthened local synagogue youth groups.[8] Brought together under the promise of an educational yet recreational program, campers were taught religious texts and prayers as part of their experience, and they were encouraged to apply what they learned to their own lives, reinventing Jewish tradition in their own images.

Songleading was an important part of the camping curriculum. Modeled initially on musical activities of German Jewish youth organizations, Zionist youth groups and American Christian Evangelical camps (see Cohen forthcoming; Sack 1940: 7), songleading (described initially as "group singing") was initially viewed by the Reform camping movement's founders as an essential element of the camping experience. In addition to reinforcing a sense of communal identity among campers, group song sessions served as opportunities for organizers to reinforce the camp's religious and political agendas— which framed a progressive vision of Reform Jewish religious and social values. The camping scene's first rabbis, who also took amateur roles as its inaugural songleaders, generally led without instruments or much musical experience; accounts of the first years of summer camping appear to credit enthusiasm rather than musical skill as a prime factor for inspiring campers to open their mouths in song. As the Reform Jewish camp program gained momentum, however, and began to expand to several regional sites throughout the United States, organizers began to hire individuals with vocal and guitar competence to take either full or partial songleading responsibilities. At first organizers sought songleaders from outside the camping system, but in time former campers filled songleading roles more and more frequently. Over the following decades, the average age of a songleader thus dropped significantly, and eventually songleaders became a group of older peers almost continuous in age with the oldest campers.

Through the collective efforts of songleaders and camp administrators, songleading and group singing become an important part of many elements of the camping experience, expanding most notably to include the musical settings for daily religious services. Songleaders further promoted the values of the genre by offering songleading classes, composing new songs to Jewish liturgical texts, and taking on personae that mirrored those of well-known musical artists in the commercial folk music industry. Campers, meanwhile, saw the developing musical style as reflective of their own sentiments both as Jews and as Americans. Through its centralized placement, songleading thus became an emblem of the Reform Jewish camp experience itself.

Within this cultural environment, the Kutz Camp Institute came to take a special role. Founded in 1965, Kutz was initially intended to be a permanent home for the movement's annual Leadership Institute, the national summer retreat for high school students that had served to launch the postwar Reform camping boom in 1948. Songleading had been an important element of this leadership experience from the start, and by the early 1960s attendees were receiving reel-to-reel tapes of songs taught and sung during each year's Institute.[9] Once the land for Kutz had been purchased and the camp sessions begun there, however, this practice took a significant new direction: the organizers of the Institute created an educational track specifically intended to instruct select campers in the techniques and repertoire of songleading. Kutz thus set itself up as a national, centralized site for the transmission of the Reform Jewish songleading tradition. High school students from around the country would come to learn the rudiments, cultural norms, and repertoire of the Reform songleading style, studying directly with experienced, hired songleaders who were themselves older peers. Upon completion of this course, students were expected to songlead on their own at camps and youth groups within their local regions. In this manner, the Reform Jewish youth movement was able to maintain both a standard of quality and a regularized technique on a national level. At the same time, the songleading track ensured that youth would continue to propagate the art form, and through this reinforce the songleader's position as a prominent member of the movement's youth culture. Nearly all the movement's most prominent songleaders would receive their seminal training and experience in this program as teenagers, and several later returned to teach the training course themselves.

The impact of the songleading track was considerable. Even among those campers *not* in the songleading program, guitars became commonplace items to bring to camp. Informal jam sessions organized by the campers would supplement scheduled songleading activities at religious services and after meals. New songs in the Jewish folk idiom became exciting commodities, composed, exchanged, and debuted at the camp; and in many cases new compositions and older "discoveries" were disseminated to the rest of the movement via recordings and personal contact originating at Kutz. Through such activities young people were able to fashion songleading into a cultural voice that addressed their needs as Reform Jews, gathering in the process an eclectic repertoire of hundreds of songs.[10] Most importantly, however, although loosely overseen by adults, most of the camp's songleading activity was relegated to a relatively narrow age range—from the youngest campers at fourteen to the hired songleaders in their early twenties.

By the time of my observation, the Kutz songleading program had instructed many hundreds of teenagers, who came to see themselves as interconnected participants in a longstanding tradition. Former students I interviewed looked back on the experience as a defining time in their lives, both in gaining deep insight into the repertoire and the style, and in finding for themselves a role of spiritual leadership.

Kutz camp thus has come to serve almost as a laboratory "gold standard" for observing the progressive activity of Reform Jewish youth songleading. Despite several reorganizations of the camp's structure, songleading appears to have retained a similar meaning, usage, and training pedagogy throughout the course of Kutz's existence. My observations of songleading at Kutz in the summer of 2000, then, are intended to be seen as part of a historic pedagogical continuum of activity and philosophy, maintained as tradition at the camp.

◆ The Guitar as an Icon of Songleading

Those who entered the Kutz Camp Institute's central building in the summer of 2000 faced a striking image: jutting out from the far wall of the main room was a line of nearly thirty guitars, brought to the program by campers and counselors and stored there as a collective property display. The sight was plainly visible (and accessible) to campers as they walked to their dorms, programs, and meals. During periods of free time, including the few-minute stretches between scheduled activity sessions, individuals would routinely come over to the wall, pull out their instruments, and start using them for

informal song gatherings or practice sessions.[11] Continuing a long-held perception at the camp, the guitar served as a primary representative of the songleading experience, and of the camp experience in general.

Despite a clearly communicated philosophy propounded by the hired songleaders that songleading did not require technical competence on an instrument, the guitar served as a dominant icon for representing music and musical
leadership at the camp. The image and sound of the guitar was omnipresent
throughout each day, and those in musical leadership roles during services,
song sessions, and other musical activities invariably performed their duties
with guitars strapped around their shoulders. The instrument had an almost
exclusive presence throughout the camp session. During my period of observation, instruments other than the guitar rarely came to light, and when they
did appear, they nearly always served in a subservient role.[12] As a result, a guitar's mere presence served as an indicator that the person holding it was in a
position of authority, or at least aiming to assume a level of authority.

The guitar's widespread popularity also sustained a culture of guitar instruction and maintenance at Kutz. Proficiency on the guitar was considered
socially prestigious; to help campers, counselors with guitar experience offered
optional classes on developing guitar-playing techniques. Campers could frequently be seen practicing guitar by themselves or in groups, and those with
particularly advanced skills often received significant attention from their
peers. The instrument itself served as a medium of communication, with
campers exchanging songs through demonstrations of the necessary chords.
When it came to learning songs, campers would either experiment with guitar chords to find a suitable accompaniment for a song, or, in the event the
song was already part of the communal repertoire, refer to Reform movement-
sponsored chord sheets that were created in a standard chords-over-words format (without a melodic line). Students who participated in these processes
commonly discussed strumming technique, chordal knowledge, and favorite
guitar models in the process. The camp, meanwhile, supported these activities
by offering sets of guitar strings and picks for sale in their canteen, alongside
the standard fare of snacks and toiletries.

Beyond the physical instrument, the guitar's image and sound were themselves important indicators of camp and Reform youth experiences. During
the camp session, guitar cases were occasionally decorated as art objects, and
several served as canvases for the airing of political beliefs through scrawlings
or slogan-bearing stickers. In another case, students asked to create a mural
of the "things they liked most about Kutz" indicated singing by drawing a
staff with musical notes and a guitar. And guitar indicators were still stron-

ger in the camp's publicity materials: in a seventeen-and-a-half-minute promotional video ("UAHC Kutz Video" 2001–2) made for the Kutz Camp Institute in the fall of 2001, shots of people playing guitars appeared twenty times,
evenly spaced throughout the film, and a soundtrack of songs that featured
acoustic guitar played prominently throughout.

Through such placement and usage, the guitar thus gained its status as a
symbol of camp singing, and, by extension, of the camp experience overall.

◆ Creating, Compiling, and Personalizing Repertoire

The guitars were used to provide chordal support for a specialized communal repertoire, comprising settings of liturgical and paraliturgical texts as well
as a number of popular Israeli and American songs. Constantly in flux, the
repertoire had been published several times since the 1960s; the most recent
compendium, released in 2000, contained 366 songs, chosen because they were
considered the most popular throughout the many national veins of songleading practice.[13] Despite the several forms in which this compendium was
released, however—including a words-only songbook, a words-and-chords
"chordster," and, in 2001, an edition that included notated melodic lines—the
repertoire itself was practiced overwhelmingly as an orally transmitted genre,
with melodies and words acquired through group learning sessions and repetition. Campers would occasionally sing selections spontaneously based on
their mood or the occasion, and during song sessions or services they would
frequently sing along unimpeded, with the texts disseminated but often
unused.

Songleaders sorted this repertoire into two general categories. Music for religious rituals consisted mostly of settings for liturgical texts, meant both to
comprise and to supplement the camp's services. Repertoire of this type was
rarely taught formally; rather, campers who did not know the melodies already would learn them through frequent exposure and informal exchange.
Music for song sessions, meanwhile, was more recreational in nature. Spanning a much more varied subject matter, it was meant for an event solely dedicated to group singing. Well-known favorites were invariably included in each
summer's active song session repertoire, yet the hired songleaders were also
expected to teach the campers a number of new songs each year. Taken together, these two categories emphasized songleading's multifaceted role in the
lives of the campers.

Campers personalized their musical world still further by supplement-
ing songs with hand motions, verbal interjections, and alternate lyrics. Called

"shtick" by songleaders, these actions were usually performed in a song session environment. Though seemingly frivolous and tolerated only mildly by adult camp staff, shtick nonetheless served an important function to the campers by reinforcing a sense of communal knowledge, ownership, and mediation of the material. As Campbell notes, these kinds of utterances beautifully illustrate the role youth play as active mediators of the traditions passed down to them (1998: 66–70). I use as an example the phrase "nutter butter peanut butter" shouted between the verse and the chorus of a popular Reform movement song titled "Not by Might, Not by Power" (see ex. 10.1).

The utterance of this line at first appeared to be little more than a silly diversion; yet one camper, in a controversial service reading, used the phrase to illustrate her cohort's sense of tradition:

> It's the middle of the song session. A popular song is being strummed on [the songleaders'] magical music maker. . . . Then that line comes . . . that one line that brims with energy, with tradition—NUTTER BUTTER PEANUT BUTTER! Traditions are what shape Judaism. Traditions range from that special Kutz camp song to family gatherings at [Passover] to the lighting of the candles on Friday nights. The best thing about traditions is that they are constantly being created, reread and re-evolved. Traditions are what makes being Jewish special, for there are thousands of them in the many faces of Judaism. Always hold fast and stay true to your traditions, even if they are as tiny as blurting out "NUTTER BUTTER PEANUT BUTTER."[14]

Placed almost defiantly on the same level with Jewish holidays, shtick thus became the epitome of Jewish youth empowerment in its ability to help young people define and assert their own local culture with a greater intensity. Consciously and energetically inventing traditions in a manner almost as self-aware as Hobsbawm's own analysis (in Hobsbawm and Ranger 1992), the campers imposed their own "youth" voices upon the musical material they knew in a manner that differentiated them from disapproving adults.

The participants also cultivated a deep relationship with the repertoire through the creation of new songs. While new songs occasionally came to light through bursts of personal inspiration, their creation also entered the camp's schedule via a recognized class overseen by a counselor with songleading experience. The extent to which the songs were inculcated into the religious fabric of the camp became evident with the class's final "project": an optional evening service at the end of the session (coincidentally on the same day that the songleading students debuted in the dining hall) at which a few of the students

---

Example 10.1 Shtick from "Not by Might, Not by Power"

Words and lyrics by Debbie Friedman (1974), based on Zechariah 4:6.
Shtick appears in square brackets.

Verse:
The children sing ["La da di dah!"]
The children dream ["Awwww." Tilt head onto hands pressed together as if
   going to sleep.]
And their tears may fall, [Show tears falling from eyes with fingers]
But you'll hear them call, [Frame face with open hands, as if to listen]
And another song will rise [Place hands low to the floor, sometimes bending
   over; slowly bring them up throughout the rest of the verse. Yell:
   "Say what?"]
Another song will rise ["Say what?"]
Another song will rise. ["Nutter Butter peanut butter!"]
Transition into clapping pattern and ululation, leading to chorus.

---

put their work on display as functional parts of a religious ritual. Notably, the
new songs did not inspire the same level of participation as Kutz's regular song
sessions or scheduled religious services, since the settings were experimental in nature, and none were familiar to the campers. Nonetheless, the early
evening ritual attracted the largest group of any optional service that session:
over thirty-two campers packed the small pagoda reserved for the occasion.
As each creator played his or her song at the appropriate time of the service,
it became clear that regardless of each song's level of "success," the teens felt
pride and accomplishment in adding their own voices to the repertoire and
personalizing the summer's musical experience.

◆ Passing on the Tradition

Serving as mediators of this world were two songleaders in their early twenties. Poised at the end of their college years, these figures acted as the musical
elders at the camp. They were responsible for choosing the summer's repertoire, leading and organizing song sessions, coordinating music for religious
services and other events, and most importantly, transmitting the songleading
tradition to campers. Both had attended the Kutz songleading program as

teens, and over subsequent years both had taken on songleader roles in a variety of settings within Reform Judaism. As a result, the two professed a healthy respect for the generations of songleaders preceding them and embraced a set of values and pedagogic techniques that had been used for years to train young people for such musical responsibilities.

As had been the case since the songleading program's beginnings, the songleaders were responsible for leading an intensive, session-long course on songleading for interested campers with some musical experience who had wanted to become songleaders in their own right.[15] In July and August 2000, this course consisted of fifteen two-hour sessions held at the same time each day, following a format closely based on Kutz songleading classes from previous years.[16] As illustrated in example 10.2, each session focused on a particular topic, including basic song teaching techniques, body language, songleading with a partner, dealing with shtick, differentiating between songleading at religious services and song sessions, distinguishing between "songleading" and "performing," and choosing repertoire to shape a song session. At the start of every class, the songleader/instructors would analyze the previous evening's after-dinner song session with the campers, pointing out what they saw as particularly effective or ineffective moments while transitioning into the day's topic. Through such discussions, the students had the opportunity to see each song session through the eyes of the songleaders, and discuss the event using an insider language and set of criteria. Following these comments, the songleader/instructors would launch into the day's lesson, often offering exaggerated demonstrations to illustrate their points and foster conversation.

By the third day of instruction, a portion of each class had been set aside for students to present individual "teaches"—songleading simulations that the instructors evaluated in front of the whole group. The teaches were progressive: each camper's first attempt involved teaching a single song; the second teach, upon permission of the songleader/instructors, would be a brief, three-song session. It is important to note that songleading students did not aim to lead only their peers. Rather, in a nod to the songleader's broad presence within Reform Judaism, songleading students worked toward developing skills for age groups they intended to work with in their own lives: as part of every teach, the songleading student being evaluated would request that the other students act a certain age (ranging from five-year-olds to teenagers) to emulate an appropriate classroom or song session situation. The importance of being able to teach a broad range of ages could also be seen in the students' first scheduled opportunity to songlead in front of a "real" group: a subset of

Example 10.2 Topics Covered in Kutz Songleading Class, July–August 2000

July 23, 2000: Introduction.

July 24: "Teaches"*—basic teaching techniques.

July 25: The difference between songleading and performing/guest songleader. *Student teaches begin.*

July 26: Body language.

July 27: Instrumental care/musicality.

July 30: Setting the environment for a song session.

July 31: "Shtick" [alternate song texts, body motions, and insertions for songs within the repertoire] and how to handle it.

August 1: Teaches at local day camp.

August 2: "Manipulating" a group.

August 4: "Shaping" or planning a song session. Guest songleader.

August 6: Music theory for songleaders: Major/minor chords; relative minor; intervals; simple chord relationships. [Electronic keyboard brought in for illustration.]

August 7: Songleading for religious services. Guest songleader.

August 8: Working with a "co"[-songleader].

August 9: First rehearsal for Aug. 10 song session, Dining Hall.

August 10: Second rehearsal for Aug. 10 song session, Dining Hall/wrap-up.

August 10, afternoon: Dress rehearsal for Aug. 10 song session, Dining Hall.

August 10, evening: Student-led song session.

* A "teach" is an evaluated exercise in which a student attempts to teach a song to the rest of the class. Often the other students are instructed by the student to simulate people of a certain age group. Afterward, the student is critiqued publicly by both instructors and peers; the instructors give the student written evaluations later.

Kutz Camp's day care program (Camp Shalom), comprising children ranging from three to seven years old. Songleading students thus learned crucial skills by practicing them in diverse environments. At the same time, the campers came to view songleading as a discipline that could be used to inspire and instruct youth of all ages.

At the end of the course, students devoted class time to prepare for their own public song session, again under the guidance of the hired songleaders.

The instructors pooled the students into sets of two or three, each with at least one guitar player. Each group chose a song they wanted to lead, practiced it together, and then presented it several times in front of the songleader/instructors, who subsequently provided critique. Eventually these songs were ordered and "shaped" into a song session, which then became the songleading students' dining hall debut. By leading the young people through a series of practical exercises and on-the-ground discussions, the curriculum (as led by the hired songleaders) thus introduced students to a taxonomy of the major theoretical issues involved in songleading, while simultaneously providing practical opportunities for students to reinforce the skills they acquired.

Learning the role of the songleader took place outside of class as well. In addition to informal student practice sessions, songleaders-in-training had the opportunity to experience songleading as a constant musical presence at the camp. To usher in the Jewish Sabbath on Friday evenings, songleaders would beckon campers from their cabins and lead them, singing, into a group circle in an open field before proceeding to the dining hall for the ritual meal. Songleaders coordinated daily with the rotating groups of students assigned to lead each day's religious services, attempting to fulfill their liturgical music requests. Several counselors with songleading experience occasionally helped lead camp song sessions, or coordinated smaller cabin singalongs. Songleaders also provided campers ways to connect the activities to those of the secular folk music industry that had paralleled songleading throughout its history: before several song sessions, for example, the hired songleaders warmed up by singing the Indigo Girls' "Strange Fire" with each other; a visiting songleader, during a concert given at the camp, transitioned from a paraliturgical song in the Reform Jewish repertoire into a song by the Dave Matthews Band, to the delight of many in the crowd; and songs such as Joni Mitchell's "Circle Game" and Harry Chapin's "Cat's in the Cradle" appeared in the movement's most recent repertoire collection in their own special section. Campers clearly caught on to this dynamic; the songleading students, for example, as if to show their understanding of this crossover after their debut performance, gathered in a separate room after their dining hall debut and celebrated by singing Don McLean's "American Pie" along with several selections from the camp repertoire (fieldnotes, Aug. 10, 2002). In this way, both campers and songleaders-in-training could gain a textured understanding of the songleading culture in a wider context. These experiences would create deeply held values and provide a blueprint for reproduction once the campers returned to their hometowns.

◆ Signs of a Bounded Tradition: The Israeli Experience

Lest songleading be seen as a "universal" manifestation of teenage experience at the Kutz Camp Institute, it is important to recognize that the culture and norms of songleading were in many ways unique outcroppings of American Reform Jewish social organizations (most notably its national youth federation). Such a boundedness of the songleading tradition could be seen most clearly by the reactions of about a dozen Israeli teenagers brought to the camp as part of an exchange program. Facing starkly different cultural and religious norms from what they knew in their home country, most of the Israelis experienced a certain level of culture shock with the camp's practices in general and balked at participating in many of the camp's activities. Songleading, however, was one of the most emphasized forms of Jewishness at the camp and thus was a site of particular friction.[17]

The Israelis, unfamiliar with the American Reform Jewish songleading aesthetic and repertoire, frequently mocked and rebelled against the practice. They initially sat together at meals and talked among themselves during the song sessions that followed, consciously appearing to pay little attention to the songleaders. When goaded by the counselors to join the rest of the campers, several responded with exaggerated clapping motions, broad and disruptive dancing moves, and mocking vocables. At other song sessions they confronted the songleaders with loud comments: when the songleaders asked everyone to turn to a particular song in their songbooks, for example, several Israelis (and a few American followers) would shout back in singsong: "Number [x]?!? That's my favorite!" Religious services were also sources of deep skepticism for several of the Israelis, who would sit docilely or passively as others participated.[18] Although this behavior abated somewhat by the end of the camp session, it never fully disappeared.

The rejection of the songleading tradition by the Israeli campers was a clear indication both that songleading had its own well-developed insider value system, and (more important) that songleading was an experience that inculcated itself through exposure to a complex series of sonic expectations within the Reform Jewish cultural system. For the Americans, songleading broadly indicated community and Jewishness; to the Israelis, songleading appeared to represent the epitome of their foreignness, and their exposure to a representation of Judaism that clashed with the sonic religious sensibilities they experienced in their home country.

◆ Whose Childhood? Intergenerational Debates over the Songleading Tradition

Even as young people were discovering new worlds (and potential sources of income) through their songleading experiences, past songleaders often criticized them for what they saw as a progressive dilution of the art form, fraught with superficial ability, a lack of knowledge, and dubious spirituality. One particularly dramatic example of this critique took place while the songleading class was rehearsing for its end-of-session debut. While some students were practicing a popular song written for the Reform Jewish songleading repertoire in the 1970s, the song's composer (who had become a professional Jewish music recording artist) stopped in unannounced. The veteran songleader silently watched the presentation as it unfolded, and then confided in me that the songleading students did not seem to understand what they were doing (fieldnotes, Aug. 10, 2002). Such a comment clearly showed a disappointed distance from the emerging youth songleading scene, but at the same time it also portrayed the importance of the composer's *own* teen years in creating a lasting, meaningful personal ideology through the songleading medium.

My discussions with other past songleaders corroborated this position. Each generally saw him- or herself as encountering songleading at a high point of its musical history and then claimed that later songleaders were less likely to understand the purpose and meaning of the songleading tradition. Their comments suggested that they felt they had acquired their deepest "truths" about the tradition as young people and subsequently kept these truths throughout their lives. On a much broader level, similar reasoning may also help explain why the songleading style and repertoire has become so popular within *adult* Reform Jewish worship over the past three decades. As attendees of the summer camps grew to take on positions of adult leadership in the movement, the musical styles they encountered as youths frequently became a model for religious music in their adult lives.

Songleading's dominance as *the* format of musical expression at Kutz and other Reform Jewish youth camps, however (almost entirely at the exclusion of all other musical forms), has caused the style to be associated inextricably with youth. Among the movement's classically trained synagogue musical professionals, particularly cantors and liturgical composers (not to mention some musicologists), there tends to be some resistance to accepting songleading as a legitimate form of spiritual expression outside of a youth setting. Many of these figures have publicly dismissed the entire songleading genre as "camp music" and "children's music," describing it using the same terms attributed to accepted anthropological narratives of adolescence: artlessness, ignorance, overly energetic tendencies, and developing—but *not* mature—identity. Song-leading, in this view, becomes appropriate as a formative "stage" in a child's musical life, but only as preparation for adapting to the musical values of the adult world.

Interestingly, this approach mirrors assumptions made in much of the an-thropological and ethnomusicological literature involving childhood.[19] The increasing dominance of songleading in *adult* Reform Jewish settings, how-ever, in conjunction with several recent academic studies, challenges the no-tion that youth must grow into an empirical adult culture, or even that the differences between youth and adult aesthetic tastes are as clearly based on "maturity" as conventional wisdom would suggest. Sociologist Nancy Lesko, for example, has portrayed general approaches to child development theory as emerging from a late-nineteenth-century construct based on equating childhood with prevalent notions of cultural primitivism (2001).[20] Studies on children within the life courses of other cultures, moreover, suggest that childhood may be as much a product of social organization as it is of so-called biological and neurological advancement.[21] Thus, it is worth considering that arguments *against* the legitimacy and artfulness of youth expression may ulti-mately be a way of keeping young people "in their place" within a communally sanctioned life continuum. According to Hirschfeld, this teleological percep-tion of culture ironically serves to mask important processes of individual cul-tural development that do not fit with such a trajectory. In its place, he offers an alternative viewpoint: "Children do not become who their elders are," he suggests. "Rather their elders become what the child—or more specifically what the architecture of the child's mind—affords" (2002: 622). It may well be, therefore, that much of what we see as musical tradition actually gains its foothold *before* adulthood, and not *because* of it.

To the youth at Kutz Camp, songleading is a competent way of life—a mix-ture of sound, setting, and movement that makes no aspirations to the adult world. Young people practice, compose music, learn and mediate Jewish tra-dition with the intention of communicating their ideas to those around them, most of whom are their peers. Handed down from older youth to younger youth, who then re-create it to fit their own purposes, the art of songleading provides the soundtrack for young people as they explore themselves, their re-ligious leanings, and their worldviews. These musical experiences, moreover, can remain a deeply held touchstone for conceiving of and practicing religious expression. Manifesting a distinct ethos and culture, songleading thus becomes an instrument for young people to realize their visions in a spiritual place they can claim as their own, and perhaps to pursue these visions over a lifetime.

Notes

1. Songleading is today practiced regularly by adults as well. Here, however, I will look primarily at the young people who propagate the tradition within a summer camp setting.

2. The study also noted different religious and ethnic groups as having varying ideas on what constituted the transition into adulthood, and when and in what order those transitions should take place.

3. Along with Campbell's work, there is a burgeoning literature in the field of music and education that is increasingly exploring ethnographic research methods.

4. The substantial costs of the Kutz camping experience were shouldered in large part either by parents or by supporting home institutions.

5. The camp hierarchy was arranged such that each level of leadership was somewhat older than the previous one. Thus, high school–aged campers were supervised by college-aged counselors and songleaders; those who organized the counselors were somewhat older; those who served as rabbinic authorities were still older.

6. Many publications and ephemera have illustrated the importance to which summer camp attendees attribute their camp experiences (see, for example, the essays in Joselit and Mittelman 1993), and camps themselves appeal to the strength of community created during camp sessions to advertise the camp's success as well as draw campers back the following year.

7. The earliest recorded camping experiences in the Reform movement actually took place at the start of September 1939. See Sack 1940.

8. It is notable that the Reform Jewish youth organization—the National Federation of Temple Youth, or NFTY (pronounced "nifty")—was founded in 1939, just a few months before the movement's first leadership retreat.

9. Personal interview with Rabbi Bennett Miller, August 21, 2000.

10. This process of song discovery, learning, and dissemination took place at all of the Reform movement's regional camps, and each developed its own regional songleading traditions (many also published their own songbooks). Kutz's position as the only movement camp with a national clientele, however, gave it an enhanced status, and made it theoretically easier for material to be disseminated on a much wider scale.

11. Occasionally campers took out guitars that were *not* their own, though this practice often caused discontent. Those who had particularly valuable guitars that they did not want to expose to possible misuse kept them in their cabins.

12. The one exception to this was a small, beat-up box piano that occupied a less conspicuous corner of the same room where all the guitars were on display. Although counselors and a rare camper occasionally tinkered around on the piano, the tinkering usually had nothing to do with the camp repertoire but more reflected a camper's piano lessons from home.

13. For songleaders, at least, the plastic nature of the repertoire could be easily seen by the format of the publication containing material specific to their needs (that is, lyrics and chord charts, known as a "chordster"): the collection consisted of loose-leaf pages collected in a three-ring binder. Additional songs could consequently be added to a local repertoire by simply putting them through a three-hole punch and adding them to appropriate parts of the chordster.

14. Daf t'filah (page accompanying Sunday evening t'filah), Aug. 6, 2000. Copy in possession of author.

15. These students were known as "songleading majors," to denote the significant amount of time they devoted to learning songleading techniques (other campers signed up for different majors, including Jewish Leadership and Jewish Studies).

16. For an example of the pedagogy used in a previous year (1993), see Schachet-Briskin 1996: 16–22. Schachet-Briskin has a clearly different approach to the material, but for the most part he covers a very similar set of skills and ideas in song-leading.

17. For a greater in-depth discussion of the cultural dissonance Israeli youths face when brought to American summer camps, see Ezrachi 1995.

18. This skepticism was voiced more vividly at another Reform camp I observed earlier that same summer. The camp had been a pioneer in bringing Israelis in, though in this case to serve as counselors for a Hebrew-only-speaking unit. After a meal during the introductory "Staff Week," the Israeli counselors introduced themselves to the rest of the camp staff by giving their name and one thing they liked. When the final counselor introduced herself, she ended with "and I like TEH-FEE-LAH," using a grossly Americanized pronunciation of the Hebrew word for prayer services. Following this, the rest of the Israeli counselors meandered back to their seats, loudly singing "la la la" to no particular tune.

19. See, for example, Minks 2002 and Hirschfeld 2002.

20. This theory is also discussed briefly in Minks 2002: 381.

21. See, for example, Bock and Sellen 2002 and the five essays their article introduces.

Afterword

Amanda Minks

Studies of music and childhood have often alternated between a focus on how children are different from adults and a focus on how groups of children in various times and places differ from each other. Perhaps children's lives have always been perceived as somehow different from adults', but neither the boundaries nor the content of childhood have been constant over time and across social, cultural, and geographical space. It is not coincidental that generational and cultural notions of difference became the object of systematic study in the eighteenth and nineteenth centuries, when new social formations emerged from shifting production systems, exploration and imperialism juxtaposed radically different ways of life, and faith in science and reason opened up human nature itself to scrutiny.

Most modern discourses on children are rooted in Enlightenment notions of childhood innocence (as opposed to Catholic and Puritan doctrines of original sin) as well as a developmental scheme linked to sociocultural evolutionism. These assumptions were foregrounded in late-nineteenth-century studies of children's songs and games, part of a larger project aimed at recovering remnants of human history. It was believed that antiquated habits—relics of past civilizations—were preserved among those most removed from rationality and modernity: Western children, women, and peasants, as well as all non-Western "others." Western children, in this view, recapitulated the stages of human development, from primitive to civilized, while non-Western others, as well as the internal others represented by women and peasants, occupied a state of arrested development (Schwartzman 1978: 46). As Judah Cohen points out in his contribution to this volume, childhood was equated with cultural primitivism. The ideological construction of nonmodern others—closer to nature than to culture, sheltered from literacy and rationality, grounded in the concrete tasks of everyday life—was crucial to the constitution of modernity (Bauman and Briggs 2003).

One of the central ways that childhood figures into the construction of modernity is in the development of the modern nation-state. Children living through European nationalisms in the nineteenth century and postcolonial nationalisms in the twentieth have been, on the one hand, crucial sources of "authentic" national culture (through their presumed conservatism) and, on the other hand, objects of educational projects for producing new kinds of citizens. In their study of this process in early twentieth-century Japan, Hermann Gottschewski and Machiko Gottschewski reveal a tension, common to modern nationalisms, between asserting an authentic or originary national difference and domesticating a cosmopolitan language of modernity—here, Western classical music. The "authentic" in this case was drawn from antiquated poetic texts and from a particular style of *warabe-uta,* vernacular children's songs, which supplanted local differences and contemporary features with an idealized rural image of Japanese childhood. The Gottschewskis suggest that the cosmopolitan approach became dominant in nation- and person-building projects through musical composition and education, but local practices in schoolyards and homes continued the transmission of regional genres.

The Gottschewskis' essay represents just one of the important areas of research this volume broaches that has received too little attention.[1] Below I discuss other contributions this volume makes to understanding the relationship between music and childhood. These intertwined areas include musical designs for socialization, adult recollections of musical practices in childhood and youth, and musical representations of and through children.

◆ Musical Designs for Socialization

Several contributors to this volume allude to the concepts of enculturation and socialization, which have been central tools in studies of music and childhood, though with varied understandings of the terms. In the 1940s the term *enculturation* was promoted by the anthropologist Melville Herskovits as "the aspects of the learning experience . . . by means of which, initially, and in later life, [man] achieves competence in his culture" (Herskovits 1948: 39, quoted in Merriam 1964). Alan Merriam, one of Herskovits's students and a founder of American ethnomusicology, subdivided the concept into the specific processes of socialization, education, and schooling. Socialization, according to Merriam, referred to "the process of social learning as it is carried on in the early years of life" (1964: 146). Education was to signify "the directed learning process, both formally and informally carried out, for the most part during childhood and adolescence—which equips the individual to take his place as an adult member of society." Merriam cited Herskovits's definition of schooling: "Those processes of teaching and learning carried on at specific times, in particular places outside the home, for definite periods, by persons especially prepared or trained for the task" (Herskovits 1948: 310; quoted in Merriam 1964: 146).

The problem with the term *enculturation,* from today's perspective, is that it reifies culture as a fixed object to be instilled in the labile minds and bodies of children in a particular community. It obscures the processual and often conflictive nature of cultural practices—which are not easily corralled in bounded communities—and it obscures the dialectical, intersubjective nature of socializing activities. As *enculturation* has fallen out of use as an explanatory tool, *socialization* has been refigured, notably in the language socialization paradigm, to encompass interactive learning contexts in any phase of the life cycle.[2] While most studies, until recently, have focused on the ways that adults socialize children, it is also clear that children socialize one another, and they socialize their elders into new roles and activities, as any new parents can attest. Making *socialization* an umbrella term for social learning has the advantage of illuminating continuities and disjunctures between formal and informal learning contexts within and across age groups.

I use the phrase "musical *designs* for socialization" because, as some of the essays in this volume attest, plans to socialize children through music do not always work out precisely as the planners intended. As Judah Cohen writes, the founders of the Kutz Camp Institute initiated song-leading traditions to promote religious and political agendas as well as a sense of camp community. They may not have foreseen the way that phrases such as "nutter butter peanut butter" would be inserted into religious songs as kids made the traditions their own. Joy Calico writes that the aim of the postwar *New German Folk Songs* was to inculcate in youth "the values of peace, cooperation, hard work, optimism, confidence, and respect for tradition" in an antifascist and socialist framework. Her investigation of the contemporary attitudes of Germans who had sung the songs in their youth suggests that the songs may be remembered for their lyrical and ideological content, but perhaps more often they are "triggers for memories," adults' nostalgic evocations of their lives as children.

The focus on musical designs also points to the fact that historical documents usually tell us more about the institutional structures and musical forms intended for socialization than about children's experiences interacting with them, or about the ultimate outcome of these encounters. For example, Susan Boynton and Isabelle Cochelin's essay paints a vivid picture of the institutional regimentation of eleventh-century child oblates, and of the central role played by music in religious education and in the ritual embodiment of institutional hierarchies. Yet, as Boynton and Cochelin remark in their conclusion, the monastic customaries from which this portrait was constructed were not written from the perspectives of the oblates. We can only surmise that the inculcation of religious ideals was not all-encompassing based on descriptions of surveillance and discipline, which signal potential acts of transgression.

What comes through in Calico's work on the *New German Folk Songs* is the indeterminacy of songs engineered to shape identity. Unforeseen events and influences may interfere with musical designs for socialization, and the meanings attached to particular songs may vary from person to person and over time. Music is undoubtedly a powerful socializing and unifying force, which is one of the reasons it is so often employed by political and religious institutions aimed at instilling particular ideologies in children and youth. However, it remains unclear to what extent music, in and of itself, can effect the transformation of subjectivity, and, crucially, to what extent subjectivities forged through music and other expressive practices endure over time. In other words, what is the long-term significance of texts, melodies, and movements internalized in childhood and youth? On one hand, repetitive bodily practices—an important part of what Bourdieu called the "habitus"—are surprisingly enduring, and these practices are often means of socializing the ideological configurations they index.[3] On the other hand, a person who genuflects, without thinking, at the appropriate moment in a Catholic mass is not necessarily a devout believer, and a person who joins in singing the national anthem at a baseball game is not necessarily a patriot.

◆ Remembering Childhood and Youth

From the perspective of adults' reflections on their musical childhoods, coherent teleologies of development often supplant a recognition of the contingency and indeterminacy of designs for socialization. This is not to say that one view is more accurate than the other, but rather that parents, teachers, or curriculum planners can never know exactly which elements learners will ultimately pick out as significant in the stories they tell about developing musical competencies and social identities. Moreover, the significant elements singled out by "rememberers" may change over time and depending on the context of their narrations of childhood.

Portraits of childhood are a common component of musical biographies and autobiographies, but they are often viewed as a transparent recounting of events rather than creative reconstructions of the past, used for more or less explicit purposes in the present (a characterization some would attribute to all historical narratives). In her essay on Senegalese griots, Patricia Tang foregrounds the instrumentality—in terms of both use-value and exchange-value—of remembered narratives of childhood. Professional members of the hereditary griot class strategically use stories about their immersion as children in the griot tradition to stake claims to ownership and authenticity. These stories help to validate the status of griots as experts in the tradition, which is crucial to commodifying their knowledge and skills as musicians, teachers, and research consultants. Tang's essay suggests the need to make explicit the processes of co-construction inherent in the biographical interview—a genre in its own right that mediates much historical research—and the struggles for control over representation that it entails.[4] In anthropological and ethnomusicological disciplinary formations, the figure of the ethnographer has been uniquely authorized to identify and mediate/translate musical and cultural authenticity. Without denying the authorial power of this role, Tang provides a more dialogic view, showing how the notion of authenticity reenters discourses among those involved in the production of tradition (both researchers and researched), and how memories of childhood become central to narrating authenticity.

The essays by Heather Willoughby and Roe-Min Kok, as well as Patricia Tang, prompt—in different ways—the question of how remembered constructions of childhood mediate personal and social histories and identities. In the narratives of Korean traditional singers presented by Willoughby, there is a focus on a sense of fate, of predetermined events and encounters that led three young girls (including a fictional character in a film) to undertake the unconventional path of becoming a *p'ansori* singer. Paradoxically, through their rigorous adherence to a musical tradition bound to the past, these singers charted new and controversial social roles for Korean women, sacrificing marriage and family in order to commit themselves to achieving the highest levels of musical performance.

As Roe-Min Kok's essay illustrates, recollections of childhood musical experiences can also be a reflexive resource for social critique. Through reconstructing memories of her childhood activities learning piano in Malaysia under the British-based Associated Board of the Royal Schools of Music, Kok provides a trenchant critique of the socialization of racial hierarchies through artistic classifications. Her essay is a compelling illustration of Bourdieu's notion of symbolic violence: "gentle, invisible violence, unrecognized as such, chosen as much as undergone . . . [which] presents itself as the most economical mode of domination because it best corresponds to the economy of the system" (Bourdieu 2003: 127). Far from constituting an autonomous realm of sublime beauty, as the pedagogues of the ABRSM would have it, the discourses of Western classical music employed in colonialist education set up a hierarchy of value that rationalizes inequality as it disguises power.

By including essays methodologically based on the practice of remembering, this volume problematizes the rigid separation of narratives of childhood constructed through historiographic and ethnographic techniques from those constructed through personal reflection and oral history. None of these approaches provides a transparent view of the lived experience of children; they are all socially and culturally mediated, although in different ways. Kok, among others, makes explicit the link between childhood memories and the construction of identity, increasingly understood as an active, open-ended process that has everything to do with the particular place and moment from which one speaks, and the pathways traveled to reach that point. Stuart Hall writes,

> Though they seem to invoke an origin in a historical past with which they continue to correspond, actually identities are about questions of using the resources of history, language and culture in the process of becoming rather than being: not "who we are" or "where we came from," so much as what we might become, how we have been represented and how that bears on how we might represent ourselves. Identities are therefore constituted within, not outside representation . . . [They are] not the so called return to roots but a coming-to-terms-with our "routes." (1996: 4)

In this view, childhood experiences and the practice of remembering do not determine identity, but they are crucial tools in its construction.

As Willoughby's and Tang's essays illustrate, remembering childhood is also a tool in the process of constructing tradition, of creatively bridging the gap between expressive utterances of the past, the present, and the future. Richard Bauman and Charles Briggs eloquently make this point in discussing the poet Arunkumar Sarkar's recollection of hearing his parents and grandparents recite poetic and religious texts as a child: "[What is foregrounded] is the experiential and social and expressive resonance that derives from the assimilation of discourse to other discourse, the ways in which utterances are aligned to the already-said and anticipate the to-be-said in the discursive realization of social—here kinship—relations through time. . . . Here, tradition is a discursive accomplishment, a symbolic, interpretive construction creating discursive links to the past, rather than an intrinsic quality of pastness inherent in a perduring textual object" (Bauman and Briggs 2003: 319). Bauman and

Briggs argue that form matters in acts of traditionalization; the particularities of shape, sound, and texture provides the resources for making connections between temporal moments. Expressive utterances, be they musical or poetic, embody both a history and a futurity, which are variously fleshed out through the generations. The links between different temporal moments of expressive production may be constructed through a "regime of textual fidelity, close alignment of the now-said to the already-said" (320). On the other hand, they may be constructed as rupture, maximizing "the intertextual distance between current and antecedent discourse." Whether they signify continuity or rupture, recollections of childhood often play a key role in the "webs of discourse" that give meaning to social and musical practices and identities.[5]

◆ Representations of and through Children

All of the essays in this volume—including this afterword—entail representations of children or childhood achieved through different methods and with different aims. An advantage of juxtaposing constructions of childhood based on ethnographic methods with constructions based on historiographic or self-reflective methods is precisely to highlight their commonality as mediated representations.

In discourses on identity and agency, the term *voice* is often used as a gloss for the authentic expression of self-representation and intentionality. For example, in a discussion of historians' search for "the voice of the child," Harry Hendrick (2000: 52) writes, "True, children are intimidated by a "dominant discourse," but it does not necessarily follow that they *have* to speak "with the voices" of this discourse. It is not inevitable: they may speak *through* the discourse, thereby altering it in subtle ways. All dominant discourses contain within them resistant themes. To suggest otherwise is to deny children any potential for their own voices." However, the essays in this volume suggest a need for a broader conception of "voice," one that is still tied to representation but not necessarily a self-representation of internal desires and identity.[6] For example, Anne McLucas's analysis of the Apache girls' coming-of-age ceremony challenges the equation of the singing or speaking voice with agency and power. Other than the sound of jingles on their dresses as they dance, the girls remain almost entirely silent during the ceremony; nevertheless, they are seen as powerful, and they may later perform influential political roles in the community. McLucas's essay also draws attention to the importance of detailed analysis of formal structure. While it is not intelligible outside of complexly interlocking social and cultural contexts, form is sometimes neglected in attempts to portray the discourses in which it is embedded. Attention to form—and to the ways that participants conceptualize it—can be a means of understanding the cultural variability of such concepts as voice and agency.

In his essay on choirboys in sixteenth-century Seville, Todd Borgerding writes that boys' voices were considered to be pure, high, sweet, clear, and natural—the epitome of vocal perfection. They were superior to women's voices, which, in spite of a high pitch range, were heard as "artificial" and "affected." As costumed performers, boys could represent male or female adults—often angels or prophets—while singing texts in a comprehensible, homophonic style that conveyed central doctrinal messages such as the mystical transformation of the Host into the body of Christ. The choirboys of Seville were not the authors or originators, but rather the *animators,* of the religious discourse to which they gave voice.[7] Their value as paid "spokespersons" for religious officials and, ultimately, for God, lay in the qualities attributed to their embodied voices, which indexed the innocence and goodness of children praised in the Bible as well as the purity and transcendence of the Host.

A very different set of representations of and through childhood is presented in Steven Huebner's essay on Ravel and Colette's *L'Enfant et les sortilèges.* Huebner analyzes the opera from the perspective of Freud's and (more surprisingly) Piaget's child development theories. Whether or not there are direct relations among them, juxtaposing "artistic" and "scientific" representations of childhood reveals the circulation of discourses that transcend the boundaries of a musical work or a scientific study. In this way *L'Enfant et les sortilèges* and Freud's and Piaget's developmental schemes are illuminated as distinctly modern imaginaries of childhood.

Huebner makes a provocative comparison between the characteristics of preoperational syncretism—posited by Piaget as a stage in child development—and common characteristics of aesthetic modernism. These characteristics include "mystical animism, flattening of the psychical and physical perspectives, isolation of the part at the expense of the whole, and concentration of one mode of perception at a time." Huebner mentions other works by Ravel, Stravinsky, and Satie in which the figure of the child becomes a "vehicle for modernist expression." It is significant that both Ravel's and Satie's musical representations of a child's perspective also involve representations of social and cultural difference. In a comment revealing the endurance of musically embodied otherness, Huebner points to the multiple, hierarchically organized cultural voices mediated by *L'Enfant et les sortileges,* producing in one passage "a cultural hodgepodge of ragtime and pentatonic *faux chinoiserie,* a tired cliché that to our ears today seems, if not vulgar, particularly lowbrow."

These essays suggest that studying musical representations of and through children may provide important insights into "the way that music has been used to construct, evoke, or mark alterity of a musical or a sociocultural kind" (Born and Hesmondhalgh 2000: 2). Following Georgina Born and David Hesmondhalgh, we might ask how Western composers' representations of childhood have drawn on other notions of social difference, and how those representations have shaped public notions of difference. Further research is needed to illuminate the construction of exoticism and authenticity through musical representations of childhood, perhaps appropriating the analytical term of *infantilism* to complement *primitivism* and *indigenism* in modernist aesthetic discourses.

Crucially, the marking of children and childhoods as different must be viewed in tandem with other forms of marking difference. In the musical and social discourses that construct different childhoods, children are represented —either directly or indirectly—as raced, classed, ethnicized, and sexed/gendered. Moreover, as social theorists of the second half of the twentieth century emphasized, there is no construction of difference outside of power relations. Even the apparently progressive framework of cultural relativism has been critiqued as a means of containing and provincializing others. Seeing beyond one's own culture and translating the cultures of others have been the privileged activities of the academic specialist; only by employing the "rational" language of social science can others participate in the discourse of cultural relativism (Bauman and Briggs 2003).

I have argued elsewhere that there is no clear line of development in musical research on childhood (Minks 2002). Contrasting paradigms coexist in public and scholarly discourses; some fall out of view for a time, only to resurface in another form. A universalist vision of childhood, highlighting children's difference from adults rather than between social groups, has been common in turn-of-the-century diffusionist research (Newell 1884), in Brailoiu's midcentury "child rhythm" thesis (Brailoiu 1954), and, not least of all, in late-twentieth-century human rights discourses (critiqued in Stephens 1995). Anthropologists and ethnomusicologists, for the most part, have focused on the social and cultural multiplicity of childhood, yet their focus, until recently, on bounded systems of socialization and enculturation has obscured the global political-economic patterns that affect even the most isolated field site and constitute the conditions of possibility for academic travel and research.

In a broad discussion of the kinds of differences constituted through music, Line Grenier (1989: 138) writes: "Music does not construct age, gender, or race as totally abstract or quasi-bureaucratic categorizations; what it does con-

tribute to constructing are specific, complex sets and patterns of social relations, processes of iteration and differentiation between historically produced
objects and subjects, through which individuals and groups define themselves
and others." Childhood, as a culturally variable frame and globally circu-
lating figure (Castañeda 2002), should be viewed not in isolation but as part
of a multidirectional web of historical and social relations (a point made by
Boynton and Cochelin in their study). The unique volume of essays presented
here helps to problematize commonsense notions of music in childhood by
outlining some of these webs of relations in which "children"—living and
imagined—are embedded that give meaning to musical practices and social
life.

Notes

1. Other innovative studies that discuss children's music or musical activities
in the context of nationalism and modernity include Kok 2003b and Anagnost
1997a and 1997b.

2. See Schieffelin and Ochs 1986; Schieffelin and Kulick 2004.

3. The habitus is a system of "durable, transposable dispositions" acquired
through habitual, embodied practices. These dispositions generate and organize a
social group's ensuing practices and representations, which are "adapted to their
outcomes without assuming a conscious aiming at ends" (Bourdieu 2003: 53).
Bourdieu provides a framework for theorizing musical practice as a realm not
only of cultural transmission, but also of the reproduction of social inequality. The
potential for social transformation is deemphasized in his work, as is a person's
capacity to reflect on and critique his or her position in a system of reproduction.

4. See Briggs 1986 and 2002.

5. For a concise discussion of anthropological approaches to tradition, see Bauman 2001.

6. This observation was informed by Amanda Weidman's 2002 study of another context—that of early recordings of South Indian classical music—in which
the singing voice came to signify something other than the identity and agency of
the singer.

7. See Goffman 1974: 517–18.

Bibliography

Abbate, Carolyn. 2001. *In Search of Opera*. Princeton, NJ: Princeton University Press.

Agawu, Kofi. 2003. *Representing African Music: Postcolonial Notes, Queries, Positions*. New York: Routledge.

Aitken, Samuel. 1897–98. *Mr. S. Aitken's Report on His Tour in Australasia & Canada 1897–1898*.

Aleshire, Peter. 2001. *Warrior Woman: The Story of Lozen, Apache Warrior and Shaman*. New York: St. Martin's.

Alexandre-Bidon, Danielle, and Didier Lett. 2000. *Children in the Middle Ages: Fifth–Fifteenth Centuries*, translated by Jody Gladding. Notre Dame, IN: Notre Dame University Press.

Althusser, Louis. 2001. "Ideology and Ideologized State Apparatuses: Notes Towards an Investigation." In *Lenin and Philosophy and Other Essays*, translated by Ben Brewster, 85–126. New York: Monthly Review.

Amit-Talai, Vered, and Helene Wulff, eds. 1995. *Youth Cultures: A Cross-cultural Perspective*. London: Routledge.

Amos, Heike. 1997. *Auferstanden aus Ruinen: Die Nationalhymne der DDR 1949 bis 1990*. Berlin: Dietz.

Anagnost, Ann. 1997a. *National Past-times: Narrative, Writing, and History in Modern China*. Durham, NC: Duke University Press.

———. 1997b. "Children and National Transcendence in China." In *Constructing China: The Interaction of Culture and Economics*, edited by Kenneth G. Lieberthal, Shuen-fu Lin, and Ernest P. Young, 195–222. Ann Arbor: Center for Chinese Studies, University of Michigan.

Andaya, Barbara Watson, and Leonard Y. Andaya. 1982. *A History of Malaysia*. London: Macmillan.

Ansorg, Leonore. 1997. *Kinder im Klassenkampf: Die Geschichte der Pionier-organisation von 1948 bis Ende der fünfziger Jahre*. Berlin: Akademie Verlag.

Appadurai, Arjun. 1990. "Disjuncture and Difference in the Global Cultural Economy." *Public Culture* 2 (2): 1–24.

Appel, Bernhard. 1994. "'Actually, Taken Directly from Family Life': Robert Schumann's *Album für die Jugend*." Translated by J. Michael Cooper. In *Schumann and His World*, edited by R. Larry Todd, 171–202. Princeton, NJ: Princeton University Press.

———. 1998. *Robert Schumanns "Album für die Jugend": Einführung und Kommentar.* Zurich: Atlantis Musik-Verlag.

Araiz, Oscar. 1989. Interview with Oscar Araiz. Program book for production of *L'Enfant et les sortilèges* at the Grand Théâtre de Genève. Bibliothèque de l'Opéra (Paris, Bibliothèque Nationale de France), *L'Enfant et les sortilèges,* dossier d'œuvre.

Ariès, Philippe. 1962. *Centuries of Childhood.* Translated by Robert Baldick. New York: Vintage Books.

Arnheim, Rudolf. 1998. "Beginning with the Child." In *Discovering Child Art: Essays in Childhood, Primitivism, and Modernism,* edited by Jonathan Fineberg, 15–26. Princeton, NJ: Princeton University Press.

Ashcroft, Bill, Gareth Griffiths, and Helen Tiffin, eds. 1989. *The Empire Writes Back: Theory and Practice in Post-Colonial Literatures.* London: Routledge.

The Associated Board of the Royal Schools of Music: Summary of the Ninety-Second Annual Report of the Board for the Year 1980.

The Associated Board of the Royal Schools of Music: Summary of the Eighty-Ninth Annual Report of the Board for the Year 1977.

The Associated Board of the Royal Schools of Music: Sixtieth Annual Report of the Board for the Year 1948.

Austern, Linda Phyllis. 1994. "'No Women Are Indeed': The Boy Actor as Vocal Seductress in Late-Sixteenth- and Early-Seventeenth-Century English Drama." In *Embodied Voices,* edited by Leslie C. Dunn and Nancy A. Jones, 83–102. Cambridge: Cambridge University Press.

———. 1998. "'Forreine Conceites and Wandering Devises': The Exotic, the Erotic, and the Feminine." In *The Exotic in Western Music,* edited by Jonathan Bellman, 26–42. Boston: Northeastern University Press.

Austin, Joe. June 2004. Review of *Encyclopedia of Children and Childhood in History and Society,* edited by Paula S. Fass. H-Net Listserv Book Review. H-Childhood@h-net.msu.edu. Available at http://www.h-net.msu.edu/reviews/showrev.cgi?path=119881097066018. Accessed August 18, 2005.

Basso, Keith H. 1990. *Western Apache Language and Culture: Essays in Linguistic Anthropology.* Tucson: University of Arizona Press.

Baudelaire, Charles-Pierre. 1925. "Morale du joujou." *L'Art romantique,* edited by Jacques Crépit. *Oeuvres,* vol. 2, 131–41. Paris: Louis Conrad.

Bauer, Sabine, Bockhorst, Hildegard, Brigitte Prautzsch, and Carla Rimbach, eds. 1993. *Woher—Wohin? Kinder- und Jugendkulturarbeit in Ostdeutschland.* Remsheid: Topprint.

Bauman, Richard. 2001. "Tradition, Anthropology of." In *International Encyclopedia of the Social and Behavioral Sciences,* edited by Neil J. Smelser and Paul B. Baltes, 15819–24. London: Elsevier.

Bauman, Richard, and Charles Briggs. 2003. *Voices of Modernity: Language Ideologies and the Politics of Inequality.* Cambridge: Cambridge University Press.

Becher, Johannes R. 1951. *Auf andere Art so große Hoffnung: Tagebuch 1950.* Berlin: Aufbau Verlag.

———. 1966–81. *Gesammelte Werke.* 18 vols. Berlin: Aufbau Verlag.

Bede the Venerable. 1960. *In Marci Evangelium Expositio. Bedae Venerabilis Opera,* vol. 2, part 3. Edited by David Hurst. Corpus christianorum series latina 120. Turnhout: Brepols.

Bell, Catherine. 1992. *Ritual Theory, Ritual Practice.* Oxford: Oxford University Press.

———. 1997. *Ritual: Perspectives and Dimensions.* Oxford: Oxford University Press.

Benedict of Nursia. 1972. *La Règle de Saint Benoît.* Introduction, translation, and notes by Albert de Vogüé. Edited by Jean Neufville. Sources chrétiennes 182. Paris: Cerf.

Berend, Nora. 1994. "La Subversion invisible: La Disparition de l'oblation irrévocable des enfants dans le droit canon." *Médiévales* 26:123–36.

Berliner, Paul F. 1994. *Thinking in Jazz.* Chicago: University of Chicago Press.

Bertos Herrera, Maria del Pilar. 1988. *Los seises en la catedral de Granada.* Maracena: Caja Provincial de Ahorros de Granada.

Betz, Albrecht. 1976. *Hanns Eisler: Musik einer Zeit, die sich eben bildet.* Munich: edition text + kritik.

Bhabha, Homi. 1985. "Sly civility," *October* 34:71–80.

Bick, Sally. 2003. "Hanns Eisler in Hollywood and Behind the Iron Curtain." *Acta Musicologica* 75 (1): 65–84.

Blacking, John. 1967. *Venda Children's Songs.* 2nd ed. Chicago: University of Chicago Press, 1995.

Bock, John, and Daniel W. Sellen. 2002. "Childhood and the Evolution of the Human Life Course: An Introduction." *Human Nature* 13:153–59.

Bohlman, Philip V. 2002. "Landscape—Region—Nation—Reich: German Folk Song in the Nexus of National Identity." In *Music and German National Identity,* edited by Celia Applegate and Pamela Potter, 105–27. Chicago: University of Chicago Press.

Bonde, Sheila, and Clark Maines. 2003. "Toward an Archeology of Ritual." In *Saint-Jean-des-Vignes in Soissons: Approaches to Its Architecture, Archaeology, and History,* edited by Sheila Bonde and Clark Maines, 255–61. Bibliotheca Victorina 15. Turnhout: Brepols.

Boquet, Denis. 1999. "De l'enfant-Dieu à l'homme-enfant: Regards sur l'enfance et la psychologie de l'adulte chez Aelred de Rievaulx (1110–1167)." *Médiévales* 36:129–43.

Borgerding, Todd. 1997. "The Motet and Spanish Religiosity, ca. 1550–1610." PhD diss., University of Michigan.

———. 1998. "Preachers, *Pronunciatio*, and Music: Hearing Rhetoric in Renaissance Sacred Polyphony." *Musical Quarterly* 82:586–98.

Born, Georgina, and David Hesmondhalgh. 2000. "Introduction: On Difference, Representation, and Appropriation in Music." In *Western Music and Its Others*, edited by Georgina Born and David Hesmondhalgh, 1–58. Berkeley: University of California Press.

Boswell, John. 1988. *The Kindness of Strangers: The Abandonment of Children in Western Europe from Late Antiquity to the Renaissance*. New York: Pantheon Books.

Bourdieu, Pierre. 2003. *The Logic of Practice*. Reprint. Stanford, CA: Stanford University Press.

Bourke, John G. 1892. *The Medicine Men of the Apache*. In U.S. Bureau of American Ethnology Ninth Annual Report, 1887–88. Washington: U.S. Government Printing Office.

Bowers, Roger. 1995. "To Chorus from Quartet: The Performing Resources for English Church Polyphony, c. 1390–1559." In *English Choral Practice, 1400–1650*, edited by John Morehen, 1–47. Cambridge: Cambridge University Press.

Boyer, Ruth McDonald, and Narcissus Duffy Gayton. 1992. *Apache Mothers and Daughters, Four Generations of a Family*. Norman: University of Oklahoma Press.

Boym, Svetlana. 2001. *The Future of Nostalgia*. New York: Basic.

Boynton, Susan. 1998. "The Liturgical Role of Children in Monastic Customaries from the Central Middle Ages." *Studia Liturgica* 28:194–209.

———. 2000. "Training for the Liturgy as a Form of Monastic Education." In *Medieval Monastic Education*, edited by Carolyn Muessig and George Ferzoco, 7–20. Leicester: Leicester University Press.

———. 2002. "Les Coutumes clunisiennes au temps d'Odilon." In *Odilon de Mercoeur, l'Auvergne et Cluny: La "Paix de Dieu" et l'Europe de l'an mil*, 193–202. Actes du colloque de Lavoûte-Chilhac. Nonette: Editions Créer.

———. 2005. "The Customaries of Bernard and Ulrich as Liturgical Sources." In *From Dead of Night to End of Day: The Medieval Customs of Cluny—Du coeur de la nuit à la fin du jour: Les Coutumes clunisiennes au Moyen Age*, edited by Susan Boynton and Isabelle Cochelin. Turnhout: Brepols.

Brailoiu, Constantin. 1954. "Le Rhythme enfantin: Notions liminaires." Republished in *Problems in Ethnomusicology*, edited and translated by A. L. Lloyd, 206–38. Cambridge: Cambridge University Press, 1984.

Briggs, Charles. 1986. *Learning How to Ask: A Sociolinguistic Appraisal of the Role of the Interview in Social Science Research*. Cambridge: Cambridge University Press.

———. 2002. "Interviewing, Power/Knowledge, and Social Inequality." In *Handbook of Interview Research: Context and Method,* edited by Jaber F. Gubrium and James A. Holstein, 911–22. Thousand Oaks, CA: Sage.

Brooke, Christopher. 1974. *The Monastic World, 1000–1300.* London: Elek.

Brooks, Lynn Matlock. 1988. *The Dances of the Processions of Seville in Spain's Golden Age.* Kassel: Edition Reichenberger.

Burrow, John Anthony. 1986. *The Ages of Man: A Study in Medieval Writing and Thought.* Oxford: Oxford University Press.

Bynum, Caroline Walker. 1995. "Why All the Fuss about the Body? A Medievalist's Perspective." *Critical Inquiry* 22 (1): 1–33.

Calico, Joy Haslam. 1999. "The Politics of Opera in the German Democratic Republic, 1945–1961." PhD diss., Duke University.

———. 2002. "'Für eine neue deutsche Nationaloper': Opera in the Discourses of Unification and Legitimation in the German Democratic Republic." In *Music and German National Identity,* edited by Celia Applegate and Pamela Potter, 190–204. Chicago: University of Chicago Press.

Calvert, Karin. 1992. *Children in the House: The Material Culture of Early Childhood, 1600–1900.* Boston: Northeastern University Press.

Campbell, Patricia Shehan. 1998. *Songs in Their Heads: Music and Its Meaning in Children's Lives.* New York: Oxford University Press.

Cannadine, David. 2001. *Ornamentalism: How the British Saw Their Empire.* Oxford: Oxford University Press.

Castañeda, Claudia. 2002. *Figurations: Child, Bodies, Worlds.* Durham, NC: Duke University Press.

Chang, Sa-hun. 1986. "Women Entertainers of the Yi Dynasty." In *Women of the Yi Dynasty,* 251–65. Seoul: Research Center for Asian Women, Sookmyong Women's University.

Chernoff, John. 1979. *African Rhythm and African Sensibility.* Chicago: University of Chicago Press.

Cho, Hae Joang. 1998. "Constructing and Deconstructing 'Koreanness.'" In *Making Majorities: Constituting the Nation in Japan, Korea, China, Malaysia, Fiji, Turkey, and the United States,* edited by Dru C. Gladney, 73–94. Stanford, CA: Stanford University Press.

———. 2002. "*Sopyonje:* Cultural and Historical Meaning." Translated by and edited by Yuh Ji-Yeon. In *Im Kwon-Taek: The Making of a Korean National Cinema,* edited by David E. James and Kyung Hyun Kim, 134–56. Detroit: Wayne State University Press.

Choi, Chungmoo. 1998. "Nationalism and Construction of Gender in Korea." In *Dangerous Women: Gender and Korean Nationalism,* edited by Elaine H. Kim and Chungmoo Choi, 9–31. New York: Routledge.

Chŏng, No-sik. 1940. *Chosŏn Ch'anggŭk-sa (History of Korean Singing-Drama).* Seoul: Tongmunsŏn.

Chŏng, Pŏm-t'ae. 2002. *Myŏngin myŏngch'ang* (*Great People, Great Singing*). Seoul: Kip'ŭnsaem.

Chopyak, James D. 1987. "The Role of Music in Mass Media, Public Education, and the Formation of a Malaysian National Culture." *Ethnomusicology* 31:431–54.

Clement of Alexandria. 1903. *Paedagogus*. Translated by Alexander Roberts and James Donaldson. The Ante-Nicene Fathers 2. New York: Charles Scribner's Sons.

Cochelin, Isabelle. 1996. "Enfants, jeunes et vieux au monastère: la perception du cycle de vie dans les sources clunisiennes (909–1156)." PhD diss., Université de Montréal.

———. 2000a. "Étude sur les hiérarchies monastiques: Le prestige de l'ancienneté et son éclipse à Cluny au XIe siècle." *Revue Mabillon* 72:5–37.

———. 2000b. "Le dur apprentissage de la virginité: Cluny, XIe siècle." In *Au cloître et dans le monde. Femmes, hommes et sociétés (IXe–XVe siècles). Mélanges en l'honneur de Paulette L'Hermite-Leclercq*, edited by Patrick Henriet and Anne-Marie Legras, 19–32. Paris: Presses de l'Université de Paris–Sorbonne.

———. 2005. "La singularité de l'œuvre de Bernard au regard de l'histoire des coutumiers." In *From Dead of Night to End of Day: The Medieval Customs of Cluny—Du coeur de la nuit à la fin du jour: Les Coutumes clunisiennes au Moyen Age*, edited by Susan Boynton and Isabelle Cochelin. Turnhout: Brepols.

Cohen, Judah M. 2006. "Singing Out for Judaism: A History of Songleaders and Songleading at Olin-Sang-Ruby Union Institute." In *A Place of Our Own: The Rise of Reform Jewish Camping*, edited by Michael M. Lorge and Gary P. Zola, 173–207. Tuscaloosa: University of Alabama Press.

Colette. 2001. "Un salon en 1900." In *Oeuvres*, 4:164–68. Bibliothèque de la Pléiade. Paris: Gallimard.

Columban. 2001. *Le opere*. Introduction by Inos Biffi and Aldo Granata. Milan: Jaca Book.

Confucius. 1998. *The Original Analects: Sayings of Confucius and His Successors* (*Lun yu*). Translation with commentary by E. Bruce Brooks and A. Taeko Brooks. New York: Columbia University Press.

Consuetudines Cluniacensium antiquiores cum redactionibus derivatis. 1983. Edited by Kassius Hallinger. *Consuetudinum saeculi X–XI–XII monumenta*. Corpus consuetudinum monasticarum 7.2. Siegburg: Franz Schmitt.

Cramer, Eugene C. 1976. "The Significance of Clef Combinations in the Music of Tomás Luis de Victoria." *American Choral Review* 18:3–11.

Crawford, Sally. 1999. *Childhood in Anglo-Saxon England*. Gloucestershire: Sutton.

Cremony, John C. 1868. *Life among the Apaches.* San Francisco: A. Roman. Repr., Lincoln: University of Nebraska Press, 1983.

Cristiani, Riccardo. 2000. "*Infirmus sum, et non possum sequi conventum.* L'esperienza della malattia nelle consuetudini cluniacensi dell'XI secolo." *Studi medievali,* 3rd ser., 41:777–807.

Csipák, Károly. 1975a. "Neue deutsche Volkslieder. Analysen." *Das Argument* 5:218–35.

———. 1975b. *Probleme der Volkstümlichkeit bei Hanns Eisler.* Munich: Katzbichler.

Cunningham, Hugh. 1998. "Histories of Childhood." *American Historical Review* 103: 1195–1208.

de Bruyn, Günter. 1991. "On the German Cultural Nation." *New German Critique* 52:60–66.

de Jong, Mayke. 1983. "Growing Up in a Carolingian Monastery: Magister Hildemar and His Oblates." *Journal of Medieval History* 9:99–128.

———. 1995. "Carolingian Monasticism: The Power of Prayer." In *The New Cambridge Medieval History.* Vol. 2, *C. 700–c. 900,* edited by Rosamond McKitterick, 622–53. Cambridge: Cambridge University Press.

———. 1996. *In Samuel's Image: Child Oblation in the Early Medieval West.* Leiden: Brill.

———. 1998. "*Imitatio morum:* The Cloister and Clerical Purity in the Carolingian World." In *Medieval Purity and Piety: Essays on Medieval Clerical Celibacy and Religious Reform,* edited by Michael Frassetto, 49–80. New York: Garland.

Demouy, Patrick. 1993. "*Les Pueri chori* de Notre Dame de Reims: Contribution à l'histoire des clergeons au Moyen Age." In *Le Clerc séculier au moyen âge,* 135–49. Paris: Publications de la Sorbonne.

Desclais Berkvam, Doris. 1981. *Enfance et maternité dans la littérature française des XIIe et XIIIe siècles.* In *Essais 8.* Paris: Champion, 1981.

———. 1983. "Nature and Norreture: A Notion of Medieval Childhood and Education." *Mediaevalia* 9:165–80.

Dobszay, László. 1995. "Pueri vociferati: Children in Eger Cathedral." In *International Musicological Society Study Group Cantus Planus: Papers Read at the Sixth Meeting, Eger, Hungary, 1993,* 93–100. Budapest: Hungarian Academy of Sciences, Institute for Musicology.

Driver, Harold Edson. 1941. *Culture Element Distributions: XVI: Girls' Puberty Rites in Western North America.* Anthropological Records 6.2. Berkeley: University of California Press.

Drucker, Philip. 1937. "The Tolowa and Their Southwest Oregon Kin." *University of California Publications in American Archaeology and Ethnology* 35:221–300.

Dubois, Jacques. 1973. "Oblato." In *Dizionario degli istituti di perfezione,* 6:654–76. 10 vols. Rome: Edizioni paoline, 1974–2003.

Dumont, Sandrine. 2004. "Enfants de choeur et vicaires de la maitrîse de Cambrai. Étude socio-anthropologique (1550–1670)." "À la recherche du chant perdu": Patrimoine, musiques et musicologie, special issue of Mélanges de Science Religieuse 61:51–70.

Dupont, Jacques. 1990. "Visages de l'enfance, sortilèges de Colette." L'Avant-scène opéra: L'Enfant et les sortilèges, L'Heure espagnole 127:23–26.

Dwars, Jens-Fietje. 1998. Abgrund des Widerspruchs: Das Leben des Johannes R. Becher. Berlin: Aufbau Verlag.

Eicker, Isabel. 1995. Kinderstücke: An Kinder adressierte und über das Thema der Kindheit komponierte Alben in der Klavierliteratur des 19. Jahrhunderts. Kassel: Gustav Bosse.

Eisler, Hanns. 1968. Gesammelte Werke. Ser. 1, vol. 18, edited by Stephanie Eisler and Manfred Grabs. Leipzig: VEB Deutsche Verlag für Musik.

———. 1975. Neue deutsche Volkslieder, edited by Manfred Grabs. Leipzig: VEB Deutscher Verlag für Musik.

———. 1982. Hanns Eisler. Musik und Politik Schriften 1948–1962, edited by Günter Mayer. Leipzig: VEB Deutscher Verlag für Musik.

Elam, Keir. 1996. "'In What Chapter of His Bosom?': Reading Shakespeare's Bodies." In Alternative Shakespeares, Vol. 2, edited by Terence Hawkes, 140–63. London: Routledge.

Elm, Susanna. 2003. "Inscriptions and Conversions—Gregory of Nazianzus on Baptism (Or. 38–40)." In Conversion in Late Antiquity and the Early Middle Ages, edited by Kenneth Mills and Anthony Grafton, 1–35. Rochester, NY: University of Rochester Press.

Enterline, Lynn. 2000. The Rhetoric of the Body from Ovid to Shakespeare. Cambridge: Cambridge University Press.

Eppstein, Ury. 1982. "The Beginnings of Western Music in Meiji-Era Japan." PhD diss., Tel Aviv University.

Ezrachi, Elan. 1995. "Encounters between American Jews and Israelis: Israelis in American Jewish Summer Camps." PhD diss., Jewish Theological Seminary of America.

Fallows, David. 1985. "The Performing Ensembles in Josquin's Sacred Music." Tijdschrift van de Vereniging voor Nedeerlandse Muziekgeschiedenis 35:32–64.

Farmer, Sharon. 2002. Surviving in Medieval Paris: Gender, Ideology, and the Daily Lives of the Poor. Ithaca, NY: Cornell University Press.

Farrer, Claire R. 1980. "Singing for Life: The Mescalero Apache Girls' Puberty Ceremony." In Southwestern Indian Ritual Drama, edited by Charlotte Frisbie, 125–60. Albuquerque: University of New Mexico Press.

———. 1994. Thunder Rides a Black Horse: Mescalero Apaches and the Mythic Present. Prospect Heights, IL: Waveland.

Fass, Paula S., ed. 2004. Encyclopedia of Children and Childhood in History and Society. New York: Macmillan.

Feld, Steven. 1992. *Sound and Sentiment.* 2nd ed. Philadelphia: University of Pennsylvania Press.

Feldman, David Henry. 1986. *Nature's Gambit: Child Prodigies and the Development of Human Potential.* Education and Psychology of the Gifted Series 9. New York: Basic Books.

Fergusson, Erna. 1933. *Dancing Gods: Indian Ceremonials of New Mexico and Arizona.* Albuquerque: University of New Mexico Press.

Fineberg, Jonathan, 1997. *The Innocent Eye: Children's Art and the Modern Artist.* Princeton, NJ: Princeton University Press.

Finnegan, Ruth. 1989. *The Hidden Musicians.* New York: Cambridge University Press.

Fiske, J. 1992. "The Cultural Economy of Fandom." In *The Adoring Audience: Fan Culture and Popular Media,* edited by Lisa A. Lewis, 30–49. London: Routledge.

Flanigan, Clifford, Kathleen Ashley, and Pamela Sheingorn. 2001. "Liturgy as Social Performance: Expanding the Definitions." In *The Liturgy of the Medieval Church,* edited by Thomas J. Heffernan and E. Ann Matter, 695–714. Kalamazoo, MI: Medieval Institute.

Fletcher, Alice. 1888. "Glimpses of Child-Life among the Omaha Indians." *Journal of American Folklore* 1:115–23.

Frisbie, Charlotte J. 1967. *Kinaaldá: A Study of the Navaho Girl's Puberty Ceremony.* Middletown, CT: Wesleyan University Press.

García, Vicente, and Miguel Querol Gavaldá, eds. 1957. *Francisco Guerrero, Opera Omnia,* vols. 1–2, *Canciones y villanescas espirituales.* Barcelona: Consejo Superior de Investigaciones Científicas, Instituto Español de Musicología.

Gaunt, Kyra D. 1997. "The Games Black Girls Play: Music, Body and 'Soul.'" PhD diss., University of Michigan.

Geidai. 1987.『東京芸術大学百年史　東京音楽学校篇　第一巻』(*History of Tokyo National University of Fine Arts and Music*), edited by a commission of the Tokyo National University of Fine Arts and Music. Tokyo Academy of Music Series 1. Tokyo: Ongaku-no-tomo-sha.

Goddard, Pliny Earle. 1909. "Gotal: A Mescalero Apache Ceremony." In *Putnam Anniversary Volume: Anthropological Essays Presented to Frederic Ward Putnam in Honor of His Seventieth Birthday, April 16, 1909, by His Friends and Associates.* New York: G. E. Stechert and Co.

Goffman, Erving. 1974. *Frame Analysis: An Essay on the Organization of Experience.* New York: Harper and Row.

Golomb, Claire. 2002. *Child Art in Context: A Cultural and Comparative Perspective.* Washington, DC: American Psychological Association.

Gondô, Atsuko (権藤敦子). 2003.「昭和初期における郷土意識とわらべうた—坊田壽眞の業績とその時代背景を中心に」(*The Consciousness of "Home" and Warabe-Uta at the Beginning of the Shôwa Era. With a Focus on the Work of*

Bôta Kazuma and His Historical Background). In 『近代音楽・歌謡の成立過程における国民性の問題』(*On Issues of National Identity in the Development Process of Modern Japanese Music*), edited by Lyou, Lin-Yu, 42–58. (平成13・14年度科学研究費補助金研究成果報告書　課題番号 13610063). Okayama: Ministry of Education, Culture, Sports, Science, and Technology.

Gonzáles-Barrionuevo, Herminio. 1992. *Los seises de Sevilla*. Seville: Editorial Castillejo.

———. 2002. *Francisco Guerrero (1528–1599). Vida y obra: La música en la catedral de Sevilla a finales del siglo*. Seville: Cabildo Metropolitano de la Catedral de Sevilla.

Goody, Esther N. 1982. *Parenthood and Social Reproduction: Fostering and Occupational Roles in West Africa*. Cambridge: Cambridge University Press.

Gottschewski, Hermann. 2003. "Gibt es einen 'japanischen Stil' in der musikalischen Interpretation? Zur japanischen Deklamation europäischer Melodik." In *Aspekte historischer und systematischer Musikforschung. Zur Symphonie im 19. Jahrhundert, zu Fragen der Musiktheorie, der Wahrnehmung von Musik und Anderes,* edited by Christoph-Hellmut Mahling and Kristina Pfarr, 549–73. Schriften zur Musikwissenschaft 8. Mainz: Are-Verlag.

Gottschewski, Hermann, and Gottschewski, Machiko. 2004. "'Poesie und Musik' —Das japanische Klavierlied um 1920." In *Musikalische Lyrik. Teil 2: Vom 19. Jahrhundert bis zur Gegenwart—Außereuropäische Perspektiven,* edited by Hermann Danuser, 364–84. Handbuch der musikalischen Gattungen 8.2. Laaber: Laaber-Verlag.

Gould, Richard A. 1979. "Tolowa." In *Handbook of North American Indians,* vol. 8, *California,* edited by Robert F. Heizer, 128–36. Washington: Smithsonian Institution.

Grabs, Manfred, ed. 1976. *Materialien zu einer Dialektik der Musik*. Leipzig: Verlag Philipp Reclam jun.

Graef, Hermann. 1959. *Palmenweihe und Palmenprozession in der lateinischen Liturgie*. Veröffentlichungen des Missionpriesterseminars St. Augustin. Siegburg: Kaldenkirchen.

Granada, Luís de. *Rhetorica ecclesiastica*. 1848. Translated by José Joaquín de Mora. Obras del V. P. M. Fray Luís de Granada. Madrid: Imprenta de M. Rivadeneyra.

Gregori i Cifré, Josep María. 1988. "Els escolans cantors de la Seu de Barcelona, 1459–1589." *Recerca musicológica* 8:46–64.

Grenier, Line. 1989. "From Diversity to Difference: The Case of Sociocultural Studies of Music." *New Formations* 9:125–42.

Guerrero, Francisco. 1589. *Canciones y villanescas espirituales*. Venice: Giacomo Vincenti.

Gunnerson, James H. 1979. "Southern Athapaskan Archeology." In *Handbook of*

North American Indians, vol. 9, *Southwest,* edited by Alfonso Ortiz, 162–69. Washington: Smithsonian Institution.

Hall, Stuart. 1996. "Introduction: Who Needs 'Identity'?" In *Questions of Cultural Identity,* edited by Stuart Hall and Paul du Gay, 1–17. London: Sage.

Hampson, Sasha. 2000. "Rhetoric or Reality? Contesting Definitions of Women in Korea." In *Women in Asia: Tradition, Modernity and Globalization,* edited by Louise Edwards and Mina Roces, 170–187. Ann Arbor: University of Michigan Press.

Hanawalt, Barbara. 1986. *The Ties That Bound: Peasant Families in Medieval England.* New York: Oxford University Press.

———. 1993. *Growing Up in Medieval London: The Experience of Childhood in History.* New York: Oxford University Press.

———. 2002. "Medievalists and the Study of Childhood." *Speculum* 77:440–60.

[Harms, William.] 2003. "Most Americans Think People Need to Be 26 to Be Considered Grown-Up." Press Release, University of Chicago. Available at http://www-news.uchicago.edu/releases/03/030509.adulthood.shtml. Accessed July 5, 2003.

Hayward, Paul A. 1994. "Suffering and Innocence in Latin Sermons for the Feast of the Holy Innocents, c. 400–800." In *The Church and Childhood: Papers Read at the 1993 Summer Meeting of the Ecclesiastical History Society,* edited by Diana Wood, 67–80. Studies in Church History 31. Oxford: Blackwell.

Heath-Gracie, G. H. 1960. *Mr. G. H. Heath-Gracie's Report, Malaya Tour 1960.*

Hebdige, Dick. *Subculture: The Meaning of Style.* New York: Routledge, 1979.

Hell, Julia. 1992. "At the Center an Absence: Foundationalist Narratives of the GDR and the Legitimatory Discourse of Antifascism." *Monatshefte* 84:23–45.

Hendrick, Harry. 2000. "The Child as a Social Actor in Historical Sources: Problems of Identification and Interpretation." In *Research with Children: Perspectives and Practices,* edited by Pia Christensen and Allison James, 36–61. London: Falmer.

Herlihy, David. 1978. "Medieval Children." In *Essays on Medieval Civilization: The Walter Prescott Webb Memorial Lectures,* edited by B. Lackner and K. R. Philp, 109–41. Austin: University of Texas Press.

Herms, Michael. 1996. "Zum Gründungsprozeß der Freien Deutschen Jugend in den Westzonen." In *Das neue Leben muß anders werden. Studien zur Gründung der FDJ,* edited by Helga Gotschlich, Michael Herms, Katharina Lange, and Gert Noack, 121–72. Berlin: Metropol Verlag.

Herrgott, Marquard, ed. 1726. *Vetus disciplina monastica.* Paris: Osmont.

Herskovits, Melville. 1948. *Man and His Works.* New York: Alfred A. Knopf.

Hesbert, Réné-Jean. 1968. *Invitatoria et antiphonae. Corpus antiphonalium officii,* vol. 3. Rerum ecclesiasticarum documenta, Series maior, Fontes 9. Rome: Herder.

Hildemar. 1880. *Expositio regulae ab Hildemaro tradita,* edited by R. Mitter-müller. Regensburg: Pustet.

Hirschfeld, Lawrence. 2002. "Why Don't Anthropologists Like Children?" *American Anthropologist* 104:611–27.

Hobsbawm, Eric, and Terrence Ranger, eds. 1992. *The Invention of Tradition.* Cambridge: Cambridge University Press.

Hoffman, Barbara G. 2001. *Griots at War: Conflict, Conciliation, and Caste in Mande.* Indiana: Indiana University Press.

Hoijer, Harry. 1938. *Chiricahua and Mescalero Apache Texts.* Chicago: University of Chicago Press.

Howe, Stephen. 2002. *Empire: A Very Short Introduction.* Oxford: Oxford University Press.

Innes, Matthew 2003. "'A Place of Discipline': Carolingian Courts and Aristo-cratic Youth." In *Court Culture in the Early Middle Ages: The Proceedings of the First Alcuin Conference,* edited by Catherine Cubitt, 59–76. Studies in the Early Middle Ages 3. Turnhout: Brepols.

Iogna-Prat, Dominique. 2002. *Order and Exclusion: Cluny and Christendom in the Face of Heresy, Judaism, and Islam (1000–1150),* translated by Graham Robert Edwards. Ithaca, NY: Cornell University Press, 2002.

Jankélévitch, Vladimir. 1956. *Ravel,* edited by Jean-Michel Nectoux. Paris: Editions du Seuil, 1995.

Jardine, Lisa. 1992. "Twins and Travesties: Gender, Dependency and Sexual Availability in *Twelfth Night.*" In *Erotic Politics: Desire on the Renaissance Stage,* edited by Susan Zimmerman, 27–38. New York: Routledge.

Jerome. 1979. *Commentaire sur S. Mathieu. Tome II (livres III–IV).* Edited and translated by Emile Bonnard. Sources chrétiennes 259. Paris: Cerf.

Jett, Stephen C. 1964. "Pueblo Indian Migrations: An Evaluation of the Possible Physical and Cultural Determinants." *American Antiquity* 29:281–300.

Joselit, Jenna Weissman, and Karen S. Mittelman, eds. 1993. *A Worthy Use of Summer: Jewish Camping in America.* Philadelphia: National Museum of American Jewish History.

Jourdan-Morhange, Hélène. 1945. *Ravel et nous: L'Homme, l'ami, le musicien.* Geneva: Editions du milieu du monde.

Kendall, Laurel. 1996. *Getting Married in Korea: Of Gender, Morality, and Modernity.* Berkeley: University of California Press.

Kim, Eun-Shil. 1993. "The Making of the Modern Female Gender: The Politics of Gender Reproduction Practices in Korea." PhD diss., University of California, Berkeley.

Kim, Yung-Chung, ed. and trans. 1976. *Women of Korea: A History from Ancient Times to 1945.* Seoul: Ewha University Press.

Kim-Renaud, Young-Key. 1994. "Sopyonje: A Journey into the Korean Soul." *Korean Culture* 15:12–16.

Kindaichi, Haruhiko, 金田一春彦. 1995.『童謡・唱歌の世界』(*The World of Dôyô and* Shôka). Tokyo: Kyôiku Shuppan.

Kindaichi, Haruhiko, 金田一春彦, and Anzai Aiko, 安西愛子. 1977.『日本の唱歌（上）・明治篇』(*The* Shôka *of Japan*). Vol. 1, *Meiji Era*, Tokyo: Kôdansha Bunko.

Kinney, Anne B. 1995. *Chinese Views of Childhood.* Honolulu: University of Hawai'i Press.

Klein, Melanie. 1950. "Infantile Anxiety-Situations Reflected in a Work of Art and in the Creative Impulse." In *Contributions to Psycho-Analysis, 1921–1945,* 227–33. London: Hogarth.

Knapp, Raymond. 1999. "Suffering Children: Perspectives on Innocence and Vulnerability in Mahler's Fourth Symphony." *Nineteenth-Century Music* 23:233–67.

Knowles, David. 1966. *From Pachomius to Ignatius: A Study in the Constitutional History of the Religious Orders.* Oxford: Clarendon.

Koch, Hans, and Joachim Mückenberger, eds. 1952. *Für den Frieden der Welt: Aus den Erfahrungen der Kulturveranstaltungen der III. Weltfestspiele der Jugend und Studenten für den Frieden in Berlin 1951.* Halle: Mitteldeutscher Verlag.

Koh, Helen H. 1995. *The Voice in Sŏp'yŏnje: Narrativization, P'ansori, and Aesthetic Landscape.* Unpublished manuscript.

Koizumi, Fumio, 小泉文夫, ed. 1969.『わらべうたの研究』(*Game Songs of Japanese Children*). Vol. 2,「研究編」*Studies of Game Songs.* Tokyo: Inaba Insatsusho.

Kojima, Tomiko, 小島美子. 1972.「唱歌調への反逆としての童謡運動」("The Children's Song Movement as Rebellion against the *Shôka* Style").『音楽教育研究』, *Ongaku kyôiku kenkyû* (*Music Education Research*) 15, no. 4: 53–61.

Kok, Roe-Min. 2003a. "Romantic Childhood, Bourgeois Commercialism, and the Music of Robert Schumann." PhD diss., Harvard University.

———. 2003b. "A 'Springtime of the Peoples': Childhood as Nationhood in Robert Schumann's *Album for the Young.*" Paper presented at the Romanticism and Nationalism in Music conference, Corfu, Greece, October 17–20.

Komoda, Haruko, 薦田治子, and Nogawa Mihoko, 野川美穂子. 2002. "Theory and Notation in Japan." In *The Garland Encyclopedia of World Music. East Asia: China, Japan, and Korea,* edited by Robert C. Provine, Tokumaru Yoshihiko, and J. Lawrence Witzleben, 565–84. New York: Routledge.

Köster, Maren. 2002. *Musik-Zeit-Geschehen: Zu den Musikverhältnissen in der SBZ/DDR 1945 bis 1952.* Saarbrücken: Pfau.

Kristeva, Julia. 2002. *Les Mots: Colette ou la chair du monde.* Vol. 3 of *Le Génie feminine: La Vie, la folie, les mots.* Paris: Fayard.

Kurtzman, Jeffrey G. 1994. "Tones, Modes, Clefs, and Pitch in Roman Cyclic Magnificats of the Sixteenth Century." *Early Music* 22:641–64.

Kwami, Robert M. 1989. "African Music Education and the School Curriculum."
PhD diss., University of London Institute of Education.

———. 1994. "Music Education in Ghana and Nigeria: A Brief Summary." *Africa*
64:544–60.

Laird, Paul R. 1997. *Toward a History of the Spanish Villancico*. Warren, Michigan:
Harmonie Park Press.

Langford, Peter. E. 1995. *Approaches to the Development of Moral Reasoning*. Hove,
UK: Lawrence Erlbaum Associates.

Langham Smith, Richard. 2000. "Ravel's Operatic Spectacles: *L'Heure and L'Enfant*." In *The Cambridge Companion to Ravel*, edited by Deborah Mawer,
188–210. Cambridge: Cambridge University Press.

Lavelli, Jorge. 1979. Program book, *L'Enfant et les sortilèges/L'Heure espagnole*,
Palais Garnier. Bibliothèque de l'Opéra (Paris, Bibliothèque Nationale de
France), *L'Enfant et les sortilèges*, dossier d'œuvre.

Lawrence, C. H. 2001. *Medieval Monasticism*. 3rd ed. Harlow: Pearsons.

Leclercq, Henri. 1936. "Oblat." In *Dictionnaire d'Archéologie chrétienne et de
Liturgie*, vol. 12, part 2: 1864–67.

León, Luis de. 1984. *The Names of Christ*. Translated by Manuel Durán and
William Kluback. New York: Paulist.

Leppert, Richard. 1995. "Music, Domesticity, and Cultural Imperialism." In
The Sight of Sound: Music, Representation, and the History of the Body, 90–117.
Berkeley: University of California Press.

Lesko, Nancy. 2001. *Act Your Age! A Cultural Construction of Adolescence*.
New York: Routledge.

Liber tramitis aevi Odilonis abbatis. 1980. Edited by Peter Dinter. Corpus
consuetudinum monasticarum 10. Siegburg: Franz Schmitt.

Liechty, Mark. 1995. "Media, Markets, and Modernization: Youth Identities
and the Experience of Modernity in Kathmandu, Nepal." In *Youth Cultures:
A Cross-Cultural Perspective*, edited by Vered Amit-Talai and Helena Wulff,
166–201. London: Routledge.

Lin, Yutang, ed. and trans. 1943. *The Wisdom of Confucius*. New York: Random
House.

Lincoln, Bruce. 1981. *Emerging from the Chrysalis: Studies in Rituals of Women's
Initiation*. Cambridge, MA: Harvard University Press.

Lion, Xavier. 1925. Review of *L'Enfant et les sortileges*. *Le Ménestrel*, April 3.

Lleo Cañal, Vicente. 1975. *Arte y espectáculo: La fiesta del Corpus Christe en Sevilla
en los siglos XVI y XVII*. Seville: Publicaciones de la Excma. Diputación
Provincial de Sevilla.

Locke, David. 1990. *Drum Damba*. Tempe, AZ: White Cliffs Media.

Lopez Calo, Jose. 1963. *La musica en la catedral de Granada en el siglo XVI*.
Granada: Fundacion Rodriguez Acosta.

Maier, Charles S. 1997. *The Crisis of Communism and the End of East Germany.* Princeton, NJ: Princeton University Press.

Mählert, Ulrich, and Stephan Gerd-Rüdiger, eds. 1996. *Blaue Hemden—Rote Fahnen: Die Geschichte der Freien Deutschen Jugend.* Opladen: Leske + Budrich.

Mangeot, A. 1925. Review of *L'Enfant et les sortilèges, Le Monde musicale,* March: 95–96.

Marcus, Ivan G. 1996. *Rituals of Childhood: Jewish Acculturation in Medieval Europe.* New Haven, CT: Yale University Press.

Marks, Julie. 1979. "'On the Road to Find Out': The Role Music Plays in Adolescent Development." In *Becoming Female: Perspectives on Development,* edited by Claire B. Kopp, 333–62. New York: Plenum.

Marnat, Marcel. 1986. *Maurice Ravel.* Paris: Fayard.

Mayer, Hans. 1991. *Der Turm von Babel: Erinnerung an eine Deutsche Demokratische Republik.* Frankfurt am Main: Suhrkamp Verlag.

McAllester, David A. 1954. *Enemy-Way Music: A Study of Social and Esthetic Values as Seen in Navaho Music.* Papers of the Peabody Museum of American Archaeology and Ethnology, Harvard University 41 (3). Cambridge, MA: Harvard University Press.

McCarthy, Marie. 2002. "Social and Cultural Contexts of Music Teaching and Learning: An Introduction." In *The New Handbook of Research on Music Teaching and Learning,* edited by Richard Colwell and Carol Richardson, 563–64. New York: Oxford University Press.

McLucas, Anne Dhu. 2000. "The Music of the Mescalero Apache Girls' Puberty Ceremony." In *Indigenous Religious Musics,* edited by Karen Ralls-Macleod and Graham Harvey, 198–209. Aldershot: Ashgate.

Merriam, Alan. 1964. *The Anthropology of Music.* Evanston, IL: Northwestern University Press.

Metz, René. 1976. "L'Enfant dans le droit canonique médiéval. Orientations de recherche." *Recueils de la Société Jean Bodin* 36:13–23. Reedited in Metz 1985.

Metz, René. 1985. *La Femme et l'enfant dans le droit canonique médiéval.* London: Variorum Reprints.

Metzer, David. 1997. "We Boys: Childhood in the Music of Charles Ives." *Nineteenth-Century Music* 21:77–95.

Mignolo, Walter D. 2000. "(Post)Occidentalism, (Post)Coloniality, and (Post)Subaltern Rationality." In *The Pre-Occupation of Postcolonial Studies,* edited by Fawzia Afzal-Khan and Kalpana Seshadri-Crooks, 86–118. Durham, NC: Duke University Press.

Milner, Christiane. 1981. "Mélanie Klein et les sortilèges de Colette." *Cahiers Colette* 5:36–44.

————. 1991. "*L'Enfant et les sortilèges:* Notice." In Colette, *Oeuvres,* 3:1333–40. Bibliothèque de la Pléiade. Paris: Gallimard.

Minks, Amanda. 2002. "From Children's Song to Expressive Practices: Old and New Directions in the Ethnomusicological Study of Children." *Ethnomusicology* 46:379–408.

Mirza, Sarah, and Margaret Strobel, eds. and trans. 1989. *Three Swahili Women: Life Histories from Mombasa, Kenya.* Bloomington: Indiana University Press.

Mishra, Vijay, and Bob Hodge. 1991. "What is Post(-)Colonialism?" *Textual Practice* 5 (3): 399–414.

Morales, Juan Luis. 1960. *El niño en la cultura española.* Alcalá de Henares: Talleres Penitenciarios.

Mueller, Renate. 2002. "Perspectives from the Sociology of Music." In *The New Handbook of Research on Music Teaching and Learning: A Project of the Music Educators National Conference,* edited by Richard Colwell and Carol Richardson, 584–603. New York: Oxford University Press.

"Musik muß hinaus ins Volk." 1954. *Musik und Gesellschaft* 4, no. 2: 1.

Naimark, Norman M. 1995. *The Russians in Germany: A History of the Soviet Zone of Occupation, 1945–1949.* Cambridge, MA: Harvard University Press.

Nebrija, Antonio. 1981. *La educación de los hijos.* Edited and translated by León Esteban Mateo and Laureano Robles. Valencia: Universidad de Valencia.

Nelson, Janet. 1994. "Parents, Children, and the Church in the Early Middle Ages." In *The Church and Childhood: Papers Read at the 1993 Summer Meeting of the Ecclesiastical History Society,* edited by Diana Wood, 81–113. Studies in Church History 31. Oxford: Blackwell.

Newell, William Wells. 1884. *Games and Songs of American Children.* New York: Dover, 1963.

Nicholas, Dan. 1939. "Mescalero Apache Girls' Puberty Ceremony." *El palacio* 46:193–204.

Nketia, J. H. Kwabena. 1973. "The Musician in Akan Society." In *The Traditional Artist in African Societies,* edited by Warren L. d'Azevedo, 79–100. Bloomington: Indiana University Press.

Opler, Morris Edward. 1965. *An Apache Life-Way: The Economic, Social, and Religious Institutions of the Chiricahua Indians.* New York: Cooper Square Publishers.

Opler, Morris Edward. 1969. *Apache Odyssey: A Journey between Two Worlds.* Lincoln: Univ. of Nebraska Press, 2002.

Oppong, Christine. 1973. *Growing Up in Dagbon.* Accra-Tema: Ghana Publishing Corporation.

Orgel, Stephen. 1989. "Nobody's Perfect; Or, Why Did the English Stage Take Boys for Women?" *South Atlantic Quarterly* 88:7–29.

Origen. *Commentary on Matthew.* 1896. Translated by Allan Menzies. The Ante-Nicene Fathers 9. New York: Christian Literature Company.

Orme, Nicholas. 2002. *Medieval Children*. New Haven, CT: Yale University Press.

Osgood, Cornelius. 1951. *The Koreans and Their Culture*. New York: Ronald.

Ott, Alexander, ed. 1954. *Leben, Singen, Kämpfen: Liederbuch der deutschen Jugend*. Berlin: Verlag Neues Leben.

Panzacchi, Cornelia. 1994. "Livelihoods of Traditional Griots in Modern Senegal." *Africa* 64:190–210.

Parakilas, James, ed. 1999. *Piano Roles: Three Hundred Years of the Piano*. New Haven, CT: Yale University Press.

Parisse, Michel. 2004. "La Tradition du monachisme féminin au haut Moyen Âge." In *Robert d'Arbrissel et la vie religieuse dans l'Ouest de la France, Actes du colloque de Fontevraud, 13–16 décembre 2001*, edited by Jacques Dalarun, 107–20. Disciplina monastica 1. Turnhout: Brepols.

Park, Chan E. 2003. *Voices from the Strawmat: Toward an Enthnography of Korean Story Singing*. Honolulu: University of Hawai'i Press and Center for Korean Studies.

Pastoureau, Michel. 1997. "Emblems of Youth: Young People in Medieval History." In *A History of Young People in the West*, vol. 1, *Ancient and Medieval Rites of Passage*, edited by G. Levi and Jean-Claude Schmitt, translated by C. Naish, 222–39. Cambridge, MA: Belknap.

Paterson, Linda. 1989. "L'enfant dans la littérature occitane avant 1230." *Cahiers de Civilisation médiévale* 32:233–45.

Patrologiae cursus completus, series latina. 1844–1866. Edited by Jacques-Paul Migne. 221 vols. Paris: Migne.

Pavlovic, Mihailo B. 1970. *Sidonie-Gabrielle Colette: Le Monde animal dans sa vie et dans sa création littéraire*. Belgrade: Faculté de Philologie de l'Université de Belgrade.

Pesic, Peter. 2001–2. "The Child and the Daemon: Mozart and Deep Play." *Nineteenth-Century Music* 25:91–107.

Peter the Venerable. 1975. "Statuta Petri Venerabilis abbatis Cluniacensis IX (1146/7)." In *Consuetudines benedictinae variae (Saec. XI–Saec. XIV)*, edited by Giles Constable, 19–106. Corpus consuetudinum monasticarum 6. Siegburg: Franz Schmitt.

Piaget, Jean. 1926. *The Child's Conception of the World*. Translated by Joan and Andrew Tomlinson. Repr., Lanham, MD: Rowman and Littlefield, 1959.

Piaget, Jean. 1932. *The Moral Judgment of the Child*. Translated by Marjorie Gabain. Repr., New York: Free Press, 1965.

Pickering, Julie. 1994. "Kim So-hi [*sic*] and Pak Tong-jin: P'ansori as a Way of Life." *Koreana: Korean Art and Culture* 8 no. 2: 58–61. Available at http://www.kofo.or.kr/koreana.

Pihl, Marshall R. 1994. *The Korean Singer of Tales*. Cambridge, MA: Harvard University and the Harvard-Yenching Institute.

Pike, David. 1992. *The Politics of Culture in Soviet-Occupied Germany, 1945–1949.* Stanford, CA: Stanford University Press.

Pollock, Linda. 1983. *Parent-Child Relations from 1500 to 1900.* Cambridge: Cambridge University Press.

Potter, Pamela M. 1998. *Most German of the Arts: Musicology and Society from the Weimar Republic to the End of Hitler's Reich.* New Haven, CT: Yale University Press.

Pulaski, Mary Ann Spencer. 1980. *Understanding Piaget: An Introduction to Children's Cognitive Development.* Rev. ed. New York: Harper and Row.

Rasmussen, Ann Marie. 1996. *Mothers and Daughters in Medieval German Literature.* Syracuse, NY: Syracuse University Press.

Ravel, Maurice. 1989. *Lettres, écrits, entretiens.* Edited by Arbie Orenstein. Paris: Flammarion.

Real, Isabelle. 2001. "Vies de saints, vie de famille. Représentations et système de parenté dans le Royaume mérovingien (481–751) d'après les sources hagiographiques." *Hagiologia* 2:384–474.

Rendle, Martha Champion. 1951. "Iroquois Women, Then and Now." In *Symposium on Local Diversity in Iroquois Culture. U.S. Bureau of Ethnology Bulletin,* edited by William N. Fenton, 149:167–80. Washington, DC: U.S. Bureau of Ethnology.

Reynaud, François. 1974. "Contribution à l'étude des danseurs et des musiciens des fêtes du Corpus Christi et de l'Assomption à Tolède aux XVIe et XVIIe siècles." *Mélanges de la Casa de Velázquez* 10:133–68.

Reynaud, François. 2002. *Les enfants de choeur de Tolède à la Renaissance: Les "clerizones" de la cathédrale et le "colegio de los infantes."* Turnhout: Brepols.

Reynolds, Christopher A. 1989. "Sacred Polyphony." In *Performance Practice: Music before 1600,* edited by Howard Mayer Brown and Stanley Sadie, 185–200. New York: W. W. Norton and Company.

Reynolds, Roger. 1999. "The Subdiaconate as a Sacred and Superior Order." In *Clerics in the Early Middle Ages: Hierarchy and Image,* 1–39. Aldershot: Variorum.

Rich, John Martin, and Joseph L. DeVitis. 1994. *Theories of Moral Development.* 2nd ed. Springfield, IL: Charles C. Thomas.

Riché, Pierre, and Danielle Alexandre-Bidon. 1994. *L'enfance au Moyen Âge.* Paris: Seuil.

Riché, Pierre. 1976. *Education and Culture in the Barbarian West: From the Sixth through the Eighth Century.* Translated from the 3rd French ed. by John J. Contreni. Columbia: University of South Carolina Press.

Riché, Pierre. 1995. *Éducation et culture dans l'occident barbare, VIe-VIIIe siècles.* 4th ed. Paris: Seuil.

Richmond, P. G. 1970. *An Introduction to Piaget.* London: Routledge and Kegan Paul.

Roa, Martin de. 1623. *Antiguedad Veneracion i fruto de las sagradas Imagenes, i reliquias. Historias i exenplos a este proposito.* Seville: Gabriel Ramos Vejarano.

Roberts, Don L. 1972. "The Ethnomusicology of the Eastern Pueblos." In *New Perspectives on the Pueblos,* edited by Alfonso Ortiz, 243–55. Albuquerque: University of New Mexico Press.

Roland-Manuel, Alexis. 1925. "Maurice Ravel ou l'esthétique de l'imposture." *La Revue musicale,* April 1, 16–21.

———. 1926. Review of *L'Enfant et les sortilèges. Le Ménestrel,* February 5.

———. 1938. *Ravel.* Repr., Paris: Mémoire du livre, 2000.

Romero, Patricia W., ed. 1988. *Life Histories of African Women.* London: Ashfield.

Ros, Carlos. 1994. *La Inmaculada y Sevilla.* Seville: Editorial Castillejo.

Rose, Tricia. 1994. *Black Noise: Black Music and Black Culture in Contemporary America.* Hanover, NH: University Press of New England.

Rouché, Jacques. 1939. "Comment M. Rouché a monté *L'Enfant et les sortilèges.*" *Le Jour,* May 15.

Sack, Eugene J. 1940. "We Discover the Camp Meeting—and Religion." *Youth Leader: A Magazine for Jewish Clubs* 8 (3): 7–12.

Said, Edward. 1978. *Orientalism.* New York: Pantheon.

———. 2000. *Out of Place: A Memoir.* New York: Vintage.

Sawasaki, Masahiko, 沢崎真彦. 1993.「『新訂尋常小学唱歌』成立への動向と編纂」("The Tendencies Toward the Establishment of the 'Revised *Shôka* for Common Schools' and Its Compilation").『音楽教育研究』 *Ongaku kyôiku kenkyû* (*Music Education Research*) 36, no. 3: 161–75.

Schachet-Briskin, Wally. 1996. "The Music of Reform Youth." MSM thesis, Hebrew Union College–Jewish Institute of Religion, School of Sacred Music.

Schebera, Jürgen. 1998. *Eisler: Eine Biographie in Texten, Bildern und Dokumenten.* Mainz: Schott.

Schieffelin, Bambi, and Don Kulick. 2004. "Language Socialization." In *Companion to Linguistic Anthropology,* edited by Alessandro Duranti, 349–68. London: Blackwell.

Schieffelin, Bambi, and Elinor Ochs. 1986. "Language Socialization." *Annual Review of Anthropology* 15:163–91.

Schroeder, Henry Joseph, eds. 1941. *Canons and Decrees of the Council of Trent.* St. Louis: B. Herder Book Co.

Schultz, James A. 1995. *The Knowledge of Childhood in the German Middle Ages, 1100–1350.* Philadelphia: University of Pennsylvania Press.

Schwartzman, Helen. 1978. *Transformations: The Anthropology of Children's Play.* New York: Plenum.

Sears, Elizabeth. 1986. *The Ages of Man: Medieval Interpretations of the Life Cycle.* Princeton, NJ: Princeton University Press.

Sebastian, Wenceslaus. 1958. "The Controversy over the Immaculate Conception from after Scotus to the End of the Eighteenth Century." In *The Dogma of the*

Immaculate Conception, edited by Edward Dennis O'Connor, 213–70. Notre Dame, IL: University of Notre Dame Press.

Shahar, Shulamith. 1990. *Childhood in the Middle Ages.* Translated by Hayah Galai. London: Routledge.

Shapiro, Anne Dhu [now Mc Lucas]. 1991. "A Critique of Current Research on Music and Gender." *World of Music* 33, no. 2: 5–13.

Shapiro, Anne Dhu [now McLucas], and Inés Talamantez. 1986. "The Mescalero Apache Girls' Puberty Ceremony: The Role of Music in Structuring Ritual Time." *Yearbook of the International Council for Traditional Music* 18:77–90.

Shapiro, Michael. 1994. *Gender in Play on the Shakespearean Stage.* Ann Arbor: University of Michigan Press.

Shimony, Annemarie. 1980. "Women of Influence and Prestige among the Native American Iroquois." In *Unspoken Worlds: Women's Religious Lives in Non-Western Cultures,* edited by Nancy Auer Falk and Rita M. Gross, 243–59. San Francisco: Harper and Row.

Shostak, Marjorie. 1981. *Nisa: The Life and Words of a !Kung Woman.* New York: Vintage Books.

Silcher, Friedrich. N.d. *Zwölf Kinderlieder für Schule und Haus . . . zwei- und dreistimmig componiert von Fr. Silcher Heft II.* Tübingen: Verlag der H. Laupp'schen Buchhandlung.

Sitwell, Gerald, trans. 1958. *St. Odo of Cluny—Being the Life of St. Odo of Cluny by John of Salerno and the Life of St. Gerald of Aurillac by St. Odo.* London: Sheed and Ward.

Slobin, Mark. 1989. *Chosen Voices: The Story of the American Cantorate.* Urbana: University of Illinois Press.

Smith, Mary. 1981. *Baba of Karo: A Woman of the Muslim Hausa.* New Haven, CT: Yale University Press.

Sonnichsen, C. L. 1973. *The Mescalero Apaches,* 2nd ed. Norman: University of Oklahoma Press.

Sŏp'yŏnje. 1993. Directed by Im Kwŏn-Taek. Performances by Kim Myông-gon, O Chông-hae, and Kim Kyu-ch'ŭl. Seoul: T'ae Hung Productions Co. Ltd.

Source Readings in Music History. 1998. Translated by William Strunk Jr. et al. Rev. ed. Edited by Leo Treitler. New York: Norton.

Southern, Richard W. 1953. *The Making of the Middle Ages.* New Haven, CT: Yale University Press.

Stallybrass, Peter. 1992. "Transvestism and the 'Body Beneath': Speculating on the Boy Actor." In *Erotic Politics: Desire on the Renaissance Stage,* edited by Susan Zimmerman, 64–83. New York: Routlege.

Stanivukovic, Goran V., ed. 2001. *Ovid and the Renaissance Body.* Toronto: University of Toronto Press.

Steblin, Rita. 1983. *A History of Key Characteristics in the Eighteenth and Early Nineteenth Centuries.* Ann Arbor: UMI Research Press.

Steinberg, Leo. 1996. *The Sexuality of Christ in Renaissance Art and in Modern Oblivion.* 2nd rev. ed. Chicago: University of Chicago Press.

Steinitz, Wolfgang. 1972. *Deutsche Volkslieder demokratischen Charakters aus sechs Jahrhunderten.* East Berlin: Akademie-Verlag.

Stephan, Alexander. 1974. "Johannes R. Becher and the Cultural Development of the GDR." *New German Critique* 2: 72–89.

Stephens, Sharon, ed. 1995. *Children and the Politics of Culture.* Princeton, NJ: Princeton University Press.

Stevenson, Robert. 1961. *Spanish Cathedral Music in the Golden Age.* Berkeley: University of California Press.

Stratton, Suzanne L. 1994. *The Immaculate Conception in Spanish Art.* Cambridge: Cambridge University Press.

Synnott, Anthony. 1988. "Little Angels, Little Devils: A Sociology of Children." In *Childhood Socialization,* edited by Gerald Handel. New York: Aldin de Gruyter.

Szego, C. K. 1999. "Musical Meaning-Making in an Intercultural Environment: The Case of Kamehameha Schools." PhD diss., University of Washington, Seattle.

———. 2002. "Music Transmission and Learning: A Conspectus of Ethnographic Research in Ethnomusicology and Music Education." In *The New Handbook of Research on Music Teaching and Learning: A Project of the Music Educators National Conference,* edited by Richard Colwell and Carol Richardson, 707–29. New York: Oxford University Press.

Talamantez, Inés. 1991. "Images of the Feminine in Apache Religious Tradition." In *After Patriarchy: Feminist Transformations of the World Religions,* edited by Paula M. Cooey, William R. Eakin, and Jay B. McDaniel, 131–45. Maryknoll, NY: Orbis Books.

———. 2000. "In the Space between Earth and Sky: Contemporary Mescalero Apache Ceremonialism." In *Native Religions and Cultures of North America, Anthropology of the Sacred,* edited by Lawrence E. Sullivan, 142–59. New York: Continuum.

———. 2001. "The Presence of Isanaklesh: The Apache Female Deity and the Path of Pollen." In *Unspoken Worlds, Women's Religious Lives,* 3rd ed., edited by Nancy Auer Falk and Rita M. Gross, 290–300. Belmont, CA: Wadsworth.

———. Forthcoming. *Isanaklesh: An Apache Coming-of-Age Ceremony.*

Talavera, Hernando. 1496. *Tractado de lo que significan las cerimonias de la misa y de lo que en cada una se deve pensar y pedir á nuestro señor.* Granada: n.p.

Tambiah, Stanley. 1979. "A Performative Approach to Ritual." *Proceedings of the British Academy* 65:113–69.

Tang, Patricia. 2001. "Masters of the Sabar: Wolof Griots in Contemporary Senegal." PhD diss., Harvard University.

Tedlock, Barbara. 1980. "Songs of the Zuni kachina Society: Composition,

Rehearsal, and Performance." In *Southwestern Indian Ritual Drama,* edited by Charlotte J. Frisbie, 7–35. Albuquerque: University of New Mexico Press.

Terrones del Caño, Francisco. 1617. *Instrucción de predicadores.* Edited by Félix Olmedo. Madrid: Espasa Calpe, 1946.

Thilman, Johannes Paul, and Max Zimmering. 1951. *Friedens- und Kampflieder für die Freie Deutsche Jugend.* Dresden: VVV Dresdener Verlag.

Thornton, Sarah. 1996. *Subcultures: Music, Media, and Cultural Capital.* Middletown, CT: Wesleyan University Press.

Tillery, Randal. 1992. "Touring Arcadia: Elements of Discursive Simulation at a Children's Summer Camp." *Cultural Anthropology* 9:374–88.

Titon, Jeff Todd. 1980. "The Life Story." *Journal of American Folklore* 93:276–92.

Trexler, Richard. 2002. "From the Mouths of Babes: Christianization by Children in Sixteenth-Century New Spain." In *Religion in Social Context in Europe and America, 1200–1700,* 250–292. Tempe: Arizona Center for Medieval and Renaissance Studies.

Tutsch, Burkhardt. 1996. *Studien zur Rezeptionsgeschichte der Consuetudines Ulrichs von Cluny.* Münster: LIT.

"UAHC Kutz Video." 2001–2. Promotional video distributed as part of CD-ROM, "Kutz Camp: The National Leadership Institute." New York: Union of American Hebrew Congregations.

Ulrich of Zell. *Antiquiores consuetudines monasterii Cluniacensis.* In *Patrologiae cursus completus, series latina* 149:635–778.

Very, Francis George. 1962. *The Spanish Corpus Christi Procession: A Literary and Folkloric Study.* Valencia: Tipografía Moderna.

Vives, Juan Luis. 1996–98. *De institutione feminae christianae.* Edited by Constantinus Matheeussen and Charles Fantazzi, translated by Charles Fantazzi. Leiden: Brill.

———. 2002. *De subventione pauperum sive de humanis necessitatibus libri II.* Edited by Constantinus Matheeussen and Charles Fantazzi. Leiden: Brill.

Wallace, Jo-Ann. 1994. "De-Scribing *The Water Babies:* 'The Child' in Post-Colonial Theory." In *De-Scribing Empire: Post-Colonialism and Textuality,* edited by Chris Tiffin and Alan Lawson, 171–84. London: Routledge.

Wallace, William J. 1978. "Music and Musical Instruments." In *Handbook of North American Indians,* vol. 8, *California,* edited by Robert F. Heizer, 8:642–48. Washington, DC: Smithsonian Institution.

Walter, Michael. 1997. *Die Freie Deutsche Jugend: Ihre Funktionen im politischen System der DDR.* Freiburg im Breisgau: Arnold Bergstraesser Institut.

Walters Robertson, Anne. 1988. *"Benedicamus Domino:* The Unwritten Tradition." *Journal of the American Musicological Society* 41:1–62.

Waterman, Richard. 1956. "Music in Australian Aboriginal Culture—Some Sociological and Psychological Implications." In *Music Therapy 1955,* edited by E. Thayer Gaston, 40–49. Proceedings of the National Association for Music Therapy 5. Lawrence, KS: National Association for Music Therapy.

Weidman, Amanda. 2002. "Gender and the Politics of Voice: Colonial Modernity and Classical Music in South India." *Cultural Anthropology* 18:194–232.

Weimann, Robert. 1996. *Authority and Representation in Early Modern Discourse.* Baltimore: Johns Hopkins University Press.

Wheeler, R. E. M. 1950. "What Matters in Archaeology: An Address to the Council for British Archaeology at Burlington House, London, 10 July, 1950," *Antiquity* 95:122–30.

Willoughby, Heather A. 2002. "The Sound of *Han: P'ansori,* Timbre and a South Korean Discourse of Sorrow and Lament." PhD diss., Columbia University.

———. 2003. "Retake: A Decade of Learning from the Movie *Sŏp'yŏnje.*" *Music and Culture* (Korea) 8: 119–43.

———. Forthcoming. "Image is Everything: Social and Physical Images of Female Performers in Korean Popular Music." In *Korean Pop Music: Riding the Wave,* edited by Keith Howard. Kent: Folkestone.

Woldering, Britta. 1998. *"Akai tori" in den Jahren 1918/1919. Die Entstehung einer modernen japanischen Kinderzeitschrift.* Europäische Hochschulschriften Reihe XXVII: Asiatische und Afrikanische Studien, Bd. 67. Frankfurt: Peter Lang.

Wollasch, Joachim. 1996. *Cluny—"Licht der Welt": Aufstieg und Niedergang der klösterlichen Gemeinschaft.* Zürich: Artemis und Winkler.

Wong, Deborah. 2001. *Sounding the Center: History and Aesthetics in Thai Buddhist Performance.* Chicago: University of Chicago Press.

Wright, Craig. 2000. "The Palm Sunday Procession in Medieval Chartres." In *The Divine Office in the Latin Middle Ages: Methodology and Source Studies, Regional Developments, Hagiography,* edited by Margot Fassler and Rebecca Baltzer, 344–71. New York: Oxford University Press.

Yardley, Anne Bagnall. 2006. *Performing Piety: Music in Medieval English Nunneries.* New York: Palgrave.

Yi, Po-hyŏng. 1973. "P'ansori." In *Survey of Korean Arts: Traditional Music.* Seoul: National Academy of Arts.

Yoffie, Leah Rachel. 1947. "Three Generations of Children's Singing Games in St. Louis." *Journal of American Folklore* 60:1–51.

Zilch, Dorle. 1994. *Millionen unter der blauen Fahne: Die FDJ Zahlen—Fakten—Tendenzen. Mitgliederbewegung und Strukturen in der FDJ-Mitgliedschaft von 1946–1989.* Rostock: Norddeutscher Hochschulschriften Verlag.

About the Authors

Todd M. Borgerding was educated at the Universities of Minnesota and Michigan. His published work includes *Gender, Sexuality, and Early Music* (Routledge, 2002) and *The Motet, Rhetoric, and Religion in Renaissance Spain* (University of Rochester Press, 2006). He is associate professor of music at the University of Wisconsin, Oshkosh.

Susan Boynton is assistant professor of historical musicology at Columbia University. Her publications, including articles on medieval liturgical poetry, monastic education, and liturgical manuscripts, have appeared in *Journal of the American Musicological Society, Journal of Medieval Latin, Sacris Erudiri, Traditio,* and *Viator.* She is the author of *Shaping a Monastic Identity: Liturgy and History at the Imperial Abbey of Farfa, 1000–1125* (Cornell University Press, 2006). With Isabelle Cochelin she directs the interdisciplinary series Disciplina Monastica, which includes their coedited volume of essays on the Cluniac customaries, *From Dead of Night to End of Day* (Brepols, 2005).

Joy Calico is assistant professor of musicology at Vanderbilt University. Her research on music and cultural politics in East Germany has been supported by the Deutscher Akademischer Austausch Dienst, the Berlin Program for Advanced German and European Studies, the NEH, and the American Academy in Berlin. She has published on that subject in many anthologies and journals, including *Music and German National Identity* (Applegate and Potter), the Eisler centennial volume published by the Akademie der Künste, *Cambridge Opera Journal,* and *Musical Quarterly.* Her essay on the student/teacher relationship between Eisler and Schoenberg is forthcoming in *The Cambridge Companion to Schoenberg,* and her book *Brecht at the Opera* will be published by the University of California Press in 2006. Before coming to Vanderbilt in 2003, she was assistant professor of musicology and coordinator of Russian and East European studies at Illinois Wesleyan University.

Isabelle Cochelin is associate professor at the Department of History and Centre for Medieval Studies of the University of Toronto, where she has taught since 1997. She is a specialist of medieval monasticism and has published on issues such as the modalities of entrance inside the monastery, education of the oblates, sexual norms imposed on adolescent monks, and the first years of Cluny. She collaborates on three international projects editing customaries, Cluniac and non-Cluniac, and, with Susan Boynton, she is also the editor of the series Disciplina Monastica, published by Brepols.

Judah M. Cohen is a Dorot Assistant Professor/Faculty Fellow in the Skirball Department of Hebrew and Judaic Studies at New York University; he will take up a position at Indiana University in fall 2006. His research interests span Jewish music and the arts within American Jewish life. Recent papers and publications of his have explored the American cantorate, the synagogue modes, Reform Jewish songleading, Jewish folk music, Jewish hip-hop culture, the legacy of Shlomo Carlebach, and musical representations of the Diary of Anne Frank. In addition, he has conducted extensive research on Jewish life and history in the Caribbean—the subject of his first book, *Through the Sands of Time: A History of the Jewish Community of St. Thomas, U.S. Virgin Islands* (Brandeis University Press, 2004). His current book project explores the meaning and process of becoming a Reform Jewish cantor in twenty-first-century America.

Hermann Gottschewski is associate professor at the graduate school of arts and sciences, University of Tokyo. He received his PhD from the University of Freiburg with a performance-analytical study (*Die Interpretation als Kunstwerk,* Laaber, 1996). He has traveled around the world as a visiting scholar at the Japan Foundation and Harvard University. His publications include works on musical performance, music theory, and the history of Western and traditional music in Japan.

Machiko Gottschewski (born Takagi) studied nutrition and psychology and has worked at several institutions in Germany as a language teacher and visitor's guide. Her main interest, however, is the traditional Japanese art of writing (calligraphy), which she learned from early childhood. She has presented her work in museums and galleries in Japan, Germany, Belgium, and the Netherlands, and she received several prizes, among them a prize of the distinguished Mainichi-shodô-ten. Two of her works were bought by the Municipal Museum of Weill am Rhein (Germany).

Steven Huebner is the author of *The Operas of Charles Gounod* (Clarendon, 1990) and *French Opera at the Fin de Siècle: Wagnerism, Nationalism, and Style* (Oxford, 1999; winner of the Prix Opus 2000). His many articles and reviews have appeared in such journals as *Nineteenth-Century Music, Journal of the American Musicological Society, Cambridge Opera Journal, Music and Letters,* and *Journal of the Royal Musical Association,* as well as in several collections of essays in English, French, and Italian. His recent articles include "Zola the Sower" (winner of the

2002 Westrup Prize), "'O Patria Mia': Patriotism, Dream, Death," "Thematic Recall in Late Nineteenth-Century Opera" and "'Striptease' as Ideology." His PhD was granted by Princeton University in 1985; since then he has taught at McGill University, where he currently holds the position of James McGill Professor.

Roe-Min Kok is assistant professor of music at McGill University in Montreal, Canada. Her research focuses on musical representations of children and childhood in European Romanticism (in particular on the music of Robert Schumann) and on the dissemination of Western classical music in the former British Empire. She is currently working on a book about social and structural intertextualities between music on the theme of childhood and the folk and fairytale tradition established by the Grimm brothers. Kok plays the piano, violin, Senegalese sabar, and Javanese gamelan; at McGill she teaches courses in both historical musicology and ethnomusicology.

Anne Dhu McLucas is professor and chair of the Department of Musicology and Ethnomusicology at the University of Oregon, where she was also dean of the School of Music for ten years. Her publications on British-Celtic-American folksong, British and American theater music, and Native American music have appeared in the *Journal of the American Musicological Society, American Music,* and *Ethnomusicology,* and *College Music Symposium,* as well as *The New Grove Dictionary of Music and Musicians, The New Grove Dictionary of Opera, The New Grove Dictionary of American Music,* and *The Garland Encyclopedia of World Music,* vol. 3, *The United States and Canada.* She is currently working on a monograph on oral tradition in American music. Since 1983, she has worked on the puberty ceremony of the Mescalero Apaches with Dr. Inés Talamantez, professor of religious studies at the University of Santa Barbara and a woman of Apache heritage.

Amanda Minks is assistant professor at the honors college at the University of Oklahoma. She holds an MA degree from Wesleyan University and a PhD from Columbia University, both in ethnomusicology. Her current research focuses on interculturality, play, and performance among Miskitu children on the Caribbean coast of Nicaragua. Amanda has received fellowships from the Mellon Foundation, the Fulbright Institute of International Education, the Wenner-Gren Foundation for Anthropological Research, and the Social Science Research Council, among others. Her publications have appeared in the journals *Ethnomusicology* and *Yearbook for Traditional Music.*

Patricia Tang is associate professor in the music and theater arts section at the Massachusetts Institute of Technology, where she teaches courses in world music and African music. She has carried out extensive research on Wolof griots in Senegal, masters of the sabar drum. Dr. Tang serves as director of Rambax, MIT's

Senegalese drumming ensemble. She is also active as a violinist and has recorded with such artists as NDER et le Setsima Group, Positive Black Soul, and Balla Tounkara.

Heather A. Willoughby received her PhD in 2002 from Columbia University's ethnomusicology program. Her dissertation, "The Sound of *Han: P'ansori,* Timbre, and a South Korean Discourse of Sorrow and Lament," considers the intersections between physical sound, ideologies, aesthetics, and practices of sound making and interpretation, and the experience and ideology of emotion, sentiment, and affect. Her recent research and publishing efforts focus on gender and image issues in Korean popular musics as well as *p'ansori* performance practices. She is currently employed as a cultural anthropologist and musicologist in the Graduate School of International Studies at Ewha Womans University in Seoul.

Index

The letter *e* following a page number denotes an example, *d* denotes a diagram, *p* denotes a photo, and *t* denotes a table.